NEBRASKA
OFF THE BEATEN PATH®

OFF THE BEATEN PATH® SERIES

EIGHTH EDITION

NEBRASKA
OFF THE BEATEN PATH®

DISCOVER YOUR FUN

DIANA LAMBDIN MEYER

Globe
Pequot
Guilford, Connecticut

All the information in this guidebook is subject to change. We recommend that you call ahead to obtain current information before traveling.

Globe Pequot

An imprint of Rowman & Littlefield

Off the Beaten Path is a registered trademark of Roman & Littlefield.

Distributed by NATIONAL BOOK NETWORK

British Library Cataloguing in Publication Information available

ISSN 1539-0845
ISBN 978-1-4930-3118-4

∞™ The paper used in this publication meets the minimum requirements of American National Standard for Information Sciences—Permanence of Paper for Printed Library Materials, ANSI/NISO Z39.48-1992.

Printed in the United States of America

About the Author

Diana Lambdin Meyer's love for Nebraska is rooted in her overall appreciation for wide open spaces, small towns and the people who make them interesting. Throw in a bit of history and the quirkiness hidden just below the surface in Nebraska, and the love story is complete.

Raised on her family grain farm and now based in Kansas City, Diana Lambdin Meyer's passion for all things Nebraska grew exponentially through her friendship with Hannah McNally, a.k.a. Mary Ethel Emanuel, the first author of *Nebraska: Off The Beaten Path*.

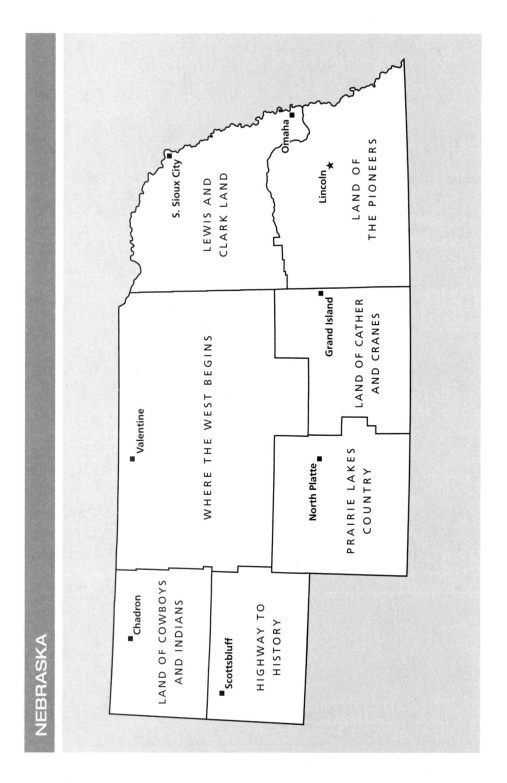

NEBRASKA

LAND OF COWBOYS
AND INDIANS

Chadron

HIGHWAY TO
HISTORY

Scottsbluff

WHERE THE WEST BEGINS

Valentine

PRAIRIE LAKES
COUNTRY

North Platte

LAND OF CATHER
AND CRANES

Grand Island

LEWIS AND
CLARK LAND

S. Sioux City

Omaha

Lincoln

LAND OF
THE PIONEERS

Contents

Introduction

After Maj. Stephen H. Long of the Army Engineers completed his expedition to the Rocky Mountains in 1819, a member of his group described the lands west of the Missouri River as the "abode of perpetual desolation." About 175 years later a late-night comedian described her New York–to–Los Angeles car trip and concluded that, after driving through Nebraska, she had proof that "the dead walk the earth."

Nebraskans are both used to and bemused by such comments about our state. And we are accustomed to living in a state offering a friendly and safe environment, abundant cultural and recreational activities, ethnic and geographic diversity, and reasonable prices. So we can easily afford to lightly shrug and smile at less-than-generous or downright inaccurate comments about Nebraska; we know better.

If you substitute Nebraska for Midwest in futurist Faith Popcorn's following comments, you'll know why this state is a good place in which to live . . . and travel: "The uncluttered, unbridled lives of Midwesterners will be the envy of the rest of the nation well into the next century. Living on the coasts used to be the aspiration, but not any longer. Today, everything that everybody wants—big family, good food, regular people, nothing hyped up—is all in the Midwest."

Nebraskans are not prone to braggadocio (the one exception is the Nebraska Cornhuskers, who won back-to-back college football championships in 1970 and 1971, in 1994 and 1995, and one more in 1997), and we are not given to gushing about the loveliness of our state and our quality of life. We accept Nebraska like we accept air; it is something so subtle, so natural that it merits little conscious consideration.

Although we are far too modest about Nebraska, we are more than willing to share. It is hoped that this book will let others in on the secrets and charm of Nebraska. Take the time to explore state parks, bicycle along portions of the Cowboy Trail (when completed it will be the nation's longest rail-to-trails path), float down the Niobrara River (one of the best canoeing rivers in the country), pull up a chair in a mom-and-pop cafe or be seated at a four-star restaurant, take a covered-wagon ride along the Oregon Trail, tee off at some of the best golf courses around according to *Golfweek* magazine, be awed at an IMAX theater, sink into a comfortable bed at a B&B, experience the intense magic of the world's largest concentration of sandhill cranes each spring, see where Kool-Aid was invented (in Hastings), lose your inhibitions by entering the cluck-off competition at the Wayne Chicken Show, take part in a cattle drive in the Sandhills, take in an opera, or stroll though the world's largest indoor rain forest at Omaha's Henry Doorly Zoo.

As you travel in Nebraska, please take the time to discover for yourself these off-the-beaten-path places. This book cannot pretend to be a comprehensive collection of all the things to see and do in Nebraska, but it is a good place to start. You'll find a variety of little-known places and a smattering of more famous attractions that should not be missed.

Your trip may be affected by the weather. Nebraskans enjoy a wide variety of climatic conditions. The highest temperature ever recorded in the state was a steamy 118 degrees Fahrenheit at Geneva in 1934 and in both Hartington and Minden in 1936. Nebraska folklorist and tall-tale collector Roger Welsch says that old-timers claim that sometimes it was so hot the hens laid hard-boiled eggs, a situation remedied by feeding them cracked ice. The coldest temperature is recorded as a numbing minus 47 degrees at Camp Clarke in 1899 and Oshkosh in 1989. Welsch reports that it was once so cold, lawyers were seen with their hands in their own pockets, and people went to church just to hear about hell.

So if you're traveling in Nebraska in the summer, bring clothes for hot weather. If it's winter, bring clothes for cold weather. In the spring or fall, which are pretty, although admittedly a bit too brief, bring something for both climates. (Residents have extensive wardrobes, with clothes suitable for every weather vagary.) Keep in mind there have been January days when it's been shorts-and-shirt weather, but there also have been occasions when late spring and early fall bring freak blizzards. And although I-80 rarely closes for winter storms, it can happen. Long-distance truckers don't call I-80 the "Snow Chi Minh Trail" for nothin', you know.

It's a good idea to travel with a Nebraska state map as you use this book. Most of the places listed are not on I-80, so you'll need a map to help you navigate. If you'd like a free packet of tourism materials, including a map and a calendar of community festivals, please call the Nebraska Division of Travel and Tourism toll-free at (800) 228-4307, or visit visitnebraska.org; the e-mail address is tourism@visitnebraska.org. All the larger cities have a convention and visitors bureau from which you can obtain additional information. Their websites are linked to the Division of Travel and Tourism, as are hundreds of other communities and attractions. Several visitor centers on I-80 are staffed from Memorial Day weekend through Labor Day weekend, and the staff there will be able to answer questions, point you in the right direction, and help you find lodging across the state.

As you drive in rural areas, don't be mystified by the "finger wave." You are likely to be greeted by fellow travelers with their index fingers raised briefly in a friendly salute. Try it yourself; you'll likely find yourself inexplicably happier.

Enjoy yourself in Nebraska. And as you learn more about us, you might come to agree with a much more accurate assessment of Nebraska than those offered by early explorers or television comics. The Rev. Val Peters, the director of Girls and Boys Town, has written, "Anyone can sit back at the seashore and be inspired because it shouts at you—so do the mountains. But the prairie only whispers. You must listen closely and not miss the message."

Helpful Information

Nebraska Association of Bed and Breakfasts
(877) 223-NABB (6222)
nebraskabb.com

Nebraska Department of Roads
1500 Highway 2
Lincoln, NE 68502
(402) 471-4567
roads.nebraska.gov
Road and weather conditions, 511

Nebraska Game and Parks Commission
2200 North Thirty-third St.
Lincoln, NE 68503-0370
(402) 471-0641
outdoornebraska.gov

Nebraska Historical Society
Fifteenth and R Streets
Lincoln, NE 68501
(402) 471-3270
nebraskahistory.org

DAILY NEWSPAPERS IN NEBRASKA

Beatrice Sun
Grand Island Independent
Hastings Tribune
Holdrege Citizen
Kearney Hub
Lincoln Journal Star
McCook Gazette
Norfolk Daily News

North Platte Telegraph
Omaha Daily Record
Omaha World-Herald
Scottsbluff Star-Herald
Sidney Sun-Telegraph
York News-Times

PUBLIC TRANSPORTATION

Only the two largest cities, Omaha and Lincoln, have fairly extensive bus routes and taxi service. A handful of communities, including Omaha, Lincoln, Nebraska City, and Kearney, have trolley lines that serve the downtown areas. Uber and Lyft are approved for operation by the Nebraska Public Service Commission in all communities, including ridesharing to Eppley Field.

Nebraska Fast Facts

- The Reuben sandwich was invented in Omaha's Blackstone Hotel.

- *Cliff's Notes* originated in Lincoln.

- Cabela's, located in Sidney, says that it has the largest and fastest growing mail-order outdoor sporting-goods business in the world.

- Nebraska measures 387 miles across. It is 459 miles diagonally from the northwest to the southeast.

- Frisbees were first tossed about in Lincoln.

- The Vise-Grip was invented in DeWitt.

- *Nebraska* comes from the Oto Indian word *Nebrathka,* meaning "flat water."

- In 1986, Nebraska was the first state to have two women, Kay Orr and Helen Boosalis, run against each other for governor.

- Nebraska ranks first in the nation for the production of alfalfa meal and great northern beans.

- Three Indian tribes, the Santee Sioux, the Omaha, and the Winnebago, have reservations in Nebraska.

- The B-29s that dropped atomic bombs on Japan, the *Enola Gay* and *Bocks Car,* were assembled at a plant in Bellevue.

- Omaha has been the home of the College World Series since 1950.

Famous Nebraskans, Born or Bred

- *Grace Abbott,* social reformer
- *Bess Streeter Aldrich,* novelist
- *Grover Cleveland Alexander,* baseball player
- *Kurt Andersen,* co-founder of *Spy* magazine
- *Fred Astaire,* actor and dancer
- *George Beadle,* Nobel Prize winner for physiology/medicine
- *Ward Bond,* actor
- *Marlon Brando,* actor
- *William Jennings Bryan,* three-time presidential candidate and prosecutor in the Scopes Monkey Trial
- *Lloyd Bucher,* Boys Town graduate and captain of the USS *Pueblo*
- *Warren Buffett,* financier and second-richest man in the United States
- *Dick Cabela,* outdoor outfitter
- *Mark Calcavecchia,* professional golfer
- *Johnny Carson,* talk-show host
- *Willa Cather,* Pulitzer Prize–winning novelist
- *Dick Cavett,* entertainer
- *Dick Cheney,* former vice president of the United States
- *Montgomery Clift,* actor
- *James Coburn,* actor
- *Buffalo Bill Cody,* Pony Express rider, scout, buffalo hunter
- *Wahoo Sam Crawford,* baseball player
- *Crazy Horse,* Oglala Sioux war chief
- *Chip Davis,* founder of Manheim Steamroller
- *Ester Renay Dean,* singer, songwriter
- *Sandy Dennis,* actress
- *Mignon Good Eberhart,* mystery novelist
- *Loren Eiseley,* naturalist and writer
- *Ruth Etting,* vaudeville performer and movie star
- *Joe Feeny,* Irish tenor on the *Lawrence Welk Show*
- *Father Edward Flanagan,* founder of Boys Town
- *Henry Fonda,* actor
- *Gerald Ford,* former president of the United States
- *Bob Gibson,* baseball player
- *Rodney Grant,* actor

- *Rollie, Will, and Joyce Hall,* founding brothers of Hallmark Cards
- *Howard Hansen,* composer and conductor
- *Robert Henri,* painter
- *L. Ron Hubbard,* founder of the Church of Scientology
- *Richard Janssen,* actor
- *Swoosie Kurtz,* actress
- *Evelyn Lincoln,* private secretary to former President John F. Kennedy
- *Harold Lloyd,* actor
- *Pierce Lyden,* actor
- *Malcolm X,* civil rights leader
- *Randy Meisner,* member of the Eagles rock group
- *Wright Morris,* novelist and photographer
- *J. Sterling Morton,* founder of Arbor Day
- *John G. Neihardt,* novelist and poet
- *Nick Nolte,* actor
- *Senator George Norris,* credited with planning the Tennessee Valley Authority
- *Rose O'Neill,* creator of the Kewpie Doll
- *Edwin Perkins,* inventor of Kool-Aid
- *Susan LaFlesche Picotte,* first female Native-American medical doctor
- *Charles Purcell,* designer of the Oakland–San Francisco Bay Bridge
- *Thurl Ravenscroft,* voice of Tony the Tiger
- *Red Cloud,* Oglala Sioux chief
- *Mari Sandoz,* novelist
- *Gale Sayers,* football player
- *William Sessions,* former director of the FBI
- *Ted Sorenson,* speechwriter/political strategist for President John F. Kennedy
- *Standing Bear,* Ponca Indian chief
- *Matthew Sweet,* rock musician
- *Robert Taylor,* actor
- *George Raymond Wagner,* better known as "Gorgeous George," professional wrestler
- *Daniel Lawrence Whitney,* a.k.a. Larry The Cable Guy, comedian
- *Evan Williams,* co-founder and former CEO of Twitter
- *Sam Yorty,* former mayor of Los Angeles
- *Daryl Zanuck,* co-founder of 20th Century-Fox

- The first paved transcontinental highway, Lincoln Highway (US 30), goes through Nebraska.

- There are approximately 2,500 lakes in the state.

- Kool-Aid was invented in Nebraska.

- The state's only Frank Lloyd Wright building is a private home in McCook.

- One of the nation's first female pilots, mail carrier Evelyn Genevieve Sharp, was from Nebraska.

- Nebraska has 23,686 miles of streams, rivers, and canals, ranking it tenth in the nation. Nebraska has more miles of river than any other state.

- Chief Crazy Horse was killed at Fort Robinson, which is now a state park.

- Most of the state sits squarely atop the huge Ogallala (also called the High Plains) Aquifer. This vast "underground sea" stretches from South Dakota to Texas.

- The world's largest elephant fossil was found in Nebraska.

- Fort Atkinson, now a state historical park, was established on a site recommended by Lewis and Clark. It was the first military fort built west of the Missouri River and had the state's first school.

- The only member of the British royalty buried in the state, Lady Evelyn Brodstone Vestey, is at perpetual rest in her hometown of Superior.

- The state is crossed by the Pony Express, the Oregon Trail, the Mormon Trail, the Ox-bow Trail, a Ponca Trail of Tears, the Sidney-Deadwood Trail, and the Texas-Ogallala Trail.

- The Lewis and Clark Trail follows Nebraska's eastern border, the Missouri River.

- The Nebraska legislature is the only nonpartisan, one-house (or unicameral) system of state government in the country.

- A sculpture by Klaus Oldenburg is located on the University of Nebraska–Lincoln campus.

- Two world-famous architects designed buildings in Lincoln: Phillip Johnson designed the Sheldon Art Gallery, and I. M. Pei designed the Wells Fargo Center.

- Black cavalry men, or "Buffalo Soldiers," were stationed at Fort Robinson during the Plains Indian Wars. They were first called Buffalo Soldiers by Native Americans because their hair reminded the Indians of buffalo hair.

- The first lawsuit in Nebraska was a dispute over stolen cheese.

- The world's first test-tube tigers were raised at the Henry Doorly Zoo in Omaha.

- Chicken pot pies were first developed by Swanson Foods in Omaha.

- The largest gathering ever of Native Americans (more than 10,000) was in 1851 at Horse Creek near Morrill.

- The world's largest collection of windmills is at the *2nd Wind Ranch* near Comstock.

Recommended Nebraska Reading for Children

My Daniel by Pam Conrad
Prairie Songs by Pam Conrad
Pioneer Girl by Andrea Warren
The Sandhill Crane by Colleen Gage
Dark Arrow by Lucille Mulcahy
Night of the Twisters by Ivy Ruckman
The Horsecatcher by Mari Sandoz
The Covered Wagon and Other Adventures by Lynn Scott
The Historical Album of Nebraska by Charles A. Wills

Land of the Pioneers

Southeast Nebraska, a lovely land of rolling hills and forested riverbanks, has witnessed several historic events that shaped the future of the West. From original homestead cabins to blazing gunfights, from architectural wonders to ethnic festivals, from the Pony Express to the Oregon Trail, the Land of the Pioneers is a rich and exciting place to discover. Historic attractions, state parks, hiking and biking trails, B&Bs in tiny towns, and deluxe hotels in cities complement your prairie experience in southeast Nebraska.

Cass County

We'll begin our southeastern tour at *Platte River State Park,* located near Louisville just south of I-80 and Highway 50. There's great hiking in the woods and a place to rest up at the lodge. Guests can stay in cabins or in a tepee village. (Tepee guests will need to bring their own sleeping bags, towels, soap, ice chests, and any other modern luxury.) Because of the rugged terrain, there are no camping facilities at Platte River State Park, but there are camping facilities at *Louisville Lakes State Recreation Area,* just a few minutes away. The restaurant at

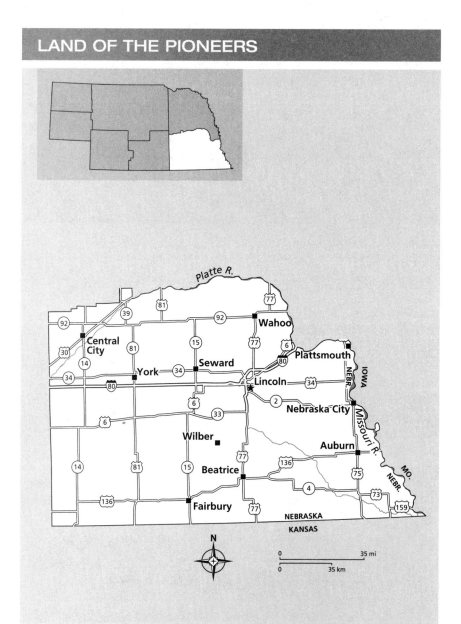

Platte R.

81

77

39

92

92

Wahoo

92

Central City

81

15

77

6

30

Plattsmouth

14

York

34

Seward

80

NEBR.

IOWA

34

80

Lincoln

34

6

2

Nebraska City

Missouri R.

6

33

Wilber

Auburn

14

81

15

77

Beatrice

136

MO.

75

NEBR.

136

4

73

Fairbury

77

159

NEBRASKA

KANSAS

N

0   35 mi

0   35 km

Platte River State Park offers buffalo entrees daily from Memorial Day through Labor Day, and on weekends through September. Activities in the park include swimming, hiking, paddle boating, tennis, archery and firearms shooting, volleyball, and horseback trail rides. A Game and Parks permit is required.

Before you get too far from Platte River State Park, please go see the one that didn't get away. At the ***Ak-Sar-Ben Aquarium and Outdoor Education Center*** at Schramm Park, there's a really scary big catfish that weighs more than 60 pounds and is 52 inches long. One snapping turtle is more than 100 years old. In other tanks are very weird-looking paddlefish and sturgeon, and lots and lots of normal-looking fish. Two snapping turtles with sharp claws occupy one tank with goldfish intended as turtle snacks. Children often report to the staff when the turtles are "fighting." But they're not fighting; they're trying quite vigorously to make little snappers. The Education Center is fun, too, with lots of critter and bird parts to learn about. There's also a movie theater where you can see all sorts of wildlife-oriented films. It's located 9 miles south of I-80, exit 436. The aquarium and center are open year-round, although it is

FAVORITE ATTRACTIONS IN SOUTHEAST NEBRASKA

(All area codes are 402.)

Edgerton Explorit Center
208 Sixteenth St.
Aurora
694-4032
edgerton.org

Glacial Till Tasting Room
1419 Silver St.
Ashland
944-2546
glacialtillvineyard.com

Homestead National Monument of America
west of Beatrice on State Highway 4
223-3514
nps.gov/home

Indian Cave State Park
7 miles northeast of Shubert
883-2575
outdoornebraska.gov/indiancave/

James Arthur Vineyards
northeast of Lincoln near Raymond
783-5255
jamesarthurvineyards.com

Rock Creek Station State Historical Park
7 miles southeast of Fairbury
729-5777
outdoornebraska.gov/rockcreekstation/

Steamboat Trace Trail
accessible from Nebraska City, Brownville, or Peru
335-3325
nemahanrd.org/steamboat_trace

closed on Tuesdays from Labor Day to Memorial Day. Admission is free. Call (402) 332-3901 or visit outdoornebraska.gov/aksarben/ for more information.

If you're staying at Platte River State Park from May through October, a short drive south will bring you to **Weeping Water** and the **Lofte Community Theater,** a setting for the "Born in a Barn" players, who produced more than 300 plays in a converted 1924 hog barn for 28 years, beginning in 1977. However, a "real" theater opened in 2006, complete with 390 seats, heat and air conditioning, and other modern amenities. Acoustics are greatly improved and assistive hearing devices are available upon request. The production schedule now includes five major shows that run from May to December each year, along with a number of special occasion programs at other times of the year. The Lofte Community Theater is on Hwy. 1 between Manley and Weeping Water. If you want to be one of the more than 12,000 people who enjoy the productions each year, call (402) 234-2553 or visit lofte.com for tickets or more information.

Weeping Water, local legend holds, gets its name from the voluminous tears shed by Native American women upon the death of their warriors after a fierce battle. They wept so long and so hard their tears began to form little streams and ultimately a larger stream. Sit quietly by the falls of the Weeping Water Creek and hear the sound of ancient grief. For the best chicken-fried steak in the world, head over to **Mom's Cafe** at 422 Main in **Plattsmouth** (junctions of Highways 66 and 34 in eastern Cass County). Of course, others argue that Mom's has the best BBQ in the world. Breakfast is served all day, and Friday nights are busy because of the Fried Fish buffet. Mom's Cafe opens at 6:30 a.m. Mon through Sat and at 7 a.m. on Sun. They close at 8 p.m. Tues through Sat and at 2 p.m. Sun and Mon. The number is (402) 296-3000.

If you're a Lewis & Clark Expedition fan, Plattsmouth has something for you. In late July 1804, the expedition reached the mouth of the Platte River, or the "Great River Platt" as indicated in the journals. Historian Stephen Ambrose noted this event as a milestone since the mouth of the Platte "was the Missouri riverman's equivalent of crossing the equator" since it meant entering a new ecosystem and territory of the Sioux. The journals mentioned the Platte's great velocity as well as the amount of sand it dumped into the Missouri River and noted "a great number of wolves" at that evening's campsite. You won't typically see wolves today, but you can stand at the Platte's mouth at **Schilling Wildlife Management Area** by going from Plattsmouth's Main Street east over railroad tracks and taking the first left onto Refuge Road. It's not hard at all to imagine the expedition and its excitement at this milestone. The phone number is (402) 296-0041.

Head back west on Highway 66 toward **South Bend,** population ninety-seven. The **Round the Bend Steakhouse** is a couple of miles north of South Bend just south of I-80 exit 426. It serves big lunches for a little money and some of the best prime rib dinners around. Its biggest claim to fame is the Testicle Festival, a feast of Rocky Mountain Oysters held annually on, ironically enough, Father's Day. The second generation of the Olson family keeps the steaks and other goodies ready at this community favorite. The phone number is (402) 944-9974; roundthebendsteakhouse.com.

If you're a golfer, you'll want to go north from South Bend toward I-80 and watch for signs to **Quarry Oaks** at 310th St./Quarry Oaks Dr. This dramatic, scenic course has craggy terrain and rolls through a burr oak forest. Many holes overlook the Platte River, and there are striking elevation changes. Fees for eighteen holes range from $65 to $75, including a cart. Call (402) 944-6000 to make a reservation for a tee time about a week ahead of time or check it out at quarryoaks.com.

If you're hungry, head next to Louisville (Highways 66 and 50) to B's Diner and Bakery at 127 Main Street. This place is known for some fabulous homemade desserts and goodies. The place is bright and cheery and smells so good. Open for breakfast and lunch. Call (402) 234-2669.

A few doors away at 209 Main Street is the Coop de Ville and Café Poulet, a combination gift shop and coffee shop. You'll find lots of locally made products by the area's talented artists, and you can munch on freshly baked cookies while enjoying specialty coffees. It's a yummy place just to hang out and relax for a while. Call (402) 234-2717.

Your next stop is **Elmwood,** the home of Bess Streeter Aldrich, one of many famous Nebraska authors. Her works include *A Lantern in Her Hand* and several other novels. She published 160 short stories (her first financial success as a writer was a $175 check for winning a 1911 short-story contest sponsored by *Ladies Home Journal*). Most of her works are about what she knew best: the lives of pioneers in her adopted state of Nebraska and her home state of Iowa. At present visitors can see her home and museum at 204 East F St., which is open for tours on Sat and Sun from 2 to 5 p.m. or by special appointment. The telephone number is (402) 994-3855. The **Bess Streeter Aldrich Museum** is housed in the Elmwood Library at 124 West D St. It contains original manuscripts, awards she won, a gift shop with her books, and a duplicate model of the bust of her that is in the Nebraska Hall of Fame in Lincoln's State Capitol Building. Learn more about special exhibits at bessstreeteraldrich.org.

It may, just maybe, be possible to actually talk to Bess Streeter Aldrich at this next location in Elmwood. If you're the kind of spirit who believes that those from another life can reach out to us in the 21st century, you will absolutely love ***The Museum of Shadows.*** Founded by Nate and Karleigh Ratterman, two passionate ghost hunters, this museum includes a collection of artifacts from around the world that are associated with the paranormal and metaphysical. Items include tribal masks from the Amazon rain forest and things collected from the catacombs of Paris. The most haunted item is a doll named Ada that moves on its own. Located at 116 North Fourth Street, the building that houses the museum was built in 1890 and once held an embalming business. (402) 297-9263; museumofshadows.com.

If you'd like to speed up the pace a bit, head west on Highway 34 and stop at ***Eagle Raceway,*** just 12 miles west of Eagle on Highway 34 or 11 miles south of exit 420 on I-80. From April through September races are held on the world's fastest ⅓-mile dirt track. Races begin on Friday and Saturday at 7:30 p.m.; the gates open at 5:30 p.m. For details call (402) 238-2595, or visit eagleraceway.com.

The very quotable Mark Twain often said of golf that it is "a good walk spoiled," but maybe that's because Samuel Clemens never played the ***Woodland Hills Golf Course,*** just west of Eagle on Highway 34. *Golf Digest* has consistently given this place five stars. It's the only course in Nebraska with this rating. If you golf, you'll know that such a good rating is rare, not just in Nebraska, but across the United States. The telephone number is (402) 475-4653, or visit woodlandhillsgolf.com.

As you're driving around Cass County, keep an eye out for colorful images painted on the sides of barns and sheds. These are traditional patterns that have appeared for years on handmade quilts. The project was launched in 2006 and maintained by student members of the Future Business Leaders of America at Elmwood-Murdoch High School. Find a map with locations and more information at embarnquilts.weebly.com.

Saunders County

The ***Willow Point Gallery and Museum*** in ***Ashland*** at 1431 Silver St. is a unique store with a waterfall, a stream, a wishing pond, fish, and native plants that makes visitors feel as though they've stepped outside from, well, the outside. See the seasons unfold at this indoor setting with nearly thirty mounted animals, including moose, black bear, mountain lion, white fox, and a huge polar bear, found among their natural habitats. Also featured is work by nationally known artist Gene Roncka, who has a series of Christmas tree ornaments on Nebraska history. Ashland is on Highway 63; take one of three I-80 exits to reach town. The hours are Mon through Sat, 10 a.m. to 6 p.m.; and Sun, noon to 4 p.m. Call (402) 944-3613.

For an experience in the real outdoors, take a walk along the 1.5 miles long Saline Ford hiking/biking trail. The parking lot at 12th and Silver Streets includes an historical marker reminding us of the many travelers who have crossed this creek before us. Located on the Mormon Trail, this very spot is where hundreds of thousands of Americans participated in the westward expansion of the U.S. The trail is paved in some places, gravel in others and ends up at Wiggenhorn City Park at 25th and Clay Streets. *Fun to note:* the entire downtown area of Ashland has free wifi, courtesy of the Chamber of Commerce.

About 30 miles northwest of Ashland is *Wahoo,* the hometown of five internationally known men, each of whom achieved prominence in vastly different fields. The five famous sons include Darryl Zanuck, co-founder of 20th Century-Fox and winner of seven Academy Awards; "Wahoo" Sam Crawford, who was named to the Baseball Hall of Fame in 1957; Clarence W. Anderson, who wrote dozens of books about horses, starting with *Billy and Blaze;* Dr. George Beadle, who won the 1958 Nobel Peace Prize for having demonstrated how genes control the basic chemistry of the living cell; and Howard Hanson, a composer/musician who headed the Eastman School of Music for forty years and won the 1946 George Foster Peabody Award for musical achievement.

Learn more about these men and the settlement of the area for free at the *Saunders County Historical Complex,* 240 North Walnut. This complex includes a museum building, a depot, a log house, a schoolhouse, a farm

FAVORITE ANNUAL EVENTS IN SOUTHEAST NEBRASKA

(Call ahead to verify dates; all area codes are 402.)

Annual Arbor Day Celebration
Nebraska City, last Friday in April
873-3000

Renaissance Festival
near Raymond, third weekend in May
783-5255

Rock Creek Trail Days
Fairbury, first weekend in June
729-5777

Homestead Days
Beatrice, last weekend in June
223-3514 or 223-2338

Czech Festival
Wilber, first full weekend in Aug
(888) 494-5237

Capital City Ribfest
Lincoln, third weekend in Aug
(888) 627-7675

Applejack Festival
Nebraska City, third weekend in Sept
873-3000

Germanfest
Syracuse, last weekend in Sept
269-7489

Star City Parade and Festival
Lincoln, second weekend in Dec
434-6900

machinery building, a caboose, and a church. All the buildings are furnished with period pieces. For those of you with an aversion to ironing, there's a really scary collection of irons through the ages. On the front of the building is a 29,490-pound rock, which at one time was part of the Twin Rocks Marker on the **Ox-Bow Trail**. The Ox-Bow Trail was an important "feeder" trail to the Oregon Trail. From April through Sept the hours are Tues through Sat, 10 a.m. to 4 p.m. From Oct through March hours are Tues through Fri, 10 a.m. to 4 p.m. Call (402) 443-3090 or visit visitsaunderscounty.org.

Stop in at the **Wahoo Bakery,** 544 North Linden St., where owner Scott Buresh makes fritters with more than just apple. Oooh, try the blueberry fritter bread, or strawberry or peach. Scott's staff turns out mountains of mouthwatering baked goods such as white rye bread, horn rolls (that's "rohlicky" if you speak Czech), and to-die-for *kolaches*. A *kolache* is a sweet bun with an indented top, loaded with fruit (even prunes!), poppy seeds, or cream cheese. Buy a lot—they're addictive. The bakery is open Tues through Sat from 6 a.m. to 4 p.m. The number is (402) 443-3387.

No stop in Wahoo would be complete without a meal at the **Wigwam Cafe** at 146 East Fifth St. This charming cafe is another chance to step into the past. Ceiling fans, exposed brick walls, booth seating, and low countertops provide an inviting setting for a great meal. The name of the cafe comes from a collection of Native American figurines. The food is pure-and-simple country cooking, from burgers to meat loaf to fried chicken and fish. Occasionally the owners, Clayton and Silvia Wade, make something different, such as Mexican food or specialties from Silvia's native Romania. Try the homemade pie. The Wigwam Cafe is open Mon and Wed through Sat from 6 a.m. to 2 p.m., and Sun from 8 a.m. to 2 p.m. They open for dinner on Fri and Sat starting at 5 p.m. You can phone them at (402) 443-5575.

As you drive by the **Saunders County Courthouse** on Highway 77, take note of a mounted torpedo surrounded by small American flags. It is displayed in memory of the men who died in the submarine USS *Wahoo*, which was sunk by the Japanese in 1943 after sinking twenty enemy ships. A plaque lists the names of the crew members who are still noted as "on patrol."

Lancaster County

The **Rogers House Bed & Breakfast,** an elegant, three-story, brick home at 2145 B St. in **Lincoln,** was built in 1914 in one of Lincoln's oldest neighborhoods as a retirement home for a prominent banker. In 1984 it became Lincoln's first B&B and the second B&B in the state. Owner Nora Houtsma's attention to detail makes a stay at this enchanting, light-filled B&B very pleasant indeed. Each of the seven rooms is decorated with antiques, and each has a private bath (four have claw-foot bathtubs and antique pedestal sinks, and three have Jacuzzis). Windows of leaded and beveled glass, French doors, polished hardwood floors, three sunrooms, and a library round out the features and amenities. The **Ricketts Folsom House,** next door at 2125 B St., is also owned by Ms. Houtsma. Its four rooms are equally as welcoming as those in the Rogers House and were renovated with the business traveler in mind; these rooms are wired for phones and laptop computers. Both the Rogers House and the Ricketts Folsom House offer a full breakfast, which can be served wherever guests prefer: in their room, in the dining room, or in the sunrooms. Room rates range from $90 to $170. For a cozy winter retreat, stay in the suite with a fireplace for $180. Children ages ten or older are welcome. Open daily except for Christmas Eve and Christmas Day. Call (402) 476-6961 or visit rogershouse inn.com.

The **Museum of the Odd,** located in a two-story pink home at 701 Y St., couldn't be more aptly named. Owner, curator, and artist Charlie Johnson has amassed an astonishing collection of oddities, covering nearly every square inch of his residence, including the floors, walls, and sometimes ceilings. The mind tends to reel with delight when presented with shelves of cartoon-character bubble-bath containers, plastic banks, toy trains, rubber animals, pulp magazines, religious icons, children's books, baseball cards, board games, Halloween and Day of the Dead trinkets, sci-fi magazines and figurines, Mardi Gras beads, and a seemingly endless explosion of ordinary items that assume oddity due to their sheer number and presentation. One visitor described the Museum of the Odd as a massive collection of "shrapnel from the twentieth century's pop-culture explosion." Be sure to call ahead to make sure Charlie will be home to admit you to his shrine to oddity. The phone number is (402) 476-6735. There's no admission charge, but donations are appreciated.

Visitors to **Bluestem Books,** at 137 South Ninth St., are invited to tarry and either read or enjoy spirited discussions in cozy, overstuffed chairs. Housed in a former art gallery in the historic Haymarket District, the bookstore contains more than 30,000 used, rare, scholarly, and out-of-print books. Specialty areas include western Americana, military history, quilting, art, literature, Nebraska history, and Nebraska authors. There are also substantial collections of science fiction, poetry, theater, and children's books. Hours are 10 a.m. to 5 p.m. Tues through Sat. The number is (402) 435-7120. The website is bluestem books.com.

After your visit to Bluestem Books, take some time to stop at other interesting places along the brick-lined streets of Lincoln's **Haymarket District.** In addition to the usual brewpubs, restaurants, galleries, and antiques stores, there's a place to buy treats for your pets and a store filled with beautiful bed linens. Ten Thousand Villages at 140 North 8th Street is a fair trade store where all products are ethically produced by people in developing nations. Buy Nebraska-made products at *From Nebraska,* at 803 Q St. *The Oven,* 201 North Eighth St., serves Indian food in one of the most simply attractive restaurants in town. Stop in for coffee at *The Mill,* 800 P St., and visit with artists at the *Burkholder Artists Cooperative,* 719 P St. Several art cooperatives and galleries in the Haymarket District hold "First Friday" open houses in the evenings on the first Friday of the month. For a listing of all of the Haymarket's businesses and special events, visit lincolnhaymarket.org or follow the district on Facebook.

Although the *Nebraska State Capitol,* Fifteenth and K Streets, is hardly off the beaten path, it is decidedly worth a visit and a free tour. It's not hard to find; in fact, at 400 feet it's the tallest building in Lincoln and is visible from up to 30 miles away. This stunning architectural masterpiece was designated the "fourth architectural wonder of the world of all time" by the American Institute of Architecture in 1948. Designed by Bertram Goodhue, the capitol is filled with incredible mosaics, murals, heavy carved doors, and a multitude of minute details that add up to a very beautiful building. (You can even get married there; the daughter of former Governor Ben Nelson wed there in October 1998.) Every piece of art inside and out is a symbolic reminder of events in the story of Nebraska and the story of humanity. The statue atop the capitol, *The Sower,* which was sculpted by Lee Lowrie, symbolizes the sowing of seeds of life for better living in the future. (Locals have an exceedingly irreverent and suggestive nickname for the capitol building; find someone with a sense of humor to ask what it is.) The statue of a pensive-looking Abraham Lincoln, facing west outside of the capitol, was done by Daniel Chester French, sculptor of the Lincoln Memorial in Washington, D.C. Don't fail to view the plains from the capitol's fourteenth-floor observation deck. Hours are Mon through Fri, 8 a.m. to 5 p.m.; Sat and holidays, 10 a.m. to 5 p.m.; and Sun, 1 to 5 p.m. For more information call (402) 471-0448. The website is capitol.nebraska.gov.

One of Lincoln's smallest bars has a big reputation in the world of blues music. Measuring only 20 feet by 90 feet, the *Zoo Bar*'s walls are lined with photographs of bands that make this downtown Lincoln bar a regular stop on their tours. Nationally and internationally famous blues acts such as Albert Collins, Luther Allison, Kinky Friedman, Marcia Ball, Gatemouth Brown, Jay McShann, Lonnie Mack, and far too many more acts to mention have all played the Zoo to wildly enthusiastic crowds. Any given night will see a capacity audience of 150 people. If the band is hot, be prepared to stand in line, but think of it as an opportunity to make some new Lincoln friends. The Zoo is often visited by famous fans of the blues when they are in town, including Wesley Snipes, and Kris Kristofferson. Former Nebraska Senator Bob Kerrey has also been known to stop in. In 1993, the Zoo Bar received the W. C. Handy Award for Best Blues Bar in the Nation from the Blues Foundation in Nashville. Although blues is the standard fare, the Zoo also books jazz, bluegrass, reggae, and rock and roll. The address is 136 North Fourteenth St. Hours are Tues to Fri, 3 p.m. to 1 a.m.; Sat, 2 p.m. to 1 a.m.; Sun, on occasion, 5 to 10 p.m. Call (402) 435-8754 or check out the upcoming bands at zoobar.com. The Zoo Bar is part of the "Beermuda Triangle" in downtown Lincoln, consisting of the Zoo Bar, *O'Rourke's, Duffy's,* and *Barrymore's* (okay, it's not three bars, it's four).

Barrymore's Lounge, with an alley entrance between O and P Streets and Thirteenth and Fourteenth Streets, is in back of the old Stuart Theater. The door is original, the same one used by Mickey Rooney and Helen Hayes during the building's former incarnation as a theater. The lounge is complete with a light board, hanging backdrops that reach ten stories to the ceiling, and dressing rooms. There's a genteel feel here, and it's a popular place for après-performance gatherings from the nearby world-class Lied Center for the Performing Arts. The phone number is (402) 476-6494.

If you're old enough to remember strapping on a pair of roller skates, or if you're a fan of in-line skating, the *National Museum of Roller Skating* in Lincoln will hold some fascination for you. See the 1819 French Petitbled, the first roller skate ever patented, and the original modern roller skate patented by James L. Plimpton in 1863. The museum has the world's largest collection of roller skates and roller-skating memorabilia, both archival and modern, ranging from wheels to toys to posters, photographs, trophies, and medals. There

Ghosts of Lincoln

Ghoulies, ghosties, and long-legged beasties: Lincoln does not lack for stories of phantoms.

The C. C. White Building on the Wesleyan University campus is said to be visited by the ghost of Miss Urania Clara Mills, an elderly music teacher who died in 1940. The apparition is clad in an ankle-length brown skirt, and she wears her hair in a bun. The Capitol Building is also haunted by the spirits of two men: one who fell to his death in 1967 while stringing Christmas lights, and another who fell from a spiral staircase, which is now closed to the public. It is said that the capitol was built on a slight rise that was sacred to the Indians, so native spirits still inhabit the site. While the ghosts may be scary, some swear the single most bone-chilling thing about the capitol is opening day of the legislative session, when lobbyists, favor seekers, and bootlickers swarm about the senators in a feeding frenzy.

are displays on roller disco, vaudeville and trick skaters, and skating animals. Tara Lipinski, 1998 Olympic gold medalist in figure skating, loaned a pair of her roller skates and a fetching outfit. Also featured are roller-skating costumes bedecked with fringe and sequins. Ask curator Deborah Wallis to tell you the story of the English guy who a long time ago wore a pair of old skates to a fancy costume ball and smashed into something expensive and extremely breakable; other people's embarrassment is always amusing. Located at 4730 South St., the museum is open Mon through Fri, 9 a.m. to 5 p.m.; closed on holidays but open on some weekends in the summer. Admission is free; donations are welcome. Call (402) 483-7551, ext. 16, or visit the museum's website at rollerskatingmuseum.com.

If you love licorice, this is your lucky day. The country's largest selection of licorice is at *Licorice International* at 803 Q St. They have more than one hundred varieties from fourteen countries. Stop in for a free sample! If you don't have time to stop, they will gladly ship your purchase. They have other tasty things, too—even a sugar-free candy from Austria. The hours are Mon through Fri, 9:30 a.m. to 6:00 p.m. and Sat, 10 a.m. to 5 p.m. The phone number is (402) 488-2230 or 800-LICORICE. The website is licorice international.com.

Pioneers Park, at South Coddington and West Van Dorn in the southwestern part of Lincoln, offers a quiet retreat to residents and travelers alike. There are duck ponds, thousands of pine trees planted by the WPA, hiking trails, a toboggan run, playgrounds, a challenging eighteen-hole golf course, picnic areas, and an amphitheater for summertime performances. Several sculptures add grace to the park. They include a huge bronze buffalo, four large sandstone columns that at one time were a part of the former Federal Treasury Building in Washington, D.C., and a bigger-than-life-size statue of Chief Red Cloud, which was approved by Native American leaders as being truly representative of the Sioux tribes. Within Pioneers Park is the 680-acre *Pioneers Park Nature Center,* with 8 miles of hiking trails through native short-grass, tallgrass, lowland prairie, wetlands, a riparian forest, wildflower areas, and herb gardens. There are two buildings with natural-history and live-animal exhibits, which are beautifully landscaped with plants that attract birds and butterflies. Here you can see a small herd of bison and elk, along with deer, wild turkey, and more. Hours at the nature center are June through Aug, Mon through Sat, 8:30 a.m. to 5 p.m., and Sun, noon to 5 p.m.; Sept through May, Mon through Sat, 8:30 a.m. to 4:30 p.m., and Sun, noon to 5 p.m. Call (402) 441-7895 or visit lincoln.ne.gov/city/parks/naturecenter.htm.

If you've got a sense of the macabre, you might consider stopping at the 190-acre *Wyuka Cemetery.* This Lincoln site is where the first post–World War

Ya Gotta Have Art

The *Sheldon Memorial Art Gallery and Sculpture Garden,* on the grounds of the University of Nebraska at Twelfth and R Streets in Lincoln, is one of those places where you can feed your mind and your soul. The emphasis of the permanent collection is on twentieth-century American art, and there's always a great temporary collection on display. However, it's a great place to visit no matter what the current exhibitions are. The building is a quiet place, airy and light filled, designed by Philip Johnson. But the best part is the sculpture garden, which is a sunken garden with little concrete seats, ponds, fountains, pretty potted plants, and, of course, some mighty fine sculpture. Even though the garden is just a few feet away from busy sidewalk traffic, somehow it remains a peaceful, sheltered setting day or night. At night you'll detect some young-and-in-love smoochers in the shadows, and during the day you can watch the sun cast shadows on the sculpture. Jazz aficionados will appreciate the Jazz in June held every Tuesday evening in the Sculpture Garden.

II serial killer is buried. For five days in 1958, nineteen-year-old Charlie Starkweather went on a killing spree with his fourteen-year-old girlfriend, Caril Ann Fugate, which left ten people dead in Lincoln and Lancaster County. Terror-stricken residents of the area seldom left their homes for those five days, and the Lincoln paper published its last extra edition during the siege. Starkweather was captured and executed; Fugate spent twenty-five years in prison. Bruce Springsteen's album *Nebraska* includes a song based on this bloodbath, and the movie *Badlands,* with Martin Sheen and Sissy Spacek, is similarly based on this tragic episode in Lincoln's history. The address at Wyuka Cemetery is 3600 O St. (O Street, by the way, is considered to be the longest, straightest main street in the world. Highway 34, which is O Street in Lincoln, runs for approximately 50 miles east to Union, Nebraska. O Street has been immortalized in verse by Allen Ginsberg, who wrote the poem "Zero Street" while visiting his friend, the novelist Karl Shapiro, who taught at the University of Nebraska.)

Close by is another wonderful collection. The *International Quilt Study Center and Museum* houses the world's largest publicly owned quilt collection. Several hundred quilts range from traditional to quite modern; they date from the 1700s to contemporary. The display of rare quilts is rotated every six months, so it's unlikely you'll ever see the same quilt twice. And if you own an old quilt and don't know its story, the center hosts regular open houses called Quilt ID Days where visitors are welcome to bring in their personal quilts for evaluation. The professionals here are often able to identify the part of the country in which the quilt was made, the time period, and pattern. They can also offer tips on better caring for your heirloom quilt. The center is located on the University of Nebraska–Lincoln campus at 1523 North Thirty-third St. Hours are Tues. through Sat, 9:30 a.m. to 4:30 p.m.; and Sun, 1:30 to 4:30 p.m. Admission is $8 for adults; free for UNL students. Call (402) 472-6549 or visit quiltstudy.org.

To see what the countryside looked like before it was altered by humankind, visit **Nine-Mile Prairie** near Lincoln. Located on West Fletcher Avenue, off Northwest Forty-eighth Street, this 230-acre area is one of the largest unplowed, virgin tallgrass prairies left in Nebraska. Almost 400 kinds of plants are known to grow on the prairie; most are native, and some are rare. More than eighty kinds of birds have been sighted in the Nine-Mile Prairie. Animals such as deer, badgers, squirrels, and mice inhabit the prairie, as do a variety of insects. When you go, remember not to pick or collect the plants, not to litter, and not to smoke. Also, bring bug repellent. Ticks are pretty bad here. The prairie is managed and studied by the UNL School of Natural Resources, so call (402) 472-9608 for more information. For a preview of what you might see, visit the website ninemileprairie.com. Although the website is not affiliated with the University, the images provided by photographer and artist Michael Farrell make a compelling statement about the beauty of the tallgrass prairie.

Another natural prairie (this one is 15 miles southwest of Lincoln or 3.1 miles south of Denton) is the **Spring Creek Prairie.** Its 800 acres include about 650 acres of tallgrass prairie; only 2 percent of the native tallgrass prairie that existed in the nineteenth century remains extant. This former farm, now owned by the Audubon Society, was spared the plow because its rock-strewn soils and steep hills of an ancient glacial moraine were suited less for farming and more for grazing. A stroll across the land will reveal wetlands, natural springs, creeks, ponds, and woodland. Wildlife may include deer, red foxes, coyotes, bobcats, badgers, beavers, and muskrats. Spring Creek is also home to several species of birds whose population has been declining; these include dickcissel, field sparrow, greater prairie chicken, Bell's vireo, and red-headed woodpecker. All this is within 75 miles of Nebraska's two largest cities and about half the state's population. You'll hardly be the first tourists; arrowheads are not uncommon, and, in places, you'll be walking in Oregon Trail ruts. Admission via the Straw Bale Visitors Center is $4 for adults, but admission is free on Tues. For more information call (402) 797-2301 or visit springcreek prairie.audubonorg.

You can't leave Lancaster County before going to the **James Arthur Vineyards** near the community of Raymond. The vineyards cover 400 acres of rolling hills and prairie grasslands. The building itself is really quite nice—it's open and inviting with a huge wraparound porch. In warm weather you can sit on the porch or walk up a hill to gazebos. In cold weather you can sink into some

Take a Bite of History

At the turn of the twentieth century, a sizable group of Germans emigrated from Russia and settled in Nebraska. Their history dates from 1770, when Catherine the Great gave free land to German settlers willing to move to Russia. The deal was sweetened with exemption from taxation and military service and the promise of freedom of language and religion for one hundred years. All good things must come to an end; burdened with high taxes and military duties, scattered groups of Germans in Russia were looking to relocate at the same time the American Midwest was open for settlement. (There's a museum in Lincoln, at 631 D St., that tells their story.) One part of their cultural heritage that they brought with them was a recipe for traditional cabbage rolls, or *runza*. As you travel across the state, you'll likely spot franchised restaurants that are called, appropriately and simply enough, Runza Restaurants. Stop in and buy a couple, both traditional and with Swiss cheese. You'll be surprised how good some hamburger, cabbage, and onions baked into what looks like a small loaf of bread can be. When you get home you can make your own *runza* from this recipe printed in **Event-Full Recipes of Nebraska** by the Nebraska Events Association.

Cabbage Rolls

Make enough of a basic yeast roll recipe to yield about twelve rolls.

For filling:
1½ lbs. hamburger
3 medium onions
½ medium head cabbage

Crumble and cook hamburger in a skillet. It shouldn't be browned but should be thoroughly cooked. Finely chop cabbage and onions, as for slaw. Cook cabbage and onions in a small amount of water until tender. Drain fat from the meat and water from the vegetables; mix vegetables and meat together and season with salt and pepper to taste.

After the dough for the rolls has risen, knead it down with flour until smooth and elastic. Using half of the dough, pull off twelve egg-size pieces. Flatten each piece of dough into a 4-inch round and place on greased cookie sheets (six to a sheet; leave 2 inches between them). Put ½ cup of the filling on each round, leaving a ¼-inch edge. Using the remainder of the dough, make twelve more rounds, then cover the filled rounds with these and pinch the edges together. Cover with towels and let rise in a warm place for about an hour. Bake in a 375-degree oven for 20 to 25 minutes, or until nicely browned. (Switch cookie sheets halfway through baking time so that tips and bottoms brown evenly.) Note: Proportions of meat and vegetables are up to individual tastes, and amounts can be varied.

comfy chairs inside by the fireplace. Buy some of the award-winning wine and some of the great cheese, meats, salmon, and trout at the gift shop, and you've got yourself a picnic. The food is very good, and the ambience is even better. To get to James Arthur from Lincoln, take Fourteenth Street north for 7 miles and turn west on Raymond Road for 2½ miles. The address is 2001 West Raymond Rd., and the phone number is (402) 783-5255; jamesarthurvineyards.com.

Otoe County

Nebraska City, one of the oldest communities in the state, was founded in the early 1850s by William Nuckolls as a trading post and a riverboat stop on the Missouri River. The city's attractions are as varied as its visitors. First is *Arbor Lodge State Historical Park and Arboretum,* a beautiful estate that was the home of J. Sterling Morton, founder of Arbor Day, which is now celebrated internationally. In 1854 a young Morton left Michigan with his new bride to take up residence in Nebraska Territory. They missed the trees of home and quickly planted trees, shrubs, and flowers around their home and added an apple orchard. A journalist by profession, Morton became the editor of Nebraska's first newspaper and used it as a way to spread the word across the territory about his tree-planting convictions. Morton's interest in trees stemmed from practical reasons: they were needed for fuel, lumber, fencing, and many other purposes. He felt that with enough trees, Nebraska could become the "Sylvan Queen of the Republic." Arbor Day became an official Nebraska holiday in 1872. Visitors to Arbor Lodge State Historical Park and Arboretum today will find a magnificent Neocolonial mansion of fifty-two rooms furnished in Victorian and Empire pieces, plus some great Stickley furniture. There's even a one-lane bowling alley. Stroll through the beautifully landscaped grounds, with a seventy-two-acre arboretum that contains 270 varieties of trees and shrubs, and a formal rose garden. The Whispering Bench, a curved bench surrounded by white pines, directly across from the Old Settlers Cabin, has been called the best place in Nebraska to sneak a kiss. The grounds are open year-round. The mansion is open daily from April through December. A Game and Parks permit is required, and a nominal admission fee is charged. Call (402) 873-7222 or visit the park's website at arbordayfarm.org. Here's one more bit of Arbor Lodge trivia: J. Sterling Morton's son, Joy, founded the Morton Salt Company.

Just across the road west from Arbor Lodge State Historical Park and Arboretum is the *Arbor Day Farm,* 100 Arbor Ave., a 235-acre working apple orchard and tree farm. This orchard is one of several in Nebraska City, which is a good reason for Nebraska City to be called the Apple Capital of Nebraska. There's something about the local soil that makes for arguably the best apples

Fall for Nebraska

The fall foliage of Nebraska is, admittedly, not nearly as famous as that in New England. But the fall colors along the heavily treed Missouri River in southeast Nebraska are very nice indeed. And a bonus: The roads, restaurants, and hotels won't be overly crowded with tourists from around the world. On any given byway it'll likely be just you and a whole lot of pretty scenery. And you won't be greeted by taciturn locals who say, "Aye-yup, you can't get there from here."

The intensity of the fall color is dictated by the amount of rainfall in the preceding months. Some years are downright spectacular, and other years are still well worth a visit. Find yourself a road anywhere just south of Nebraska City all the way down to Indian Cave State Park near the river, take your time, and enjoy your surroundings. The Southeast Nebraska Visitors Guide includes a "Country Lanes Scenic and Fall Foliage Tour" page with a map for your convenience. The guide also recommends this slow-paced tour in the early spring, when the redbud and plum trees are in bloom. Call the Nebraska Tourism Division at (800) 228-4307 to get a free copy of the guide.

in the world. If you're in town in the fall, be sure to pick up some apple cider. You can buy apple pies and nature-related items at the gift shop. During apple season you can watch as apples are sorted and boxed. Pies are available seasonally. Do not miss the experience of the Tree House Trail where you get to be above the canopy of trees. Hours are Mon through Sat, 9 a.m. to 5 p.m.; and Sun, noon to 5 p.m.; closed Christmas, Thanksgiving, and Easter. For more information call (402) 873-8717 or visit arbordayfarm.org.

No visit to southeast Nebraska would be complete without a stop at the ***Missouri River Basin Lewis & Clark Interpretive Trails and Visitors Center*** just outside of Nebraska City. The center is a lovely building high atop a bluff overlooking the Missouri River. It is the only museum in the nation to focus on the more than 400 scientific discoveries of flora (178 plants) and fauna (122 animals) made at President Thomas Jefferson's direction by the Corps of Discovery from 1803–1806. Marking the entrance is a huge sculpture by Tom Palmerton called *Pointing the Way* depicting Lewis and Clark and the Newfoundland dog, Seaman, that accompanied the Corps. (Don't fret that the Newfie doesn't look much like Newfies look now. The breed has evolved over the past 200 years to the more familiar larger and fluffier dog we know today. The dog in the sculpture does indeed look like Newfies looked two centuries ago.) The center also has a life-size replica of the keelboat used by the Corps of Discovery. Hands-on exploration affords visitors the opportunity to relive some of the Corps' daily scientific activities such as plant specimen collecting, map making, and celestial readings. There is an admission fee; pay it, it's well worth it. And take time to explore a number of the trails in the park and along the banks of the Missouri River. The hours are Mon through Sat, 10 a.m. to 7 p.m., and Sun, noon to 6 p.m. The hours may be adjusted seasonally. The address is 100 Valmont Dr., just west of the Missouri River off Highway 2. The phone number is (402) 874-9900. The website is mrb-lewisandclarkcenter.org.

Fun note about Nebraska City—a portion of the 2002 movie *About Schmidt*, starring Jack Nicholson, was shot here.

Located 28 miles southeast of Lincoln on Highway 2, Unadilla was named after the community of the same name in New York. *Unadilla* is an Iroquois word meaning "a place of meeting." The Groundhog Day Festival is not a bad place to meet some new friends. And while you're in town, take a hike at the nearby Deacon Prairie, where in warmer months you might spy a Western fringe prairie orchid, which is on the endangered species list. ***Mayhew Cabin and Historical Village Foundation,*** at 2012 Fourth Corso in Nebraska City, was once the westernmost branch of the Underground Railroad, which operated to help slaves reach free territory in the 1800s prior to the Civil War. The site was initially named after John Brown, who believed that slavery was a sin against Christianity and could only be resolved through armed conflict. His most famous raid took place in October 1859 at Harpers Ferry, West Virginia. He was convicted of treason and hanged three months later. It is believed that he made several visits to Nebraska City in the 1850s. Nebraska City's location on the edge of free territory and near the site of the Missouri River crossing made it an integral part of the Underground Railroad. The cabin on site was built in 1855 and has been authenticated by the Nebraska State Historical Society as one of the oldest buildings still standing in Nebraska. A hand-dug cave under the cabin was built under the ruse that it would be a root cellar for a new "vegetarian society." A tunnel from the cave leads to South Table Creek, where slaves could slip away down the creek bed. In addition to the cabin and cave, the historical village has several historical structures from the area, including a train depot and an AME church whose congregation dates to the 1870s. Mayhew Cabin and Historical Village is open April through Oct 31, Mon through Sat, 11 a.m. to 5:30 p.m. and Sun noon to 4 p.m. However, the site coordinates a number of programs throughout the region during Black History Month. Admission is $3 for adults and $1 for children age twelve and under. The telephone number is (402) 873-3115 or visit the website at mayhewcabin.org.

The ***Arbor Day Farm Lied Conference Center,*** at 2700 Sylvan Rd. in Nebraska City, offers deluxe accommodations in a beautiful Adirondack-style lodge. Situated on 260 acres of the Arbor Day Farm, it serves as an

Unadilla, Punxsutawney West

Whether or not Punxsutawney Phil sees the shadow of his furry little head, the Otoe County community of *Unadilla* has a celebration on the first Saturday in February. In 1988 Unadilla was officially proclaimed the Groundhog Capital of Nebraska. What's a name without a festival, you may well ask. The Groundhog Festival, held in the tiny downtown district, consists of a wild game feed, flea market, groundhog poker tournament, and, weather permitting, a parade. The weather is a factor, one would assume, because it's probably not much fun riding in a convertible on frigid days when the wind comes sweeping down the plains. Such an experience would give new meaning to "a smile frozen on her face."

environmental-education resource for the National Arbor Day Foundation. The lodge features 144 rooms on three levels, fine dining, a cocktail lounge, a lap-size heated pool, exercise equipment, a fitness center, bike rentals, golf, carriage rides, and hiking trails. The building's heating and cooling systems are powered by an ultramodern energy plant fueled by wood chips. The rooms are lovely, and prices vary throughout the year from $109 to $189 for a single room. To make reservations, call (800) 546-LIED (5433) or (402) 873-8733. Visit the website atliedlodge.com.

Another great place to stay in Nebraska City is the ***Whispering Pines B&B*** at 2018 Sixth Ave. (Steamwagon Road). The 1878 Victorian, two-story brick house sits on six and a half acres of trees, fish ponds, and flower gardens. Jeanna Stavas, who bought the inn in 2005, has remodeled to provide private baths with each of the four themed bedrooms in the house and added modern comforts among the many antiques. A fifth room is down the hill in an old horse barn, very private and secluded. Relax on the veranda, soak in the hot tub, play a game of croquet, or help with the community puzzle. Jeanna has a passion for food and offers cooking classes and concerts featuring local musicians. Even if you don't spend the night, it's fun to come for an evening of dinner and music. Rates range from $109 to $150. To make reservations, call (402) 873-5850 or visit bbwhisperingpines.com. Jeanna likes to stay in touch with guests and friends via Twitter @NebraskaCityBNB and on Facebook/Whispering Pines Bed and Breakfast.

Johnson County

The Johnson County Courthouse and town square in ***Tecumseh,*** at the junction of Highways 50 and 136, were featured as the location for the filming of

Amerika, a popular television mini-series filmed in the 1980s. The town square was chosen for good reason. It's an adorable Norman Rockwell kind of community filled with residents who take pride in their town.

The *Ramsey Family Fountain* is an old-fashioned soda fountain and café known for great soups and sandwiches—just a comfortable kind of place where Beverly and Wilbur Ramsey welcome you like family. Take a look at all of the pictures on the wall. Those are people from Johnson County who have served in the U.S. military. Ramsey's is located at 155 South Third Street; (402) 335-1235. Ramsey's is just open for lunch every day between 10 a.m. and 2 p.m.

Just around the square from Ramsey's is the *Johnson County Historical Museum* at 289 Clay Street. Among the interesting items of note is a large exhibit on the Orphan Train that brought children to Tecumseh for adoption. This was a period in U.S. history before child service agencies, so a religious organization in New York that cared for orphaned and abandoned children sent them west on trains to be adopted by those needing farm labor. It was a tough time that resulted in many children finding good homes. The museum also has a large exhibit on those from the area who served in the military. Of particular interest is an exhibit about Tecumseh native Clarence Hupka who served on the U.S.S. *Indianapolis* during WWII. The *Indianapolis* is notable in military history for delivering the atomic bomb to Pacific island of Tinian before it was dropped on Hiroshima. The *Indianapolis* sank after being hit by Japanese torpedoes, throwing 1,200 sailors in the water to be devoured by sharks. Clarence Hupka was one of 317 sailors who survived the ordeal. As of the most recent publishing of this book, Hupka still lives in Tecumseh. The museum is open Tues. through Sat., 10 a.m.–2 p.m. Call (402) 853-3614.

Head north out of Tecumseh on Hwy. 50 to the village of *Cook.* The community has two parks—Windmill Memorial Park and Triangle Park that are connected by a charming covered bridge. Although not historic, the 42-foot-long bridge is made of old barn wood found in the county and constructed by volunteers. It is the only covered bridge in Nebraska that you can drive across. Either park makes a lovely spot for a picnic with the bridge as a scenic backdrop.

Nemaha County

You might have imagined there would be a Podunk, Nebraska, and indeed, there was. The times have changed, however, and so has the name of the town. The former Podunk is now *Brock* and is in northern Nemaha County on Highway 67.

Head about 12 miles northwest to **Auburn**, which has been called the antiques capital of southeast Nebraska. (According to a promotional brochure, it's also referred to as Nebraska's Oldest Tree City, U.S.A., and Home of the World's Largest Leaf.) This pleasant little town, with a population of 3,500, has six antiques stores. If you've been looking for that one-of-a-kind piece of china to complete your collection, a Roy Rogers doll, or a metal doorstop, this could very well be your lucky day. If you work up an appetite while antiques shopping, there's a very nice restaurant called **Arbor Manor Steakhouse** at 1617 Central Ave. Four first-floor rooms in a 1908 Victorian home are the setting for some great steaks, which are cut up right in the kitchen. The homemade soup is a family recipe passed down over the years. Owners Rick and Amy Clark added an outdoor gazebo bar, where on Wednesday in summer months, they have beer and brat parties. Hours are Mon through Sat, 5 to 9 p.m.; phone (402) 274-3663. The Clarks also have a twenty-nine-room motel at the back of the restaurant with rates ranging from $67 to $79; arbormanorsteakhouseand motel.com.

Coryell Park is an unexpected pleasure, located in the middle of farm fields. This privately owned park was the original homestead of Richard Coryell, and part of it was converted into a 32-acre free park for public use in 1934. Mr. Coryell only asked one thing of those enjoying his gift to this community and that is "civility, decency and good order from all, that we may enjoy its blessings."

These blessings include enclosed picnic shelters, playgrounds, a basketball court, two social halls, a re-created homestead log cabin, and an incredible stone chapel, which is often used for weddings. A lovely creek weaves through the property that may be crossed by three covered bridges, inspired by those historic and famous bridges in Madison County, Iowa. To get to Coryell Park, take Highway 136 until you're 7 miles west of Auburn, turn north, and go 3 miles. The park closes at sunset. Reservations for large groups can be made by calling (402) 856-2875.

Brownville, east of Auburn on Highway 136 on the Missouri River, might give Rome a run for its money; Brownville is also known as the City of Seven Hills. Brownville was settled in 1854 and became a major steamboat landing, river crossing, overland freighting terminus, and grain-milling center. The entire town is on the National Register of Historic Places. It has more museums, historic homes and sites, galleries, and craft and antiques shops than you can shake a stick at.

Brownville has an impressive reputation for its literary arts programs. It seems there's always a theatrical program under way, a musical performance, poetry reading, or art show of some sort. Much of this has always been in the

Bad Name, Good Idea

There was once a site near Auburn with a name that is currently very politically incorrect and insensitive. The 125,000-acre *Half-Breed Tract* was set aside by the government in 1830, per the Prairie Du Chien Treaty, specifically for abandoned children born to fur traders and their Native American wives. As adults, these mixed-blood descendants often had difficulty in establishing a claim to tribal lands and thus were compensated with land between the Little Nemaha and Missouri Rivers. The owners were not required to live on the land, and much of it was ultimately sold to white settlers. A historical marker is located ¾ mile east of Auburn on Highway 136.

fiber of Brownville, but it all became focused when Brownville was designated Booktown USA. The designation came from Richard Booth, a British bibliophile who revitalized a small town in Wales when he opened a used book store that grew to epic proportions. Brownville is one of only three Booktowns in the United States. The designation comes from the number of books in the community per capita. And indeed you'll find lots of books everywhere.

The Lyceum at 228 Main St. is home to about 60,000 books. It's a wonderful old building that is also a lovely café serving excellent food and wine while hosting book readings and other literary events. Come in and enjoy a cup of coffee and a piece of pie and just browse through the rooms full of books. Hours are daily from 10 a.m. to 8 p.m. The phone number is (402) 825-4321.

You'll find even more books, too many to count or even estimate the number, at *The Antiquarium.* The building at 309 Water St. was once the old Brownville High School and it's where the Nebraska Teachers Association was founded. Tom Rudloff owns the business, which he moved to Brownville from an old warehouse in Omaha. He has a lovely collection of chess sets from around the world, and he's ready to sit down for a game at a moment's notice. He hosts chess tournaments and exhibits art. Tom has done a lovely job of restoring this old building. Call him at (402) 825-3171 because his hours aren't set in stone. Visit theantiquarium.webs.com for more history and information.

A nice museum is the *Captain Bailey House/Brownville Museum,* at Fourth and Main Streets. This seven-gabled Gothic Revival house was built of bricks made in Brownville. The house is full of antiques, and it even comes with a ghost. When Mrs. Bailey was found dead of poisoned ice cream, suspicion fell on a woman who was said to be overly fond of Captain Bailey. When the newly spouseless Captain Bailey failed to return her affections, he was also found dead from poisoned food. Listen carefully and you may hear the rustling of petticoats or creaking footsteps. The Captain Bailey House is open on weekends early in May and Sept through mid-Oct from 1 to 5 p.m. and daily in June through Aug from 1 to 5 p.m. Admission is free. The number is (402) 825-6001.

Also on Main Street is the ***Whiskey Run Creek Vineyards & Winery,*** where you can stop for a toast in a century-old barn situated over a creek. Hours are 10 a.m. to 5 p.m. daily. The number is (402) 825-4601. Visit the website at whiskeyruncreek.com.

The ***Brownville Village Theater*** was originally the Christian Church and now draws worshipers of live theater. The oldest in the state, this fourteen-week summer repertory theater is supported by Lincoln's Nebraska Wesleyan University. Performances begin the first Saturday in June. Each person is not only an actor but also serves as a technician, working on scenery, properties, costumes, light and sound, box office, makeup, and house management. The theater presents at least six shows, in alternating sequence, which draw audiences from hundreds of miles away. The Brownville Village Theater is 1 block south of Main Street at College Street. Reservations are highly encouraged. For more information, call (402) 825-4121 after June 1. Visit the website at brown villevillagetheatre.org.

Brownville's connection to the river is preserved at the ***Captain Meriwether Lewis Museum of River History,*** a steam-powered, side-wheel

OTHER ATTRACTIONS WORTH SEEING IN SOUTHEAST NEBRASKA

(All area codes are 402.)

ASHLAND

Mahoney State Park
28500 West Park Hwy. I-80 exit 426
944-2523
outdoornebraska.gov/mahoney/

Strategic Air and Space Museum
I-80 exit 426
944-3100
sacmuseum.org

Wildlife Safari Park
I-80 exit 426
944-9453
wildlifesafaripark.com

Wildwood Center Historic House and the Barn Art Gallery
420 Steinhart Park Rd.
Nebraska City
873-6340
wildwoodhistoriccenter.org

GREENWOOD

Bakers Candy Factory
831 South Baker St.
I-80 exit 420
789-2700
Bakerscandies.com

vessel that helped channelize the unpredictable, wild, and often dangerous Missouri River. Visitors will see what role this massive dredge played in taming the Missouri and will also learn about the geology of the Missouri River basin. Giant steam engines and boilers show how the vessel worked; dining halls, sleeping quarters, and the pilothouse show where the fifty-two-man crew worked. Open weekends only. Call (402) 825-6001 or visit lewisdredge.org for more information.

Also on the Brownville waterfront is *The River Inn,* a former casino riverboat that Jane and Randall Smith have renovated to become a floatel—a floating hotel. There are eighteen staterooms with a balcony and big Adirondack-style chairs to sit in and enjoy the river view. The rooms include a mini-fridge stocked with Whiskey Run Creek wine and a microwave and popcorn. You'll love the bathroom fixtures—very artsy, very practical, and just a lot of fun. The boat has a little fitness area, several common areas for gathering with family and friends. The $120 per night rate is for two people and includes breakfast. Call Jane and Randall at (402) 825-6441 or check out details at river-inn-resort.com.

Bring your bicycle or hiking stick to fully experience the 21-mile *Steamboat Trace Trail,* which starts south of Brownville and extends north through spectacular river-country scenery almost all the way to Nebraska City. Hike or bike, or (like me) amble along the trail; I guarantee you'll agree it's quite lovely. For information call (402) 335-3325 or visit nemahanrd.org.

Richardson County

One of the more interesting characters in Nebraska history was Joseph Deroin, the son of French trader Amable Deroin and an Otoe Indian woman. He claimed land on the Half-Breed Tract, which covers land in what is now Nemaha and Richardson County. Deroin established a trading post on the Missouri River and laid out the village of St. Deroin. He had three wives, has been described as "overbearing and tyrannical," and apparently came to view the village as his fiefdom. He was killed while trying to "collect" $6 for a pig from settler James Biddow. According to local legend, Deroin was buried astride his horse in the town cemetery. Another colorful graveyard legend holds that A. J. Ritter lost an arm while "fishing" with dynamite. His arm was buried before the rest of him, and sometimes, on certain nights, Mr. Ritter rises one-armed from his grave, searching for his lost arm. St. Deroin, at one time home to 300 people, was abandoned when the Missouri River channel shifted course and a cholera outbreak claimed many lives. By the 1920s all that remained was a one-room school. St. Deroin is part of Indian Cave State Park and welcomes visitors to the school, a reconstructed log cabin, and a general store. Living-history demonstrations on weekends in summer and fall bring the village back to life, and a Halloween hayride really brings those characters back to life.

The pristine **Indian Cave State Park,** 2 miles north and 5 miles east of **Shubert,** is named for a large sandstone cave that has the only known Native American petroglyphs in Nebraska. The park has more than 3,000 acres of land along the Missouri River, of which more than 2,300 are heavily forested. It is particularly beautiful in autumn when the leaves turn. There are 20 miles of hiking trails, with Adirondack shelters for backpackers, year-round primitive camping, modern camping year-round, horseback trails, and Missouri River fishing. The park's visitor center is open Memorial Day weekend through Oct, 9 a.m. to 5 p.m. Living-history programs are scheduled on weekends. Riverboat tours are available over Labor Day weekend. Cross-country skiing and sledding are popular winter activities in the park. A park permit is required. Call (402) 883-2575 or visit outdoornebraska.gov/indiancave/.

East and south of Shubert is the very small town of **Barada** (population twenty-four), which was named after yet another colorful Nebraska figure. Antoine Barada was the son of a French nobleman who spotted the "most beautiful woman in the world" smiling at him from a window above a Paris street. He couldn't get her out of his mind and returned to the house only to discover that she was a Native American who had returned home to her "buffalo and campfires." He knew nothing of her but her name, Taeglena, but he sold his possessions and came to America to roam the huge stretches of the Louisiana Territory looking for her. For ten years he worked as a trapper and a hunter, all the while searching Native American villages for his beloved. One fateful day he heard her name said by an old woman outside a tepee; inside was the woman for whom he had given up everything. They married and had several children, including Antoine, who became famous for his extraordinary strength. He could snap a canoe paddle in half, was said to pound a post into the ground so hard it struck water and created a 50-foot fountain (well, okay, this may be more folklore than fact), lifted a barrel of flour weighing 1,500 or 1,800 pounds (sources differ), and won a wrestling match by pinching his opponent with his toes until the opponent gave up in pain. He worked with a fur-trading company and tried to strike it rich in California. He settled down in Barada on his parents' land and lived there with his wife until his death in 1885. He is buried in the Barada cemetery.

Does all this talk of superhuman physical strength make you hungry? Then your next stop should be **Rulo,** on Highway 159, and the **Camp Rulo River Club** for a delicious meal of deep-fat-fried catfish or carp. Watch the Missouri River roll by and imagine Native Americans in canoes or Lewis and Clark in keelboats floating past. Camp Rulo River Club is open Wed through Sun, 5 to 9 p.m.; is open for lunch on Fri and Sat; and is closed on Mon and Tues and may close early on winter nights. The telephone number is (402) 245-4096.

Pawnee County

Pawnee County is an outdoor enthusiast's paradise, with 2,238 acres in wildlife-management areas. The area is famous for its game-bird population. You'll find pheasant, quail, dove, wild turkey, and prairie chicken. (Nebraska hosts the largest population of greater prairie chickens remaining in North America.) Deer and other small mammals are also easily observed. **Burchard Lake** (north and east of the community of **Burchard,** on Highway 4) offers year-round fishing, camping, picnic areas, and hiking around a 150-acre lake. Of special interest to birders is the curious "booming," or mating ritual, of the prairie chickens, who puff themselves up and drum on the ground. The booming occurs in February, March, and April. Blinds have been set up in the park so that visitors can watch this delightful spectacle without disturbing the birds. Take heed of the signs, which caution visitors not to bother the prairie chickens.

History enthusiasts will also find plenty of attractions in Pawnee County. The **Pawnee City Historical Society Museum,** located on the east edge of **Pawnee City** on Highway 8, has nineteen buildings that are chock-full of pioneer furnishing and memorabilia. Buildings include an 1881 school, reputed to be the country's smallest schoolhouse and which has a picture of George Washington, whose painted eyes seem to follow you around the room; an 1857 log cabin; and the home of David Butler, Nebraska's first governor. Don't miss the hand-built experimental tailwind airplane. One building contains more than 800 kinds of barbed wire, one of the largest barbed-wire collections in the Midwest. You may scoff at the idea of barbed wire, but barbed wire is one of the main reasons farm country is just that instead of ranch country. Pioneer farmers put up barbed wire to keep ranchers' livestock out of their crops. Barbed wire meant the end of large herds of free-roaming animals, signaled the end of lengthy cattle drives, and pretty much put a cease-and-desist order on the wild days of the Old West. The museum is open April through Oct, Tues through Sat, 9 a.m. to 4 p.m., Nov through Mar, Thurs, 9 a.m. to 4 p.m., or by appointment. Call (402) 852-3131 or visit pawneecountyhistory.com. Donations are appreciated.

Wouldn't we all be wealthier if we had kept all of our childhood toys? My brother had one of those cast iron John Deere tractors that he pedaled around, racing me and my sister in a red sports car. Those things are worth a fortune now, and if you don't believe it, visit **The Pedal Clinic** at 701 I St. in Pawnee City. This is the former Presbyterian Church building where Bill and Elsie Sunneberg have about 500 old pedal toys on display, things they have picked up at auctions around Nebraska and restored. "People are always saying, 'Oh, I wonder what happened to my tractor like that,'" Elsie says. "Well, we probably bought it at a sale." They also have a couple of real cars and tractors that date to the 1920s that they drive in local parades. The Sunnebergs don't keep regular hours, so you need to call (402) 852-2655 to make sure they are open. They don't charge admission either, but please leave a nice donation so they can keep this wonderful collection available for the public.

a note for film buffs

In 1997, the Swiss filmmaker Karl Saurer made a documentary about Swiss immigrants who settled in Steinauer. A note for linguists: Some people pronounce the name of the town as "Steener," while others say "Stinehour." Both are correct—go figure.

If you're looking for a divine place to stay in Pawnee County, the ***Convent House B&B,*** at 311 East Hickory in ***Steinauer,*** is the answer to your prayers. This two-story, square brick house was home to Benedictine nuns before becoming a B&B in 1993. About the only reminder of the convent days is a Barbie doll, dressed like a nun, in the hallway. The rooms are small (nuns are not generally given to creature comforts) but very cozy. Guests can prepare meals in the kitchen if they choose. The rooms cost $80. The inn is open year-round, including holidays. Children are welcome, too. Call (402) 869-2230 or make reservations online at conventhousebb.com.

Just west of the B&B is ***St. Anthony's Catholic Church.*** The church has many stained-glass windows, including a stunning rose-petal window that is said to rival those of churches in Europe.

Gage County

Homestead National Monument of America, 4½ miles west of Beatrice on Nebraska Route 4, is a tribute to the hundreds of thousands of individuals from around the world who responded to the cry of "Free Land" with the signing of the Homestead Act of 1862 that practically gave away land to those who agreed to live on it and improve it. The park is located on the original 160 acres deeded to Daniel Freeman, who is widely considered to be the first applicant to a claim, doing so in Brownville just minutes after midnight on January 1, 1862. Many individuals mistakenly think of "homesteaders" as those who broke the prairie in places like Kansas, Nebraska, and the Dakotas. But in fact, homesteading took place in 30 states and continued until the 1950s in Alaska.

An interpretive center, opened in 2005 and shaped like a plow that broke the sod here, tells of the political and social implications of the Homestead Act, the challenges for the homesteaders, and the issues of the American Indians who were displaced by the Homestead Act.

A walking trail through a restored prairie takes you past the graves of Daniel and Agnes Freeman to the educational center. Here is where a restored cabin, a one-room frontier schoolhouse, and numerous artifacts used in the daily lives of homesteaders are on display and visitors can participate in hands-on activities like quilting and broommaking. The second weekend of June, the city and park celebrate Homestead Days, which includes a naturalization ceremony of new American citizens on the grounds of the national park. The park is open weekdays from 8:30 a.m. to 5 p.m. and weekends from 9 a.m. to 5 p.m. It is closed on Thanksgiving, Christmas, and New Year's. For more information call (402) 223-3514 or visit the website at nps.gov/home.

The *Gage County Historical Museum,* at Second and Court Streets in *Beatrice,* is housed in a brick 1906 Burlington Railroad depot. The Neoclassical Revival style of the depot was chosen to reflect the community's growth and affluence. Its collections feature historic artifacts from several towns in Gage County and displays on rural life and the development of the railroad. Children like the caboose on the grounds. There's a little exhibit about the young

These Are My People

In a safe corner of a dark closet in my brother's house is a beat-up, faded old steamer trunk, handed down through the generations of Lambdins who came to this country, like so many others, in search of land to call their own. The trunk contains yellowed letters to and from my ancestors, a Bible, a spoon, and a pair of wool gloves. These items have significance only to our family, and, to us, they are priceless. Within those stacks of musty papers and pictures is a copy of the original land grant awarded to my great-great-grandfather, Wilford Lambdin, who fulfilled his obligations to the United States government by homesteading 160 acres in Grant County, Arkansas, in the 1880s. About 40 of those acres are still in the family.

I hadn't thought of that trunk in a long time, or of my great-great-grandfather, until I visited the Homestead National Monument. The education center has huge banners on its exterior with the pictures and names of famous people who are the descendants of homesteaders. As you sign your name in the guest book, you are asked if you are the descendant of a homesteader. I am. As I walk through this park, looking into the eyes of homesteaders, hearing their stories, and learning of their lives through these exhibits, I feel more connected here than almost any other place in the world, besides our family farm. Although I've never met them before, their stories are my story. These are my people.

Vote Me In!

You can check out more than books at the **Beatrice Public Library,** 100 North Sixteenth St. You can check out the story of **Clara Colby,** one of the pivotal players in the national movement for women's suffrage. In 1872 Clara and Leonard Colby moved to "the little western town." Leonard started a law practice and promoted real estate ventures. His better half started a public library and community theater. In 1877 the early suffragette Elizabeth Cady Stanton came to Beatrice for a library lecture. A year later Susan B. Anthony, perhaps the most famous suffragette of all, attended the Gage County Fair.

The die was cast; Clara Colby became a suffragette. By 1883 she was the editor and publisher of *The Woman's Tribune,* now recognized as one of the primary women's-rights newspapers of the era. By the next year Clara's efforts were recognized by the National Woman Suffrage Association as its "official house organ" and began reaching a national audience for her Beatrice-based publication. American women were granted the constitutional right to vote in 1920 after decades of often acrimonious debate. A complete exhibit about Clara Colby is at the Gage County Historical Society Museum, but the library is a lovely stop anyway for its bronze sculptures and other art.

woman named Beatrice for whom the town is named and why it is pronounced as such (bee·A·tris). The annual Industry Days, held the last Sunday in April, features living-history demonstrations of steam- and gas-powered equipment. A special component of Industry Days is the exhibit of Dempster products made in Beatrice. On permanent display is memorabilia of actor Robert Taylor, who grew up in the area as did Oscar-winning special effects artist John Fulton. Open March 1 through Thanksgiving, Mon through Sat, 9 a.m. to noon and 1 to 5 p.m., and Sun, 1:30 to 5 p.m. Donations are welcome. For more information call (402) 228-1679 or visit gagecountymuseum.info.

Two miles southwest of the town of **Filley** is the **Filley Stone Barn,** which is a part of the Gage County Historical Society complex. This large barn was built by Elijah Filley in 1874, when he became so disgruntled with grasshoppers that he created a structure to keep the pesky critters out. Built of limestone and rock, the barn has four levels and a threshing floor strong enough to "hold a herd of elephants." On the first Saturday of October, the barn is the site of Harvestfest, one of those "step-back-in-time" events where you can see people harvest corn the old-fashioned way, make brooms, and other chores from days gone by. For more information call (402) 228-1679.

For a thoroughly international experience in Beatrice, try a meal at the **Black Crow Restaurant,** at 405 Court St. This beautiful restaurant offers fare that is a far cry from country cooking. Owner and pastry chef Ray Arter trained in Paris and worked at Andiamo's in New York City. He met his wife and co-owner, Kate Ratigan, while they were both working at a restaurant in Vail. The menu frequently features items like rack of lamb with creamy Dijon sauce, pan-seared salmon piccata with capers, roast pork loin with mushrooms and red wine sauce, and creamy garlic polenta. Fresh oysters, fish, and mussels are not your typical small-town offering. The decor is elegant, but you need not be; the attire is casual. Ethnic meals include German, Cajun, Polish, Russian, or Caribbean. The bar is well stocked with imported beer, fine wines, and specialty liquors. The Black Crow is open Tues through Sat. Reservations are recommended. Lunch is served from 11:30 a.m. to 2 p.m.; dinner is from 5:30 to 10 p.m. The telephone number is (402) 228-7200, or visit blackcrowrestaurant.com.

Butler, Seward, and Polk Counties

If you come across three ladies in a broken-down old convertible in **Butler County,** think of the movie *To Wong Foo, Thanks for Everything, Julie Newmar,* which starred Patrick Swayze, Wesley Snipes, and John Leguizamo. This movie was filmed on location in **Loma,** a town so small it isn't even on the map. Loma used to be a thriving community with several businesses, but when the railroad stopped running, it dwindled in population. The only business in town, and one of the few buildings, is the **Loma Tavern,** complete with hitching post for as many as a dozen horses outside. Take the time to enjoy the beautiful view of the surrounding countryside; it's one of the reasons Universal Studios chose to film here. Loma is north of Highway 66 between Valparaiso and Dwight; watch for the small road sign. The Loma Tavern is open from about 7 a.m. to 1 a.m., seven days a week. Come Sundays for a live polka band. Give them a call at (402) 278-2758. About the only other thing in town is **St. Luke's Czech Catholic Shrine,** which pays homage to the Czech immigrants who settled in this area. This picturesque church was built in 1912 and celebrates mass about six times a year. The schedule can be found at holytrinitybrainard.com/st-luke-czech-shrine.

North and west of Loma on Highway 15 is David City, seat of Butler County. David City is notable as the birthplace in 1891 of J. C. Hall, who moved to Kansas City in 1910 and started what is now Hallmark Cards.

Another David City notable is artist Dale Nichols. In 2007, a group of his fans opened the **Bone Creek Museum of Agrarian Art,** which houses an extensive collection of his work; you'll also find material from Thomas Hart Benton, John Steuart Curry, and Beth van Hoesen, and the Fortune Magazine cover collection. Located at 575 E St., admission is free; open Wed through Sun. Call (402) 367-4488 or visit bonecreek.org.

If you're driving along I-80 and stop at one of the rest stops near the town of **Seward** on the Fourth of July and the highway patrol approaches your vehicle, don't worry, you are probably not in trouble.

Seward, a pretty little college town north of I-80 at exit 379, is known as Nebraska's official Fourth of July City. The party on Independence Day here is really one of the best in the state and is attended by about 50,000 people. And the highway patrol gets in on the celebration by "kidnapping" a family to be guests of honor for the day. If kidnapped, you get to be the grand marshals of the parade, get free food all day long, a huge gift basket with lots of goodies, and more.

Another fun thing at this celebration is the breakfast recognizing people who have been married 50 years or longer. Usually more than 100 couples show up. The longest anyone has been married is 72 years.

The **Polk County** community of **Stromsburg** is known as the Swedish Capital of Nebraska. It hosts a colorful Swedish Days festival every year in June, which offers a sweet little carnival and a rowdy beer garden. In other words, something for everyone. Details can be found at theswedishfestival.com. Stromsburg is located about 20 miles north of the York exit on I-80.

York and Fillmore Counties

Plan on spending some time eating in York and Fillmore Counties. In the town of **York** (take the I-80 exit north at Highway 81), you'll find great food at **Chances R,** 124 West Fifth St. Although it is a very pretty place with paneling, nice lighting, and lots of brass, you won't care what it looks like once your order has come. You'll be too busy enjoying your food! Order the chicken and judge for yourself if they do indeed have some of the best pan-fried chicken you've ever eaten. The Sunday brunch is also worthy of the drive. Check out other menu items at chancesryork.com/menu. We guarantee that you will leave with that "Oh sheesh, I ate too much" feeling. The restaurant is open Mon through Sat from 6 a.m. to midnight and Sun and holidays from 8 a.m. to 11 p.m. The telephone number is (402) 362-7755.

How can you not go to a place called House of Meats? There aren't a lot of old-fashioned butcher shops remaining in the state, so there's a certain amount of nostalgia involved in a visit here. We're all so used to plunking down our money at distressingly huge supermarkets or big-box stores with everything from school supplies to lawn chairs that we have a serious disconnect on how the food we eat gets to our dinner plate. This is meat, pure and simple. You might not be equipped to leave with a bunch of steaks, chicken, pork, fish, or traditional Czech sausage, but you might be prepared to choose from good selection of deli cheese for a nosh. The **Milligan House of Meats** is open

York's Annual Peep Show

For decades, York was known as the egg production capital of the United States. Numerous hatcheries produced millions of eggs, shipping them around the country. So think little chicks, Easter eggs, and that sort of thing.

York is also the home of Fred Niblo, one of four founding members of the Motion Picture Academy of Arts and Sciences, the Academy Awards. This all comes together. Hang in there with me.

In the meantime, a wild and crazy woman from Lincoln who had a lively sense of humor became enamored with those seasonal marshmallow candies, a harbinger of spring, called Peeps. They come in pinks and yellows and lavenders and greens and everyone buys them because they are so nice to tuck into Easter baskets, but nobody I know really eats them. But my wild and crazy friend found a purpose for Peeps other than being stuffed in Easter baskets.

Taking off on another harbinger of spring, the Academy Awards (are you making the connection now?), this crazy lady hosted a party she called *A Peep Show.* Guests in attendance were required to bring a tableaux or scene from a nominated movie incorporating Peeps in the scene. Soon, the Academy Award connection disappeared and the Peep Show could re-create any current event that could be captured by little marshmallow chickies and bunnies.

The cruel hands of fate and a disease called cancer took my crazy friend from us way too soon, but her Peep Show lives on in York. Each spring, the Chamber of Commerce hosts a Peep Show, and it's just as crazy as you can imagine, only on a grander scale. There are Peep wardrobes, Peep songs and videos, and Peeps participating in all facets of life. If you can't attend, you can Adopt-A-Peep and you'll receive a Peep in a plastic egg, along with instructions for the care and feeding of your Peep. A portion of the proceeds benefit the local animal shelter. And that would make my friend very, very happy.

To adopt your very own Peep, call (402) 362-5531 or visit the York Chamber website at yorkchamber.org.

Mon through Fri, 8:30 a.m. to 5:30 p.m. and Sat from 8:30 a.m. to noon. The address is 514 Main, and the phone number is (402) 629-4333.

Saline County

When you're in **Wilber,** you're in Czech country and you know it by the storefront signs written in Czech and the music that fills the streets much of the day. Wilber is the National Czech Capital and was designated as such by an act of Congress. Wilber is located at the junction of Nebraska Highways 103 and 41. When you drive into town, you might feel as if you've driven into a small

European village. Visitors are encouraged to "Czech" into the two-story brick **Hotel Wilber,** at Second and Wilson Streets. The most famous visitor to Wilber was Bobby Kennedy, who stopped on a whistle-stop tour during his presidential campaign. In the lobby, the original red-oak woodwork, pressed-tin ceiling, and old oak phone booth evoke images of a bygone era. An old-world-style pub and restaurant and a private beer garden await guests in this century-old B&B. There are ten rooms; rates range from $65 to $85. The rate includes a full, home-cooked breakfast on Sunday and a midnight snack (although "midnight" generally means 8 p.m.). Call (402) 821-2020 for more information.

If your stay at the Hotel Wilber piques your curiosity about all things Czech, take the time to visit the Wilber **Czech Museum,** at 102 West Third St. It contains an outstanding collection of Czech dolls, dishes, laces, and costumes, plus replicas of early immigrant homes and businesses. Visitors are likely to find several women working on quilts in the afternoon sun that streams through the windows. You can also buy a number of books, including a *Love Those Dumplings* cookbook and *Czechoslovak Wit and Wisdom.* You might want to pick up *A Poetic History of Wilber,* a 135-page poem written by Irma Anna Freeouf Ourecky, probably the coolest person in town. Donations are accepted. The museum is open daily March through December 1, except on holidays, from 1 to 4 p.m. The number is (402) 821-2183.

Throughout town, you'll find businesses selling *kolace,* a Czech pastry, and traditional Czech crafts. The Wilber Czech Craft Shop at 216 West Third Street has the best selection of lace, Christmas décor, costumes and more. The store closes during January, February and March, but you can always call (402) 821-2166 if you need something right away. Also, if you're in town on the first weekend of August, it'd be well worth your time to experience the **Czech Festival.** Parades, polka bands, Catholic masses, beer gardens, a carnival, and a plethora of brightly costumed Czech queens from across the nation are just part of the fun. The schedule is posted at nebraskaczechsofwilber.com.

Jefferson County

Jefferson County's history includes all the drama and action of the Old West, with chapters on Kit Carson, John C. Fremont, the Oregon Trail, the Pony Express, and Wild Bill Hickok. **Rock Creek Station State Historical Park,** six miles east of **Fairbury** in rural Jefferson County, is where James Butler "Wild Bill" Hickok started his reputation as a ruthless gun-slinger. One hot July day in 1861, for reasons that have never been determined, Wild Bill fatally shot David McCanles (the owner of Rock Creek Station) and wounded two others in cold blood. Legend has it he went on to kill dozens of people before his own death at age 39 in Deadwood, South Dakota, holding the now-famous Dead Man's Hand of aces and eights during a poker game. Hickok's fame was assured by glorified, exaggerated written accounts of his derring-do in dime novels of the time. At present, Rock Creek Station is an excellent park that covers 350 acres of prairie hilltops, timber-studded creek bottoms, and rugged ravines. This is the first publicly owned site along the Oregon Trail where deep wagon ruts are clearly visible. A visitor center contains artifacts from the days of the Oregon Trail and the Pony Express. Rides in an ox-drawn covered wagon help visitors comprehend the slow and uncomfortable nature of the nineteenth century's mode of travel. The grounds are open year-round for day use. The visitor center is open weekends starting in mid-April and daily from May 1 to mid-Sept. A park permit is required. For more information call (402) 729-5777 or visit outdoornebraska.gov/rockcreekstation.

Another fascinating rural Jefferson County site, 8 miles north and west of Fairbury, is the *marked grave of George Winslow,* one of the rare marked Oregon Trail graves. Winslow is one of the estimated 350,000 people (or one out of seventeen of those persons who started westward) who died on the Oregon/California Trails before reaching his or her destination. According to Merrill J. Mattes' *The Great Platte River Road,* the most common cause of death by far was Asiatic cholera. Drownings when wagons or ferries tipped over were the second-most-common cause of death. Other significant causes of death were being crushed by wagon wheels (many died of head injuries since they slept under the wagons), sustaining fatal injuries while handling domestic animals (becoming snarled in harnesses), and stampedes. Another common cause of death was by accidental gunshot. George Winslow, who had hoped to take advantage of the discovery of gold in California, was a victim of cholera on June 7, 1849. The month before his death, he wrote a letter to his wife in Massachusetts. It read, in part: "I do not worry about myself—then why do you for me? The reports of the gold region here are as encouraging as they are in Massachusetts. Just imagine yourself seeing me return with from $10,000 to $100,000. Your loving husband, George Winslow." A brown rock placed in the marker is the original stone placed on his grave by his brothers-in-law and uncle at the time of his death.

Still more pioneer history is evident in *Steele City,* population 61. Visitors may tour the restored 1880s bank, built from bricks kilned locally, which now houses a museum, a stone blacksmith and stone livery stable, windmills, and old machinery shops, which are open Sun, 2 to 4 p.m., from Memorial Day weekend through the third Sunday in September. Don't miss the uniquely beautiful stone 1881 Baptist Church. The town's population swells to nearly 10,000 on the third weekend of September for the annual Steele City Flea Market.

Located southeast of Fairbury on Nebraska Hwy. 8, Steele City is widely known in some communities as the U.S. terminus of the Keystone Pipeline. More than 600,000 barrels of Canadian crude oil arrive here each day before it is redistributed across the U.S. via other pipelines. If approved, the Keystone XL Pipeline will also pass through Steele City.

Down the road on Hwy. 8 is **Odell,** home of the small, but enjoyable **Old West Trails Center** at 301 Main Street in what was originally the First Commercial Bank of Odell. The focal point is a massive mural created by local artist Dave Reiser, but other exhibits also tell the story of the many pioneers who passed through this area on their way west. The museum is open limited hours on the weekends, so it's best to call ahead at (402) 766-3700.

Keep your eyes open while you're in the area because you just might find an **Odell diamond.** The "diamonds" are actually curious quartz crystals, which are generally pink or clear, measure about ¹⁄₁₆ inch thick, and are perfectly diamond shaped. Three and a half miles south of Odell, on Highway 8, is Diamond Lake Wildlife Management Area where, with a sharp eye and some luck, you'll pick up one of these geologic mementos. Many can still be found even though most of the diamond area was covered with water when a dam was built.

Thayer County

Road-weary travelers can set themselves down on the **world's largest porch swing** in **Hebron.** Well, the swing is not actually on a porch, it's in the city park. But it is big, and it will seat more than twenty adults. After you've rested on the porch swing, explore Thayer County and its well-marked **Oregon Trail** route. Two miles north of Hebron, on Highway 81, is the largest stone marker on the Oregon Trail. As you follow the route, you'll see markers for the location of Thompson's Station, an early trading post, and foundations from the Kiowa Ranch, where early settlers gathered for protection from Native American raids. Remember, when you are on Highway 81 you are on the Pan American Highway, which extends from Winnipeg, Canada, to the southern tip of Chile at Tierra Del Fuego. It is the longest stretch of continuous highway through the Americas.

Also in Hebron is Arrowhead Gardens, an affiliate of the Nebraska State-wide Arboretum.

Merrick and Hamilton Counties

Central City, in **Merrick County,** was at one time called Lone Tree because of a solitary large cottonwood that grew on the banks of the Platte River on the Ox-Bow and California Trails. The tree died as hundreds of tourists either carved their names on it or carried off bits of it as souvenirs. Central City, 20 miles north of I-80 on Highway 14, was the birthplace, in 1910, of acclaimed novelist and photographer Wright Morris. Morris won the Mark Twain Award, the Commonwealth Award for Distinguished Service in Literature, an honorary life membership in the Western Literature Association, and the Mari Sandoz Award for his writing. His photographs have been shown around the world and more than a dozen are on display at his childhood home at 304 D St. The **Lone Tree Literary Society** owns the home and offers it for tours by appointment and for special events. The organization also has access to the Cahow Barbershop in nearby Chapman, a renovated site that is mentioned frequently in Morris' work. He is buried in the cemetery in Chapman. Call (308) 946-3719 or visit wright morris.org for special events. The literary society hosts frequent writing and photography contests with great cash prizes for themes about life in Nebraska.

Aurora, 4 miles north of I-80 at Highway 14 in **Hamilton County,** has two fine museums that should not be missed. The **Plainsman Museum,** 210 Sixteenth St., has a rotunda with eight larger-than-life murals that depict important events in the settling of the Plains. It has an original log cabin, a sod house, a Victorian home, and an early farm home. It has a collection of Native American artifacts and an interesting display about a white Civil War officer, Gen. Delavon Bates, who led a troop of black Union soldiers before settling in Aurora. The movie *Glory* with Denzel Washington and Matthew Broderick is said to be based on his military service. The museum is open all year, Tues–Sat, 9 a.m. to 4 p.m., except major holidays. There's an admission fee. For more information call (402) 694-6531 or visit the museum's website at plainsmanmuseum.org.

Connected to the Plainsman Museum is the **Edgerton Explorit Center,** at 208 Sixteenth St., which is considered to be Nebraska's premier hands-on science center, featuring great interactive displays for people of all ages. This museum is named in honor of hometown boy Dr. Harold Edgerton, who invented the strobe light. With the strobe light Dr. Edgerton is said to have "stopped time" with his now-famous photographs of a bullet piercing an apple and a single drop of milk splashing up to make a beautiful corona. Dr. Edgerton also worked with Jacques Cousteau on the *Calypso* with his sonar device that picked up remains of the Civil War gunship *Monitor* and other famous vessels thought lost forever. All of that is important, but doesn't sound as much fun as making bubbles, does it? That's one of the hands-on scientific demonstrations at Explorit, along with activities to make eggs explode with air pressure, or figure out how a thing like dried ice can actually freeze things. Hours are Mon through Sat, 9 a.m. to 5 p.m.; Sun, 1 to 5 p.m. Admission is charged. Call (402) 694-4032 or visit edgerton.org.

Clay County

You might say that **Clay County** is for the birds—for migrating waterfowl, to be more specific. Clay County is part of the Rainwater Basin, comprised of seventeen south-central counties in an area critical to migrating waterfowl. Sink–like depressions with clay–like bottoms collect rain or runoff water to create natural marshes and lakes in this wetlands area. Most marshes or lakes cover from one to forty acres, but some are as large as 1,000 acres. By 1981 less than 10 percent of the original 4,000 wetlands remained intact; nine of every ten were destroyed either by draining or filling them to make the land more suitable to agriculture. The remaining wetlands, and the nearby Platte River, host one of the most spectacular congregations of migratory birds found on the entire planet. More than a half million sandhill cranes and nearly ten million ducks and geese pause here for several weeks, from late February through early April. Clay County has thirteen waterfowl-production areas, lagoons, and wildlife management areas. Two of the largest, offering breathtaking views of hundreds of thousands of ducks and geese, are the **Harvard Waterfowl Production Area,** east of the community of **Harvard,** and the **Massie Waterfowl Production Area,** south of **Clay Center.**

A large number of Russian German families settled near **Sutton** in eastern Clay County in the 1870s. The **Sutton Historical Society,** located in a 1908-era home at 309 North Way St. and in the house next door, which dates to 1879, documents the history of the Russian German community. The group has also relocated the old Wolfe School, a one-room schoolhouse from near Fairfield, to property behind the museum building. The collection and exhibits are growing every day and include a veteran's room honoring two Medal of Honor winners from Sutton. Hours are Sun from 2 to 5 p.m., but volunteers are around many other times during the week. Feel free to stop in if you see someone there, but Historical Society treasurer Jerry Johnson warns that he may give you a dust mop to help out. Call Jerry for more information at (402) 773-0222.

At 120 South Saunders St. downtown, it may appear that several storefronts have been renovated to the 1920s or so. But upon looking closer, it's primarily a mural across a storefront where Chris Lebe stores a Model A car. He just wants everyone to be able see it and enjoy it like he does. For a closer look, call (402) 773-0283.

If you like ghost stories and ghost towns, go west on Hwy. 41 from Clay Center about 9 miles and watch for signs to Spring Ranch via a county road. Spring Ranch was a little supply center on the Oregon Trail that functioned as a community until the 1940s. Look closely and you'll find the foundations of some old buildings, but it's the bridge over the Little Blue River that locals say is haunted. On March 15, 1885, two siblings, Tom Jones and Elizabeth Taylor, were lynched from the bridge by a mob after several scandalous situations involving Elizabeth, as well as disputes over land and timber rights in the area. It is believed that Elizabeth was the only woman ever lynched in Nebraska.

Nuckolls County

In August 1864 the Sioux and the Cheyenne raided 400 miles of emigrant trails and white settlements. Several sites in Nuckolls County were struck, including "The Narrows," whose name indicates that there was only room for one wagon at a time to pass between the bluffs and the river. More than fifty people were killed, hundreds of freight wagons were destroyed, and women and children were captured. The Indians held the area for several weeks before the U.S. Army intervened. At present, visitors can follow the well-marked route of the trails and learn more from historical markers in Nuckolls County.

If you look for *Angus* on a map, you won't find it (it was 9 miles north of Nora on the Little Blue River), but at one time it was the home of an early-day automobile manufacturing site. The *Angus Automobile Company* began producing the Fuller Car in 1907. The company manufactured several models for three years before closing. A five-passenger touring car, which sold for $2,500, was the top-of-the-line model.

Superior, at the junction of Highways 14 and 8 in southern Nuckolls County, is the birthplace and final resting place of Evelyn Brodstone Vestey. Her story is the quintessential hometown-girl-does-good. The daughter of immigrant parents and childhood friend of Pulitzer–Prize winner Willa Cather, Evelyn graduated from high school at age fourteen, studied stenography and accounting after high school, and in 1895 moved to Chicago, where she earned $12 a week as a stenographer at Vestey Cold Storage. Ultimately, she became an executive of the company and earned $250,000, making her the highest-paid female executive in the world in the 1920s. She traveled internationally, establishing business contacts and settling labor disputes. As a romantic postscript to her career, she accepted Lord William Vestey's proposal of marriage and became Lady Vestey. Throughout her life she remained in close contact with family and friends in Superior. Even in her death she maintains contact with Superior; she's buried in the local cemetery and is, in all likelihood, the only member of British royalty buried in Nebraska. Each Memorial Day weekend the *Lady Vestey Victorian Festival* offers tours of many of the seventy Victorian homes in Superior. The festival also features a tour of a porcelain doll store, a Victorian fashion show, a high tea, and rousing croquet matches. As a result, Superior now calls itself the Victorian Capital of Nebraska.

There's another royalty of sorts in Superior. Very much alive, grinning widely, and sometimes wearing a provocative plaid kilt to formal occasions, native son Lew Hunter is a screenwriting guru. Before "retiring" to Superior, Hunter enjoyed a successful entertainment-industry career at Columbia, Lorimar, Paramount, Disney, NBC, ABC, and CBS as a writer, producer, and executive. He came into his own when he started teaching screenwriting at the University of California, Los Angeles. The list of directors and writers he coached could easily fill several episodes of *Entertainment Tonight*. A few years back he moved home with his wife, Pamela, and started the ***Superior Screenwriting Colony.*** Twice a year screenwriters and potential screenwriters from around the world converge for lessons from Lew. Students live in a huge restored Victorian house where yummy meals are provided by Pamela. On the first night, at a getting-to-know-one-another party, sauerkraut pizza from a local bar and grill has become a Colony favorite. If you've got a screenplay in you yearning to be free, this is the place to get hands-on attention and direction from the best. If you want to know more about Lew's classes (he also travels to teach in England and Eastern Europe), give him a call at (402) 879-3617. Lew's website is lewhunter.com.

Places to Stay in Southeast Nebraska

(All area codes are 402 except where noted otherwise.)

LINCOLN

Rogers House Bed & Breakfast
2145 B St.
476-6961
rogershouseinn.com

NEBRASKA CITY

Arbor Day Farm Lied Conference Center
2700 Sylvan Rd.
873-8733
liedlodge.org

Whispering Pines B&B
Twenty-first Street and Sixth Avenue
873-5850
bbwhisperingpines.com

PAWNEE CITY

My Blue Heaven B&B
1041 Fifth Street
852-3131
bbonline.com/ne/blueheaven

STEINAUER

Convent House B&B
311 East Hickory
869-2230
conventhousebbt.com

WILBER

Hotel Wilber
Second and Wilson Streets
821-2020

HELPFUL SOUTHEAST NEBRASKA WEBSITES

Beatrice
beatricechamber.com

Brownville
brownville-ne.com

Fairbury
fairburyne.gov

Lincoln
lincoln.org

Nebraska City
nebraskacity.com

Plattsmouth
plattsmouthchamber.com

Superior
cityofsuperior.org/chamber

Wahoo
wahoo.ne.us

Wilber
wilberchamberofcommerce.com

York
yorkvisitors.org

Places to Eat in Southeast Nebraska

(All area codes are 402.)

BEATRICE

Scott's Back Alley Eatery (barbecue)
513 Court St.
223-5011
backalleybbq.com

EMERALD

Merle's Food and Drink
(American)
8250 West O St.
474-6435
merlesinemerald.com

LINCOLN

Cornhusker Hotel
(Continental)
333 South Thirteenth St.
474-7474

El Toro (Mexican)
2600 South Forty-eighth
St., Suite 17
488-3939

Grateful Bread (bakery)
1625 South
Seventeenth St.
474-0101

Imperial Palace (Chinese)
707 North Twenty-seventh
St.
474-2688

Lazlo's Brewery & Grill
(American)
210 North Seventh St.
434-5636
lazlosbreweryandgrill.com

Lee's Restaurant
(fried chicken)
1940 West Van Dorn
477-4339
leeschickenlincoln.com

The Mill (coffeehouse)
800 P St.
475-5522
Millcoffee.com

Virginia's Travelers Cafe
(diner)
3820 Cornhusker Hwy.
464-9885

Yia Yia's (pizza)
1423 O St.
477-9166

PLATTSMOUTH

Mom's Cafe (American)
422 Main St.
296-3000

Lewis and Clark Land

Northeast Nebraska, with its rolling, green hills, is defined by the Missouri River on the northern and eastern borders and extends to agricultural lands in the south and the Sandhills area on the west. Some of the earliest recorded historical events in the state occurred in northeast Nebraska. In 1720, a Spanish expedition under the command of Col. Pedro de Vallasur was attacked by Pawnee Indians along the Platte River. French explorers Paul and Peter Mallet crossed the area in 1739–40. Lewis and Clark explored this part of the Louisiana Purchase in 1804. Fur trader Manuel Lisa established a trading post in 1812 in present-day Washington County for the St. Louis Missouri Fur Company. In 1820, the first army base west of the Missouri River, Fort Atkinson, was established to dissuade British interest and to foster settlement of the area. The Mormon Trail crosses northeast Nebraska north of the Platte River, and the old Lincoln Highway, the first transcontinental route for cars, roughly follows the path of Highway 34 across northeast Nebraska. Take advantage of the history as well as the interesting cities and small towns of this beautiful part of Nebraska.

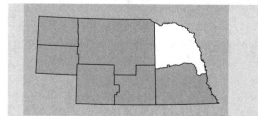

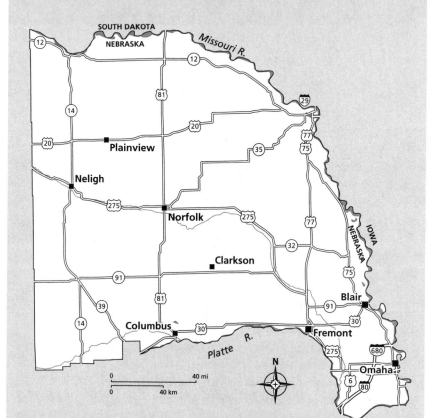

SOUTH DAKOTA
NEBRASKA

Missouri R.

12

12

81

20

14

35

77
75

20

Plainview

Neligh

275

Norfolk

275

77

IOWA
NEBRASKA

32

75

Clarkson

91

Blair

81

91

30

39

Columbus

30

Fremont

14

Platte R.

275

680

N

6

Omaha

80

0   40 mi
0   40 km

29

Douglas County

Omaha is Nebraska's largest city, with a population of more than 500,000 within the city limits and more than 900,000 in the metropolitan area. More than a 1.1 million people live within a 50-mile radius of this dynamic and energetic city. The *Old Market,* east of downtown near the Missouri River, is a beautiful area of redeveloped warehouses on brick streets, which belie its Midwestern setting. Delighted visitors often exclaim that the Old Market could be in New York, or Chicago, or New Orleans, or even Europe. Boutiques, clothing stores, bookstores, an artists' cooperative and gallery, antiques stores, galleries, brew pubs, bars with live music, florists, coffee shops, record stores, and live theater are all available in the Old Market. You'll also find one of the few remaining hat makers in the United States. Restaurant experiences run the gamut from exceedingly elegant to very casual, with prices set accordingly.

Just east of the Old Market, the Riverfront and Lewis & Clark Landing offers dining, strolling, and biking. Take a gondola ride at the nearby *Heartland of America Park.* While you're in Omaha you might want to take in a couple of nightspots featuring indie music. Move over Seattle, Omaha is fast becoming known as a hub for indie and alternative music. Omaha's reputation as a burgeoning art center is reflected in an artists' center and studio spaces called the *Hot Shops Art Center* at 1301 Nicholas St. near the Old Market. More than 80 studio artists work here, but the focal point is the bronze sculptors', blacksmiths', and tile workers' studio. The center offers classes throughout the year and hosts two open houses, one the first weekend in December and the other the first weekend in May. But the public is welcome to come in any time and watch the artists work. Call (402) 342-6452 or visit hotshopsartcenter.com.

Omaha is a veritable restaurant mecca. All over town you'll find steak houses, Italian, Creole, Greek, Persian, Southwestern, Mexican, French, Chinese, burger places, pizza places (try Zio's), and pasta places. You can't throw a stick without hitting a great restaurant, coffee shop, or ice cream parlor.

Because Omaha is the largest city in Nebraska, there are many attractions that are more than worth a visit. This book is for off-the-beaten path sites, but a few key attractions will be mentioned briefly. The *Henry Doorly Zoo,* 3701 South Tenth St., is consistently ranked as among the very best zoos in the United States. If you need a testimonial, *Family Fun* magazine ranked the zoo as the best family spot in America, ahead of both Walt Disney World and Disneyland. The annual number of visitors, approximately 1.6 million, is as large as the entire population of the state! This incredible zoo covers 104 acres and has the world's largest enclosed rain forest, a free-flight aviary, a truly wonderful aquarium, where you walk through a glasslike tunnel as sharks and

FAVORITE ATTRACTIONS IN NORTHEAST NEBRASKA

(All area codes are 402 unless noted otherwise.)

Ashfall Fossil Beds State Historical Park
2 miles west and 6 miles north of Royal
893-2000
ashfall.unl.edu

Cuthills Vineyards
3 miles west on H&N Blvd.
Pierce
329-6774
cuthills.com

Fontenelle Forest Nature Center
1111 North Bellevue Blvd.
Bellevue
731-3140
fontenelleforest.org

John G. Neihardt Center
Elm and Washington Streets
Bancroft
648-3388
neihardtcenter.org

Louis E. May Museum
1643 North Nye Ave.
Fremont
721-4515
maymuseum.com

Reeder Originals Art Gallery
115 Norfolk Ave.
Norfolk
379-0611

manta rays swim around you, an IMAX theater, and North America's largest cat complex. The Desert Dome has a daylight and nocturnal display. A large gorilla complex that allows gorillas to roam free while humans are behind glass and six African elephants that roam on 28 acres of grasslands are among the highlights, but every aspect of this zoo sets the highest bar for education about and care for animals and their habitats. The zoo is open daily from 8:30 a.m. to 5 p.m. in the summer months and 10 a.m. to 4 p.m. in the winter months. The zoo is closed on Thanksgiving and Christmas. Admission is adjusted seasonally to entice you to enjoy the animals even in the winter months. Call (402) 733-8401 or visit the website at omahazoo.com.

Just north of the zoo is *Lauritzen Gardens—Omaha's Botanical Center.* The visitor center is beautiful, with a huge seasonal flower display, a cafe, a great gift shop, and a light-filled library furnished with Mission furniture. The outside boasts 100 acres with18 stunning garden areas. The rose garden, when in bloom, is a highlight. The model railroad garden, which is open May through October, has seven model railroads running and continues to grow. They are open daily (except winter holidays) from 9 a.m. to 5 p.m., and the summer garden twilight strolls allow for opportunities to see the gardens until 8 p.m. The address is 100 Bancroft St. Admission fluctuates with the season, but, believe me, there's plenty to see here even in the dead of a Nebraska winter. The phone number is (402) 346-4002, or visit lauritzengardens.org. Follow the garden on Facebook and Twitter for special admission prices and programs.

Another great attraction is the *Joslyn Art Museum* at 2200 Dodge St. It has one of the nation's finest Western art collections (with a large collection of Swiss artist Karl Bodmer's watercolors and prints, which were made during his 1832–34 journey to the Missouri River frontier) plus classic and modern works. The collection is all housed in a beautiful Italian marble building and includes Rembrandts, Jackson Pollocks, and other masters of art. A sculpture garden and Children's Discovery Garden, filled with bright, colorful, and imaginative sculpture designed to inspire creativity in young people, are among the outdoor treasures. The garden is always free. If you visit on the first Friday of the month, take advantage of "First Friday JAM," which includes music, cocktails, and hors d'oeuvres. The museum is open Tues through Sat from 10 a.m. to 4 p.m. and Sun from noon to 4 p.m. It is closed on Mon and major holidays. Admission is free. Browse Joslyn's website, joslyn.org, or call (402) 342-3300.

Girls and Boys Town, at 137th and West Dodge Road, is a lovely stop for a variety of reasons. Started in 1917 as a shelter for homeless boys by Father Edward J. Flanagan, Girls and Boys Town is now home to youths of both sexes: in August 2000 the residents voted to change the name to Girls and Boys Town. The fascinating history of Girls and Boys Town is told in the nicely designed Hall of History. Be sure to see Spencer Tracy's portrayal of Father Flanagan for which he won the Best Actor Academy Award in the 1938 movie *Boys Town.* The visitor center has a gift shop and cafeteria. A particularly fun spot in the visitor center is the Stamp Collection Center. In addition to serving as a fund-raiser for Girls and Boys Town programs, this showcases stamps designed by children over the years. The grounds are peaceful and inspirational, especially the rose garden, adjacent to Father Flanagan's house. The Bible Garden, which features 150 plants mentioned in the Bible, is shaped like a Gothic stained glass window. The entire village is now a National Historic Landmark District. Open daily from 7:30 a.m. to 4:30 p.m. Call (800) 625-1400 or (402) 498-1140 or visit boystown.org.

Sports lovers may like to plan a trip to Omaha for a Lancers hockey game (lancers.com) or a baseball game with the Omaha Storm Chasers (m.milb.com/t541), a minor-league farm team of the American League Kansas City Royals. By far the biggest sporting event in Omaha is the NCAA College World Series for about 10 days each June at the TD AmeriTrade Park. This tournament has showcased the best in college baseball in Omaha since 1950. For tickets and information about the many activities that take place throughout Omaha at this time, visit cwsomaha.com.

Omaha is also home to a delightful variety of cultural activities that include symphony, opera, ballet, community theater (the **Omaha Community Playhouse** is the largest in the country and is where Marlon Brando and Henry Fonda first trod the stage), dinner theater, and cutting-edge original productions from nationally acclaimed theaters. For more information on these and other attractions in Omaha, please contact Visit Omaha at (866) 937-6624, (402) 444-4660, or visitomaha.com.

El Museo Latino is a labor of love for executive director Magdelana García. After completing a master's degree in museum science, she was offered a job at the Guggenheim Museum in New York City but chose instead to return to Omaha (where she had moved with her family from Mexico City at the age of ten) to start one of the few Latino cultural museums in the Midwest. García and a dedicated crew of volunteers transformed a former printing business into gallery space in just thirty-four days to open on Cinco de Mayo in 1993. Since then they've moved to a larger space at 4701 South Twenty-fifth St. to allow for additional exhibitions, classrooms, and space for the resident dance troupe. Changing exhibitions in the gallery feature artwork created by people from other countries as well as works of local Latino artists. The museum is open Mon, Wed, and Fri from 10 a.m. to 5 p.m.; Tues and Thurs from 1 to 5 p.m.; and Sat from 10 a.m. to 2 p.m. Admission is $5 for adults and $4 for seniors and students. Call (402) 731-1137 or visit elmuseolatino.org.

If you like jazz, you'll love the **Love's Jazz and Arts Center** at 2510 North Twenty-fourth St. This facility, which opened in 2005, is named for Preston Love, a prominent alto saxophonist from Omaha. Through workshops, exhibits, and special programs, the museum and center showcase the history and culture of African Americans in the arts. The center is open Tues through Sat 11 a.m. to 5 p.m. Admission is $10 for adults and $7 for students. Call (402) 502-5291 or find out about special programs and exhibits at ljac.org.

Joe Tess Place, at 5424 South Twenty-fourth St., has been around since the 1930s and is still going strong. The neighborhood favorite is known for fresh carp and catfish flown in from freshwater lakes around the Midwest. As you enter Joe Tess Place, you're greeted by a big fountain and pond filled with live fish, and the walls, bathrooms, even the ceilings are covered with fish décor. Other than that, things are pretty simple at Joe Tess Place. If you don't like fish, there's also chicken on the menu, and some pretty fabulous desserts like pineapple upside down cake and a buttery Bundt cake. The only thing that has changed in nearly 80 years is the recent switch to trans fat–free cooking oils for the fried items. The live fish market, open Tuesday through Saturday, is hugely popular, as is the take-out window. Joe Tess Place is open every day except Mon, starting at 11 a.m. Most nights, they close at 9 p.m., but on Fri and Sat, they're open until 10 p.m. The telephone number is (402) 733-4638, and the website is joetessplace.com.

While you're in south Omaha on Twenty-fourth Street, be sure to check out the international flavor of the area. There are lots of Mexican restaurants (*El Alamo,* at 4917 South Twenty-fourth St., and the nearby *American G.I. Forum,* at 2002 N St., are wonderful) and bakeries, a German restaurant, a Vietnamese restaurant, a Salvadoran/Mexican restaurant, and plenty of American-style restaurants.

The *General Crook House,* at Thirtieth and Fort Streets, provides an interesting stop for history aficionados and plant lovers alike. Brig. Gen. George Crook, who had his headquarters at Fort Omaha, lived in this large Victorian brick home from 1878 to 1882 while serving as commander of the Department of the Platte. General Crook distinguished himself in the Civil War and later became known as a famous Native American fighter. He became involved in the trial of Standing Bear, a Ponca chief who was arrested in Nebraska after illegally leaving Indian Territory (Oklahoma) while attempting to fulfill his oldest son's dying request: to be buried at home on traditional Ponca lands in northeast Nebraska. Although General Crook was named a defendant for the

ANNUAL EVENTS IN NORTHEAST NEBRASKA

(Call ahead to verify dates; all area codes are 402 unless noted otherwise.)

Great American Comedy Festival
Norfolk, mid-June
374-8004
greatamericancomedyfestival.com

Czech Festival & Rodeo
Clarkson, third weekend in June
892-3331 or 649-8777

Bluegrass Festival
Lyons, July 4th
687-2710

John C. Fremont Days
Fremont, second weekend in July
727-9428
Johncfremontdays.org

Chicken Show
Wayne (an eggstravaganza eggstrordinaire), mid-July
375-2240
chickenshow.com

Powwow
Winnebago, late July
878-3100

Last Fling 'til Spring Car Show
West Point, third weekend of Sept
372-3390
roadgems.com

Holiday Lights Festival
Omaha, late Nov through Dec
345-5401, ext 105
holidaylightsfestival.org

U.S. government, his sympathies were solidly on the side of Standing Bear and the twenty-nine other Poncas who were arrested with him. During the 1879 trial Standing Bear made the following emotional appeal: "My hand is not the color of yours. But if I pierce it, I shall feel pain. If you pierce your hand, you also feel pain. The blood that will flow from mine will be the same color as yours. I am a man. The same God made us both." The trial resulted in a court decision (astonishing for the times) that a Native American was indeed a "person" under the law, with the right of habeas corpus protection. General Crook's house is restored to its original poshness. The grounds are a monument to the Victorian-era passion for gardening. The incredibly manicured Victorian Garden is the only one to be found in the area. In bloom most of the growing season, there are hundreds of exotic plants and flowers with names like rugosa rose, love-lies-bleeding, and elephant ears. Afternoon teas, which must be scheduled in advance, are a delightfully authentic way to experience the home and garden. The house is open Mon through Fri from 10 a.m. to 4 p.m. and Sat and Sun from 1 to 4 p.m. Admission is $6 for adults, $5 for seniors and for children ages six to twelve. Call (402) 455-9990. The website is douglascohistory.org/crook-house-museum.

Another important historical site is the ***Mormon Pioneer Winter Quarters and Mormon Pioneer Cemetery,*** at North Ridge Drive (Thirty-second Street) and State Street. This settlement, near the town of Florence in north Omaha, was home to up to 4,000 Mormons who wintered here to make preparations for their continued trip west after being forced from Nauvoo, Illinois, in 1846. More than 800 lots were laid out with log cabins, soddies, and dugout dwellings. Part of the water-powered gristmill they built still stands. More than 600 people, mostly infants and the elderly, died during the exceedingly harsh winter of 1846. They also died from a lack of fresh fruits and vegetables and from diseases of biblical proportions. The visitor center and cemetery recount the dramatic story of a strong-willed people who were determined at all costs to reach a promised land where they could freely practice their religion. The beautiful visitor center is open year-round from 9 a.m. to 9 p.m. If you're visiting around Christmas, do not miss the display of dozens of intricate gingerbread houses. There is no admission fee, and the telephone number is (402) 453-9372. Learn more at lds.org/locations/mormon-trail-center-at-historic-winter-quarters.

Malcolm Little, a baby boy born in Omaha in 1925, eventually became internationally known as Malcolm X, a leader in the fight for the racial equality of African Americans. The ***Malcolm X Birthsite,*** at 3448 Pinkney St., consists of eleven acres that now include a small welcome center and a historic marker that commemorates his life and work. An outdoor amphitheater is used for

OTHER ATTRACTIONS WORTH SEEING IN NORTHEAST NEBRASKA

(All area codes are 402.)

GENOA

Genoa Indian School
107 North Walnut
993-6636 or 993-6055
This school once sprawled across 160 acres and had 600 students. It operated for fifty years and closed in 1934, but the shop building has been restored and is open to visitors.

NIOBRARA

Niobrara State Park
857-3373
Enjoy scenic wonder and float trips on the Missouri River.
outdoornebraska.gov/niobrara/

OMAHA

Bemis Center for Contemporary Arts
724 South Twelfth St.
341-7130
bemiscenter.org

Durham Western Heritage Museum
801 South Tenth St.
444-5071
durhammuseum.org

Freedom Park
2497 Freedom Park Rd.
345-1959
omaha.net/places/freedom-park
(Don't miss the USS *Hazard* minesweeper and the USS *Marlin* SST-2 submarine.)

Omaha Children's Museum
500 South Twentieth St.
342-6164
ocm.org

Omaha River City Star Riverboat
Miller's Landing on the Riverfront
Relax and enjoy the Missouri River on this lovely paddleboat.
(866) 227-7827
rivercitystar.com

programs about racial equality. There is no admission fee. Call (402) 455-9200 and keep up with news on the construction of a community center at malcolm xfoundation.org.

Another national leader born in Omaha was Leslie Lynch King, who would become the thirty-eighth president of the United States. Born in 1913, his parents divorced when he was two years old; his mother, Dorothy King, moved to Michigan and ultimately married Mr. Gerald Rudolf Ford, who adopted the boy and gave him his name. ***President Gerald Ford's Birthsite,*** at Thirty-second Avenue and Woolworth Avenue, is now a small park with the colorful Betty Ford Rose Garden, White House memorabilia, a replica of the house where Ford was born (it was razed after being heavily damaged in a 1971 fire), and displays on Nebraska history. The telephone number is (402) 444-5920, which can be called on weekdays. Hours are 7:30 a.m. to dusk daily. Admission is free.

In west Omaha you'll find a "jewel" of a store. **Borsheim's,** in Regency Court at 120 Regency Parkway, is the largest single-unit retail jewelry store in the country, and also the one with the greatest volume. In addition to jewelry you'll find fine gifts—for yourself or that special someone—that include silver, crystal, china, watches, and decorative items. Borsheim's started small in 1870 and grew to its present position due to a well-deserved reputation for quality, selection, and good prices. It has customers from all over the world. It is now owned by Berkshire Hathaway Corporation, which is headed by investment wizard and Omaha resident Warren Buffett, the second-richest man in America. The richest man in America, Bill Gates, bought his wife's engagement ring from Borsheim's. The hours are Mon and Thurs, 10 a.m. to 8 p.m.; Tues, Wed, and Fri, 10 a.m. to 6 p.m.; and Sat, 10 a.m. to 5:30 p.m. Call (402) 391-0400 or (800) 642-4438 for a complimentary catalog. borsheims.com is the website that showcases much of the store's offerings.

If you're an outdoors kind of person, or if you want to stretch your legs on some great forested trails (who said Nebraska doesn't have trees?), consider a stop at the **Neale Woods Nature Center,** 14323 Edith Marie Ave. The Neale Woods Nature Center is a 554-acre environmental oasis of hilltop forests, native prairies, and riverside woodlands along the Missouri River. There are 9 miles of trails, live animal exhibits, displays on plant and animal life, and a butterfly garden. Nebraska's largest observatory, with eight telescopes, provides stargazing and astronomy programs. Hours are Mon through Sun from 8 a.m. to 5 p.m. The nature center is not staffed, so admission of $5 for adults, $4 for seniors, and $3 for children is by the honor system. The telephone number is (402) 731-3140.

Sarpy County

Bellevue, south of Omaha, Nebraska's oldest community, started in 1822 when the Missouri Fur Company established a permanent post here. It got its name from Manuel Lisa, a Spanish explorer who liked the scenery and dubbed it "Belle View." Other early visitors were Karl Bodmer (the Swiss artist whose work is on display at Joslyn Art Museum in Omaha), explorers Maj. Steven Long and Gen. John C. Fremont, and Kit Carson. Free and guided weekday tours of several historic sites, including a log cabin built in the 1830s (making it one of the oldest intact structures in Nebraska), a railroad depot, Fontenelle Bank (built in 1857 and the state's oldest public building), the Presbyterian Church, and an early cemetery with the grave of Big Elk, the last full-blooded chief of the Omaha tribe, can be arranged by calling the Sarpy County Tourism Office at (402) 332-5771, or visit gosarpy.com. They like it if you can call ahead of time.

The ***Fontenelle Forest Nature Center,*** at 1111 North Bellevue Blvd., provides another chance to experience nature. It has 26 miles of hiking trails (1 mile of which is an equal-access boardwalk) on 1,300 acres and serves as a wildlife and environmental sanctuary that provides lots of glimpses of woodland creatures. The center, with 26,000 feet of exhibits, is open daily from 8 a.m. to 5 p.m. The admission fee is $9.50 for adults, $8.50 for seniors, and $7.50 for children ages three through eleven. Call (402) 731-3140 for more information. The website is fontenelleforest.org.

Washington County

Washington County is the location of the first U.S. military post west of the Missouri River. ***Fort Atkinson,*** now a state historical park, was built in 1820 on the recommendation of reports from the Lewis and Clark expedition. The Lewis & Clark Expedition Bicentennial observation in 2004 was marked by impressive sculptures installed in two locations at the park. (Both pieces are courtesy of the Washington County Historical Association.) Near the visitor center is a life-sized re-creation of the first official meeting between the Expedition and Native Americans. The bronze sculpture, called *First Council,* depicts that historic meeting on August 3, 1804, with figures of Lewis and Clark, two Otoe-Missouria chiefs, an interpreter, and the Newfoundland dog, Seaman. A second installation, down the bluff via a wooded path, is a large silver disk representing a compass atop which rests a peace pipe and a feather. This second piece is located about as close to the actual site of that meeting as anyone can determine. Fort Atkinson State Park is located just off Highway 75 in the town of ***Fort Calhoun.*** Fort Atkinson was built to keep Canadians and the French and Spanish out of the territory, to protect the early fur trade and river traffic, and to foster relations with Native Americans. Perhaps this last function did not manifest itself; when the soldiers left in 1827, the Native Americans burned the fort to the ground, and nearly thirty years later the early settlers of Fort Calhoun salvaged what little they could for building materials. At its peak Fort Atkinson had a school (the first in Nebraska) and a library, a kiln, a brickyard, and a sawmill. Farming also produced food for the 1,000 soldiers and their families. The crops and vegetables produced came as somewhat of a surprise—after all, this was supposed to be the Great American Desert. In any case, nothing was left but a field until local citizens rallied to have the site saved in the 1960s, and the Nebraska Game and Parks Commission joined the effort. Archaeological digs, conducted in the 1970s by the Nebraska Historical Society, led to the discovery of the location of the original buildings. The present buildings are located on the same spot and look just as the originals once did. Fort Atkinson State Historical Park makes history come alive—the visitor center has displays and interpretive materials, and periodic living-history demonstrations are held throughout the summer. Park grounds are open year-round, and the visitor center is open daily from 8 a.m. to 5 p.m. during the summer and on weekends in Sept and Oct from 10 a.m. to 5 p.m. A park entry permit is available on site. For details call (402) 468-5611 or visitoutdoornebraska.gov/fortatkinson/. North of Fort Atkinson State Historical Park is the **DeSoto National Wildlife Refuge,** east of Blair across the Missouri River on Highway 30. The refuge encompasses land in both Nebraska and Iowa. In spring and fall the refuge is host to thousands of migratory ducks and geese. Bald eagles are not uncommon. In the fall, between 300,000 and 600,000 snow geese and blue geese make a stop on their southward migration between their Hudson Bay nesting grounds in Canada and their Gulf Coast homes. (Where do you think the term "snowbird," for people who head south from cold climes for the winter, came from?) Glass-enclosed viewing provides comfy seating for wildlife observers. If you prefer, you can get out and hike or drive around the grounds. The visitor center has informative wildlife displays and videos, and it also has a beautifully designed museum with artifacts from the steamboat *Bertrand,* which sank in the Missouri River in 1865 on its way to supply mining camps in the Montana Territory. It was discovered in 1968, and most of the salvaged items, which were encased and preserved in Missouri mud, are on display. The 200,000 reclaimed objects—everything from canned goods to liquor, clothes, shoes, buttons, cooking utensils, cutlery, dishes, and mining equipment—are showcased in this wonderful museum. The entry fee is $3 per vehicle unless you have a duck stamp or someone in your car has a federal recreation passport. The refuge is open daily except for federal holidays. For more information call the visitor center between 9 a.m. and 4:30 p.m. at (712) 388-4800.

Blair, west of the DeSoto National Wildlife Refuge on Highways 91 and 75, is the site of the **Tower of the Four Winds** in Black Elk/Neihardt Park, which overlooks the Dana College campus. Built to promote world peace, brotherhood, and humanity, the tower portrays the message of Black Elk, an Oglala Sioux holy man and visionary. He is said to have envisioned a radiant person with outstretched arms in a blessing to all people in front of the tree of life. The 45-foot tower, made from native rock and covered with a 50,000-piece mosaic, represents the messiah-like figure of Black Elk's vision. Learn more about it benpark.org. (See the listing for Bancroft in Cuming County for additional information about Black Elk and John Neihardt.)

Dodge County

Fremont, located at the junction of Highways 77 and 30, is an attractive community of approximately 26,000 situated near the Platte River. It was named for Gen. John C. Fremont, an early explorer of the West who earned the nickname of the "Great Pathfinder." If you prefer your path to end at an antiques store, the downtown area is thick with them. Spend some time doing your own exploring, and you'll see why Fremont is becoming known as the antiques capital of eastern Nebraska. Seven antiques stores represent nearly one hundred dealers and include **Dime Store Days** (402-727-0580), with forty dealers at 109 East Sixth; **Park Avenue Antiques** (402-721-1157), with twenty-five dealers, at Fifth and Park; and **Yankee Peddlers West** (402-721-7800), with antiques, art, and books, at 141 East Sixth.

Nebraska has a wonderful heritage of quilting, and one of the best shops in the state for fabrics and finished quilts is **Country Traditions** in Fremont. Owner Leslie Main is the leader of the Nebraska Independent Fabric Shops, and her 4,000-square-foot building at 413 Main St. is filled with more than 4,000 bolts of fabric and some intriguing gifts for quilters. She has also coordinated the statewide shop hop for three years, so she can tell you just about anything you want to know about quilting in Nebraska. The shop is open seven days a week. Call Leslie and her staff at (402) 721-7752 or browse a bit at country traditionsonline.com.

Bryson's Airboat Tours started when a guy just wanted to do something nice for a little girl with cancer. She had never been on an airboat and wanted to ride on one before she died. Mr. Bryson had a small boat for his own personal use and took that little girl on the ride of her life. And then another child wanted to ride and another cancer patient. And before long, the Brysons had bought commercial airboats and begun this wonderful sightseeing business along the Platte River. An airboat is a very ecologically sound manner to explore the river because of the minimal disruption of the water and it doesn't seem to frighten the wildlife. The Brysons can take as many as eleven people on one boat, and it's very accessible for those in wheelchairs or with mobility issues. They have a great little picnic spot on a sandbar where guests can play volleyball, barbecue, and enjoy the beauty of the Platte River. Rates vary and the Brysons will work with you for whatever you want to do. Call them at (402) 968-8534 or visit brysonsairboattours.com.

Before leaving Dodge County, take Highway 91 west from just north of Scribner to the village of **Dodge,** the Baseball Capital of Nebraska. But you won't find much evidence of baseball unless it's a summer night and the home team is challenging what will likely be the loser. Dodge has had a semi-pro team since the 1940s, and a number of players today have retired in Dodge after time spent in the major leagues, simply because the spirit of baseball is so strong here. Check the schedule at leaguelineup.com/dcbl.

While in Dodge, stop at *Eat,* a great restaurant housed in a former bank building, which sat empty for about sixty years after the Great Depression closed many banks. You pay your bill, of course, at a teller window. And before you leave, go into the vault to check out the antiques and crafts. Eat is open seven days a week, 8 a.m. to 2 p.m., except on Friday and Saturdays when they stay open until 8 p.m. The telephone number is (402) 693-2292.

Burt and Thurston Counties

Oakland, on Highways 77 and 32 in *Burt County,* is a pretty little town of about 1,200 people with a decidedly Swedish heritage. Many homes display the traditional Swedish *dahla* horses, and the downtown area has businesses and street signs replete with Swedish touches. While you're in Oakland, take a *Troll Stroll* in the park along a path lined with wooden trolls or visit the *Swedish Heritage Center,* at 301 North Charde Ave. Swedish crystal, linens, and needlework brought by pioneers are among the articles on display. The Heritage Center is open Tues and Thurs afternoons and Sat mornings. Call (402) 685-5101 if you'd like to visit at another time.

Thurston County is rich in Native American culture and history. It is the site of the *Omaha Indian Reservation* and the *Winnebago Indian Reservation.* The Omaha Tribe of Nebraska hosts an annual powwow in *Macy,* on Highway 75, during the first full moon in August. It is the oldest continuous harvest celebration in the state (the first recorded one was held in 1805). The

River Lair

Robber's Cave used to be bigger, but time and erosion have turned it into just a small cutout in the sandy banks of the Missouri. It is said to be where river pirates ambushed trading vessels, stealing furs and supplies. It is also said to have once been a hideout of Jesse and Frank James after fleeing the disastrous raid on a Northfield, Minnesota, bank. But at least two other places in South Dakota make the same claim, so take Jesse James lore with a grain of salt. To get there, take Highway 75 Southeast of Winnebago for 4 miles, then turn east 1½ miles on County Road 852. The trail to the river and the cave is there, which can be muddy. The trail is on private tribal land, but locals fish there.

powwow begins on Thursday and ends on Sunday. For more information on the Omaha Tribe of Nebraska, call (402) 837-5391.

Overlooking the Missouri River near Macy is *Blackbird Hill,* the burial site of the Omaha Chief Blackbird. Nearby is *Robber's Cave,* in a sandstone bluff, which, legend holds, was the hideout for river bandits and the notorious James gang. The Winnebago Tribe of Nebraska hosts an annual powwow in Veterans Park in *Winnebago,* on Highway 77, on the last full weekend in July for four full days. For more information about the Winnebago Tribe of Nebraska, call (402) 878-2272. There is an admission charge for both powwows.

The community of *Walthill,* on Highway 77, has a very interesting museum at the *Dr. Susan LaFlesche Picotte Center.* Dr. Picotte was the nation's first Native American woman to become a medical doctor. The daughter of a chief who believed that learning the ways of the whites was a means of survival, Dr. Picotte was educated in the East and came home to dedicate her life to working among her people in the early 1900s. She practiced medicine in the hospital that now is a museum on the National Register of Historic Places as well as a National Historic Landmark. Each September the Susan LaFlesche Picotte Day is held to honor her work, with speakers, cultural activities, and exhibits. The Picotte Center is available for tours. Call (402) to arrange one; they're free.

lovers'leap

Visit *Blackbird Hill* and you may see a ghost or two. Legend has it that two men loved the same woman. The preferred man went hunting, and those who went with him returned to say that he accidentally drowned in the Missouri. The woman married the other man. Some years went by, and one day the presumed-drowned man returned. The husband feared his wife would leave him, so he cut her throat and leapt from Blackbird Hill. Some say the area where she bled to death never grew grass again. As for the worried husband, can you hear that plaintive and oh-so-faint ghostly moaning?

Dakota and Dixon Counties

The *O'Conner House Museum Complex,* 2 miles east of *Homer* off Highway 77 on a gravel road in *Dakota County,* makes a pleasant stop in northeast Nebraska. The O'Conner House is a luxurious fourteen-room mansion that took ten years to complete between 1865 and 1875. It has a curved staircase, a large Italian marble fireplace, and eight bedrooms on the second floor. The O'Conner House has a special summer social in July, elaborate decorations in each room for the Christmas Tour, and Open House on the first and second

Tomb with a View

Blackbird Hill is the final resting place of Omaha Chief Blackbird. An outstanding warrior and even greater negotiator with early French and Spanish traders, he became a rich man from the fur trade, as did many in his tribe. However, his dealings with the white man also earned him a few enemies. It is said that he was taught by traders how to use arsenic and thus was able to rule through intimidation—after "predicting" terrible deaths for his enemies. He died, ironically enough, from a white man's disease when a smallpox epidemic swept through the tribe in the early 1800s. As he lay dying, he asked that his body be placed upon his favorite horse and that together they be buried on a bluff to enable them to view a 30-mile stretch of the Missouri River. Lewis and Clark passed by in 1804 and mentioned this site in their journals. In 1832 the painter George Catlin climbed up and took it upon himself to root around, whereupon he found a human skull presumed to be that of Chief Blackbird. The skull is now at the Smithsonian. Blackbird Hill is off Highway 75 between Decatur (the second-oldest town in the state) and Macy. Watch for signs leading east to the Missouri River and Blackbird Hill.

weekends in November. The one-room Combs School, located next to the mansion, is where modern kids are taught readin', 'ritin', and 'rithmetic, and it is where a typical pioneer school day is re-created, which is authentic down to lunch from a syrup-pail bucket. West of the school is the Museum-Machinery Building, which houses antique farm machinery and office equipment. All the sites are open for visitors each Sun from 2 to 4 p.m. in June, July, and Aug; donations accepted. Living-history classes are offered at the Combs School in May. For more information contact the Dakota County Historical Society at (402) 698-2538; dakotacountyhistoricalsociety.com.

Wakefield has a great theater company that's been around since 1992. And if you're in town when the **Little Red Hen Theatre** has a production, do make time to enjoy the show. Four major plays are produced each year, and fine-arts activities are offered year-round at 316 Main St. The telephone number for the Little Red Hen Theatre is (402) 287-2818, or visit littleredhentheatre.com.

To get to **Dixon,** your next stop, from Wakefield, you'll need to do a little backtracking. Go south 2 miles on Highway 16, turn west on Highway 35, go 8 miles to Highway 15, and then turn north for another 11 miles. Hungry now? Then stop for burgers and pizza at **Euni's Palace** at Second and Conway. Owner Euni Diediker says that you can't miss it, since there are only two businesses in the entire town—hers and the grain elevator. On busy Sunday evenings you might have to wait a bit for one of her famous pizzas. Choose from hamburger, sausage, pepperoni, combo, or supreme. The average American consumes approximately forty-six slices of pizza a year; make it a point to have several of them at Euni's. When asked why people come from hundreds of miles away to eat her pizzas, Euni simply says, "Because they're good." They must be, since her little pizza oven has been known to crank out nearly fifty pizzas in one night. She's closed on Monday, but open for lunch and dinner the rest of the week. Euni's original restaurant burned down in 1987, and not long after that the only gas station burned, too. So make sure you're not running on empty. The gas station has not been rebuilt. Euni's telephone number is (402) 584-9309 or you can look her up on Facebook.

Now you'll find yourself not only stuffed with pizza, but in a quandary. This is because you'll want to eat again just a few miles away at **Bob's Bar** in **Martinsburg.** Martinsburg is northeast of Dixon on Highways 9 and 16. The claim to fame at Bob's Bar is a huge hamburger, weighing in at nearly a pound. You needn't ask "Where's the beef?" but you might well be tempted to ask "Where's the plate?" since it will have pretty much disappeared under the burger. Like Euni's, people come from miles around for the food, although the waitress claims there's no secret to the burger's preparation. "We just cook it," she said. One suspects she might be related to modest-about-the-food Euni. But it's obvious from the number of patrons that there's something indefinably magic going on in the kitchen of this old two-story building. Bob's is open every single day from 7:30 a.m. to 1 a.m., even on holidays. The number is (402) 945-2995.

Dixon County offers outdoor activities at **Ponca State Park,** on the Missouri near the community of **Ponca** (take 26E 2 miles north out of town). The park overlooks the only unchannelized section of the Missouri, giving a glimpse of the untamed river before

theansweris outthere

Watch the nighttime summer sky. Do you feel like someone, or something, is watching back? In August 1977 a man claimed he was abducted by aliens in a UFO right outside of Pender in Thurston County. After the ship landed he lost his memory, but he does recall being in a white room with black-and-white patterns on the floor, walls, and ceiling. He claims a telepathic voice asked about science, religion, and math. Truth or fiction? You decide.

dams changed its wild ways forever. Make it a point to learn about the river (and Lewis and Clark) at the gorgeous Missouri National Recreational River Resource and Education Center. There's an interpretive display gallery, a laboratory, and a hiking trail linking it to the community of Ponca. Whether you rent a fully equipped cabin with a screened-in porch or rough it at a campsite, you'll find the park, with its 1,400 acres, to be a stupendously pretty place to hike wooded trails, ride a horse to the Three-State Overlook, swim in the pool, or have a picnic. A park permit is necessary and can be purchased on site. The telephone number is (402) 755-2284. The Web address is outdoornebraska .gov/ponca/.

Knox County

In south-central Knox County (3 miles north of Highway 59) is tiny *Winnetoon,* inhabited by fifty-nine people, a couple of dogs, and one stripper. The stripper is the lady who strips and refinishes antique furniture at the *Winnetoon Mini-Mall.* The mini-mall sells antiques of all kinds, handcrafted items, and a surprisingly good selection of natural-food items. Check out the Privy Path with its outhouse collection. The mall is open year-round, Mon through Fri from 8 a.m. to 4 p.m., Fri from 6 to 9 p.m., and Sat from 8 a.m. to 4 p.m.—or "by chance or appointment." The telephone number is (402) 847-3368.

Your next stop is west of the town of *Niobrara.* Near there you'll see the buffalo—and the elk—roam at the *Kreycik Riverview Elk Farm.* Many farmers and ranchers in Nebraska have diversified from traditional crops and livestock, and the Kreyciks are no exception. They have developed a passion for elk and buffalo, the alternative "crop," plus a great tourist attraction. From mid-May through September you can take a covered-wagon ride through three different pastures: one with buffalo, one with elk cows, and one with elk bulls. If you go in August you can hear the bull elk's bugle, a strangely high-pitched call that the girl elks must like a whole bunch. Lots of people go to the mountains to hear the elks bugle—they needn't bother, since we've got it right here in Nebraska. Tours are offered May through October. If you hunt, the Kreyciks also offer elk hunting in the fall. If you're not a hunter, the gift shop sells frozen

Smoke on the Water

There is a volcano in Nebraska. Or at least there was at one time what seemed to be a volcano. The *Ionia Volcano* was located north of **Newcastle** in Dixon County. Five miles north of town is the site that Lewis and Clark recorded in their journals as a volcano, complete with fire and smoke, on a river bluff. This apparent volcanic activity is now believed to have been a decomposition of iron pyrite beds when they came into steamy contact with the river. The volcano was a cause of concern and consternation among early settlers. In 1878 the bluff was washed away, as were all reports of fire and smoke. A historical marker in Newcastle's Pfister Park explains the volcano and provides directions to the site. If you drive there, you won't see a very impressive volcano anymore, but there is a very impressive view from the bluff, where you can see three states: Nebraska, South Dakota, and Iowa.

elk meat. To get to there from Highway 12, go south on the oiled road across from the Niobrara State Park (there's a sign). Follow the oiled road until it ends, at which point you'll be heading west. Continue west until you see a cemetery on a hill (there's another sign), and follow that road south down the hill to the Kreyciks'. Visit nebraskaelktours.com.

Niobrara, at the junction of Highways 12 and 14, has a great place for those with an appreciation of Native American art and history. The **Ponca Tribal Museum and Library** contains artifacts from the tribe's history such as photo archives plus artwork and a gift shop. The museum is open Mon through Fri from 8 a.m. to 4 p.m. Located on the main street through town, the museum's street address is 88915 521 Ave.; the number is (402) 857-3519 and the website is poncatribe-ne.org/Museum.

In 2003 the Ponca Tribal Agency constructed an **earth lodge** typical of those used by the tribe for centuries. There is a 34-foot-wide central living area, sleeping areas, and a 20-foot-long entryway. It is located just west of Niobrara off Highway 12; watch for signs that say PONCA AGENCY. Tours are offered Monday through Saturday or by appointment and can be arranged through the Ponca Tribe Museum. There's no fee for anyone, but please consider leaving a donation.

Here's another interesting thing about the community of Niobrara. The whole dang town has been relocated and rebuilt—twice. In 1881 catastrophic floods covered the town three times; the soggy townspeople wisely decided to pick up their homes and businesses to move to higher ground. Things were dry for decades until the late 1950s, when the construction of the Gavins Point Dam created the Lewis and Clark Lake, which in turn raised the groundwater level, which in turn flooded basements with consistent and dismaying regularity. The community voted to relocate yet again in the 1970s. The federal government paid for this move to the tune of $14.5 million. Compare this to the cost of $40,000 for the 1881 move.

From Niobrara go east on Highway 12 and you'll come to the **Santee Sioux Indian Reservation,** which has been home to the Santee Sioux since 1868. The annual powwow is traditionally held the last weekend in June in the community of Santee on S54D, off Highway 12. For more information call (402) 857-2772 or visit santeesiouxnation.net.

Continue east on Highway 12, and you'll come to **Crofton.** This town is known as the "friendliest little town by a dam site" because of its proximity to **Lewis and Clark Lake** and **Gavins Point Dam.** The **Crofton Lakeview Golf Course** was once named as one of the sixty-five "golfiest" spots in America by *Golf* magazine, and the magazine said the course "epitomizes the spirit of golf."

Seeking Private Shannon

Consider this a Lewis and Clark scavenger hunt of sorts. Here's the background: In 1804, eighteen-year-old Private George Shannon got lost in northeast Nebraska while searching for stray horses with the expedition. He survived, hungry and frightened, for sixteen days before a serendipitous reunion with the expedition. Today sixteen communities in northeast Nebraska have created the Shannon Trail.

Thirteen of these communities have installed wooden chainsaw-carved depictions of Private Shannon. Each time you find a statue you get a passport stamp; if you collect all twelve, you get a free poster. Participating communities are Wynot, St. James, Bow Valley, St. Helena, Hartington, Crofton, Lindy, Santee, Niobrara, Verdigre, Center, Winnetoon (the home base of the late Joe Serres, the chainsaw artist who created the statues), Creighton, Bloomfield, and Wausa. The trail is very popular among geocachers and a selfie with Private Shannon is a must for everyone's Facebook page. For more information call (402) 667-6557 or visit shannontrail.com. And good luck!

When you're in Crofton, plan on spending the night at the **Historic Argo Hotel** at 211 West Kansas St. At first glance, the sturdy brick building, built in 1912, looks fairly institutional. However, once you step inside you're engulfed in a warm, spacious lobby with a tin ceiling, wood accents, and lots of windows. This historic hotel has been extensively refurbished; all thirteen rooms have brass beds, ceiling fans, central air, cable TV, wireless Internet, and telephones. The honeymoon suite has a four-poster bed and a bath with a Jacuzzi. The rooms come with a dinner package (there's a remarkable restaurant in the hotel) if you like, or you can just have a continental breakfast. Elegant eight-course meals can be followed by a cigar from the well-stocked humidor in the "smoking room" (bar). Each of the four bathrooms has both a claw-foot tub and a modern shower. There's talk of a resident ghost, but it has been rumored to appear only in the basement—where you won't be. The places you will want to visit are the attractive, well-stocked bar in the back and the dance floor in the front. To make a reservation for dinner (the hotel is especially busy in the summer) or to book a room, call (402) 388-2400 or visit at historicargohotel.com. You can also book hot air balloon rides over the Missouri River here.

Cuming and Stanton Counties

Bancroft, on Highways 51 and 16 in **Cuming County,** is a place where you can learn about Nebraska's Poet Laureate, John G. Neihardt, at the **John G.**

Neihardt Center. Neihardt is most famous for his book *Black Elk Speaks,* which has been translated into dozens of languages and recounts the visions of his friend, the Oglala holy man and visionary Black Elk. A prolific writer and prodigious scholar, Neihardt finished his first book at the age of sixteen. He wrote nearly thirty books of poetry, fiction, and philosophy. After teaching in country schools, Neihardt moved to Bancroft in 1900, where he worked as a trader with the Omaha tribe and became an authority on its traditions and customs. The center, at the corner of Elm and Washington Streets, has a Sacred Hoop Prayer Garden, a little building where Neihardt wrote, and a modern visitor center with interesting exhibits and films about his life and work. The hours are Mon through Fri from 9 a.m. to 5 p.m. and Sat and Sun from 1 to 5 p.m. Donations are accepted. Call (402) 648-3388 or (888) 777-4667.

From Bancroft you'll be heading west now into **Stanton County** and one of the best meals in the state. You're going to the little community of **Stanton** (population 1,549), at the junction of Highways 57 and 24, and the **Uptown Brewery** at 801 Tenth St. There are not enough superlative words to describe this place. The restaurant is the winner of several international food awards and dozens of area awards, and it is the only Nebraska restaurant outside of Omaha or Lincoln to have a three-diamond rating from the Automobile Association of America. Owners Rosalind Lamson and Adam Staib use only fresh and natural foods; nothing is canned, precooked, or processed, and you won't find sugar, refined salt, or lard on the premises. You may think this would lead to a boring menu, but you'd be dead wrong. The food is wonderful beyond belief. You could start with appetizers like herring a la Russe, venison sausage, or caviar. A friend who lived in Japan said the Uptown has the best tempura ever. For entrees there's the fresh Chilean sea bass, filet mignon, mesquite pork steak, prime rib, scallops Coquille Saint-Jacques, roast duck Grand Marnier . . . and that's just the beginning. Do try the Italian peppercorn steak with asiago cheese and beef Wellington sauce. There are also soups (my favorite is the Normandy tomato bisque) and pastas to die for. The desserts render me senseless with pleasure. Roz and Adam add items to the menu, seemingly daily, depending on where and when they can find the best and freshest, most natural foods available. If you've seen the movie *Nebraska*, starring Bruce Dern and Will Forte, the karaoke scene was shot right here in the dining room. Another scene was shot in the Uptown bathroom, so you gotta check that out! The Uptown Brewery is in a renovated 1906 building that has had incarnations as a barrel house, warehouse, feed store, package store, and other restaurants. Don't worry about being underdressed; blue jeans and T-shirts are fine, but do get all decked out if you have a special occasion to celebrate. Reservations are not necessary. The phone number is (402) 439-5100.

Golfers will enjoy the nine-hole **Elkhorn Acres** golf course in Stanton. Two miles northwest of Stanton is one of the largest lakes in northeast Nebraska at the **Maskethine Recreation Area.** The lake is surrounded by a 300-acre wildlife-management area and includes an arboretum. The area is open to seasonal hunting, fishing, swimming, boating, and camping.

Beemer is also a great place to whip your golf game into shape. The **Indian Trails Country Club** golf course, at 1128 River Rd., is locally popular and draws visitors from far away as well. Try not to get distracted by the panoramic view of the wooded Elkhorn Valley. The greens are crowned, slick, and have subtle breaks. According to *Golfing Nebraska,* "An unusual hazard comes into play on the 10. If you go over the green, you're in the graveyard." The phone number is (402) 528-3404; the website is indiantrailsclub.com.

Pierce County

Just west of **Pierce** (Highways 13 and 98), you'll come to **Cuthills Vineyards,** Nebraska's first winery. Cuthills is 3 miles west of Pierce and north of Willow Creek State Recreation Area. The prizewinning wine is produced by vineyard manager and wine maker Ed Swanson, who named the vineyard after the "cuthills" formed by glaciers that at one time scoured the area. A picturesque 1920s barn has been completely renovated to house the wine-making equipment (the grapes are crushed mechanically, so rid yourself of the notion of barefoot stompers) and a beautiful shop, where you can taste and buy the wine. After just a few years of production, Swanson now produces 25,000 bottles of wine. The wine pairs well with food, and its reputation is growing as quickly as the grape vines. Swanson currently produces semidry, semisweet, and sweet wine. A tasty mead (ask Ed's wife, Holly, to tell you the tradition of mead as a gift for newlyweds and the genesis of the word honeymoon) has been added to the line, as well as dry and sparkling wines. The shop also has great items such as smoked salmon, grape wreaths, wooden wine boxes, wine glasses, wine biscuits, mustards, grape seed oil (tasty and good for you), corkscrews, baskets, T-shirts, candles, fudge sauces with wine, and more. You can also find some lovely handmade jewelry created by Holly. Enjoy a self-guided walking tour of the vineyards at your leisure. Baco, the dog (named after a grape variety), will likely greet your arrival with tail-thumping but well-restrained glee. Cuthills Vineyards is open from Jan through April, Fri through Sun, 1 to 5 p.m.; and May through Dec, Wed through Sat, 11 a.m. to 6 p.m., and Sun 1 to 6 p.m. They are closed on all holidays. The telephone number is (402) 329-6774. The website is cuthills.com, and they invite friends to follow them on Facebook.

If you're one of those people who is afraid of clowns, you might want to skip **Plainview,** otherwise known as Nebraska's Klown Kapital. (Nebraska has a capital for everything, if you haven't noticed.)

Northwest of Pierce on Highways 13 and 20, Plainview, is the home of the **Klown Doll Museum,** housed in a nicely renovated gas station on Highway 20, with more than 4,700 clowns on display. So, you ask, why do you spell it with a K? "Because we can," says museum manager Mary Hamilton. There's a Klown Karnival in July, complete with a Klown Band. The museum is open every day from Memorial Day to Labor Day or by appointment. Call (402) 582-4433 or visit klowndollmuseum.com.

Antelope County

When you see the **Plantation House B&B** in **Elgin,** you might wonder if you're in Nebraska or Georgia. The B&B is a huge twenty-five-room, Southern-style mansion that offers genuine Midwestern hospitality. Five rooms, all with private baths, are wonderfully appointed and can be yours from $85 to $120. Or you can stay in the small cottage on the four-acre grounds. Relax in the parlor with a book, dream by the fire in the family room, or lock yourself away in the private, two-person whirlpool room Owners Leonard and Judith Orlowski make a groan-inducing breakfast that includes delectables such as French toast, chocolate pancakes, potato and cheese frittatas, omelettes, meats, muffins, and fresh fruit. Children are welcome. No credit cards. The B&B is at 401 Plantation St. To make a reservation, call (402) 843-2287 or (888) 446-2287. The website is plantation-house.com.

The community of **Neligh,** north of Elgin on Highways 14 and 275, gives you an example of an old-fashioned "daily grind" at the **Neligh Mills State Historical Site.** This flour mill on the Elkhorn River, at the corner of N and Wylie Streets, is one of the oldest examples of a water-powered mill in the United States. Built in 1873, it is now a branch museum of the State Historical Society. This is the only nineteenth-century flour mill in the state, and it still has all the original equipment. It's a fun tour and a peaceful place to watch the river flow by. The mill is open from May 1 through Labor Day. Hours are Mon through Sat from 8 a.m. to 5 p.m. and Sun from 1:30 to 5 p.m. From Labor Day weekend through May, the mill is open 1 to 5 p.m. Mon through Fri. There is a $3 admission fee. The telephone number is (402) 887-4303; nebraskahistory.org/sites/mill.

Neligh has one of the last remaining drive-in theaters in the state. If you have fond memories of smooching in a car on humid summer nights or if you'd like to create some similar fond memories, grab your sweetie and buy some tickets to the **T-K Drive-In.** Or bring your kids and try to convince them you never did any such smooching and they shouldn't either when the puberty whammy hits them. It doesn't really matter what's playing (it's always family fare); just be there between April and September on a Thursday, Friday, or Saturday evening. The phone number is (402) 887-5212; nelighdriveintheater.com.

In Neligh you can go from moving pictures to still life with animals. The **Pierson Wildlife Museum Learning Center,** housed in a former church at 205 East Fifth St., is a collection of one hundred full-body mounts and fifty shoulder mounts of creatures from four continents. According to Safari Club International, this museum has "one of the largest and most impressive private collections in the country." The collection was donated by retired Neligh physician and hunter Dr. Kenneth Pierson and his wife, Margaret. Hours are Sun through Fri, 1 to 5 p.m.; and Sat 10 a.m. to 5 p.m. Admission is $5 for adults, $4 for senior citizens, and $3 for children five years old and up. The number is (402) 877-4212; the website is piersonwildlifemuseumneligh.com.

You won't have to drive far to get back to prehistory. **Antelope County** has one of world's finest archaeological sites. **Ashfall Fossil Beds State Historical Park** is 2 miles west and 6 miles north off Highway 20 on a well-marked turnoff between Royal and Orchard. About ten million years ago, a massive volcanic eruption in what is now Idaho sent a deadly cloud spewing ash down on a watering hole in the savanna-like region of what would become Nebraska. The ash suffocated and then buried creatures great and small, from birds to rhinoceros. Today there remains an astonishingly detailed tableau of death, which is being unearthed by paleontologists. You can watch as they sift and sort in the covered Rhino Barn. They will explain the intact and fossilized skeletal remains and make the tragedy real again after all these years. Visitors are endlessly fascinated, as they should be, by the fossilized skeleton of a tiny rhino fetus, still protected by its mother's rib cage, as they died together so long ago. Two of the rhino fossils are named after Sandy, a staffer, and Justin, her son. The visitor center and interpretive facility have equally fascinating exhibits on what the birds and mammals looked like, what they ate (grain seeds in stomachs became fossilized, too), and how they lived. As an added bonus to the enjoyable learning experience, the park is located high on a hill, and you can see for many scenic miles across the rolling plains. Nature trails interpret the area's current plant and animal life. It was named a National Natural Landmark in 2006. This one-of-a-kind attraction is truly off the beaten path, and you'd be remiss to pass it up. A small admission fee is charged in addition to the park entry permit. Pay it; it's worth it, and it'll help keep the place open and able to build more trails. Besides, how often do you get to see something that *National Geographic* has called the "Pompeii of the Plains"? The park opens

May 1 and has hours Tues through Sat, 10 a.m. to 4 p.m. Expanded hours run from Memorial Day weekend through Labor Day weekend, Mon through Sat, 9 a.m. to 5 p.m.; and Sun, 11 a.m. to 5 p.m. After Labor Day through mid-Oct it's open Tues through Sat, 10 a.m. to 4 p.m.; and Sun, 1 to 4 p.m. The telephone number is (402) 893-2000, and the website is ashfall.unl.edu.

Clearwater is a little town of less than 400 people with an extraordinary number of them contributing some really creative products to our world. One of them is Brenda Switzer, but she'll tell you that her husband, Tom, and son, Brian, are the talented ones. But Brenda got the ball rolling when she quit her job nearly 20 years ago wanting to do something more creative with her life. Today, the family is *Iron Creations & Country,* making some fabulous art out of recycled farm implements, such as old disc blades, tractor seats, and pieces of scrap iron. They make yard art, interesting mailbox posts, business signs, interior art for rustic homes. Their shop is the barn on their farm, a few miles out of town, but it's worth the drive. Each December, they host an open house on their farm, inviting as many as twenty others local artisans. Get directions from the website, switzerironcreations.com, or call for direction at (402) 485-2537.

I grew up on a family farm and just about everything at one time or another, including the kids and the dogs, got painted John Deere green as a result of my dad's meticulous care of his preferred farm implements. There's still an old refrigerator in the shop that's a combination of John Deere green and yellow. It's not that my dad had to have his shop color-coordinated, but he often gave us a spray gun to keep us entertained while he worked. Mother didn't necessarily appreciate his method of child care.

Duaine Filsinger needs that refrigerator in his little museum in Clearwater. He worked for a John Deere dealership most of his adult life and collected all

The Ponca Trail of Tears

When the Ponca Tribe was forcibly removed from land along the Niobrara River to Indian Territory (now Oklahoma) in 1877, the route became known as the *Ponca Trail of Tears.* The Ponca were forced to move because an error in the 1868 Treaty of Fort Laramie gave land already belonging to the Ponca to the Dakota Sioux. The arduous journey was marked by hunger, illness, and many deaths. White Buffalo Girl, the daughter of Black Elk and Moon Hawk, died near the community of Neligh. The community gave her a Christian burial, cared for her grave, and in 1913 erected a stone monument for her. A historical marker in the Neligh Cemetery in Antelope County, high on a hill with a dramatic view, tells the story of the Ponca Trail of Tears. Feasibility studies are underway to declare this 500-mile path a National Historic Trail.

sorts of John Deere memorabilia, including about twenty of those classic pedal tractors, which he now has in a little place he calls **Filsinger's Deere Shed.** There's not an exact address. Just get on First Street and head west until you see it. Duaine doesn't charge people to look around his collection, but he sure would appreciate you calling before you show up, just to make sure he is there. Call (402) 485-2275.

Madison County

Norfolk is where the former late-night host Johnny Carson spent most of his growing-up years. A sign identifies his home on South 13th Street, but it is a private residence and not available for touring. He donated a bunch of his memorabilia, including several of his Emmys, to the **Elkhorn Valley Museum and Research Center** at 515 Queen City Blvd. The museum has taken advantage of Mr. Carson's generosity by creating an impressive gallery that includes a set of the *Tonight Show* and other interactive displays. The museum also offers a look at an old movie theater, and it has a large collection of Elkhorn Valley historical items and genealogy materials. Most everyone who goes to the museum is in awe of the enormous Square Turn Tractor—it's the only surviving and operating tractor of its kind in the world. Many people are surprised to learn that the Hall family who eventually started Hallmark Cards first operated a stationery business in Norfolk. Some of Hallmark's original Valentine's Day cards are among the exhibits. And the guy who was the voice of Tony the Tiger—is also from Norfolk. It's a very well done museum; you should go. Hours are Tues through Sat, 10 a.m. to 5 p.m. Admission is $6 for adults and $3 for children. Contacts are (402) 371-3886 or elkhornvalleymuseum.org.

The **Willetta Lueshen Bird Library** is in the same building. This hands-on learning center has more than 1,200 books about birds and nature. A large glass wall looks out onto a very pretty little garden with a whole bunch of birdfeeders.

Throughout Norfolk and this part of Nebraska, you'll find a number of colorful, expressive murals covering the sides of buildings and the interiors of churches. A very popular one, added in 2014, is the many faces of Johnny Carson, located at 3rd and Norfolk Avenue. You'll find another one with lions and tigers on the side of the Western Office building at 435 Norfolk Avenue. These were all painted by the very talented Karl Reeder, who lived in Norfolk for more than two decades and operated an art gallery here. Karl and his wife, Brenda, have moved to Colorado now, but not before making Nebraska a much more colorful place.

No stop in Norfolk would be complete without visiting the ***Norfolk Arts Center*** at 305 North Fifth St. It's a beautifully designed structure with lots of light and great open spaces. There's a small permanent collection with monthly new exhibits from around the state. The sculpture garden is pretty wonderful, too, but check the calendar for special events like family game night, productions of the Kids Theatre, and jazz music night. Hours are Tues through Fri, 10 a.m. to 6 p.m.; and Sat 10 a.m. to 4 p.m. The phone number is (402) 371-7199. Check out the beautiful artwork at norfolkartscenter.org. The center also has a presence on Facebook to keep you up to date on classes, exhibits, and special events.

If you want to stretch your legs or take a bike ride, head on over to ***TaHaZouka Park*** on the south side of town on Hwy. 81. First of all, the city park has great camping, picnicking, and a disc golf course, among other pleasant amenities. But this is also the trailhead of the ***Cowboy Trail,*** which will be the longest rail-to-trail conversion in the United States when it's fully completed. The whole thing will be 320 miles, but this completed stretch runs 195 miles to Valentine. It's all crushed limestone and pleasant for walking, running, or biking, but no motorized vehicles are allowed. If you don't want to pedal that far, at least go about four miles to the Broken Bridge. Not only is it a beautiful, scenic area, but it is a place over the Elkhorn River mentioned in Johnny Carson's biography as one of his favorite childhood swimming holes. Call (402) 471-5511 for more information on the Cowboy Trail; and for more information on TaHaZouka Park, call (402) 844-2180.

Continue south on Highway 81 for 13 miles to ***Madison*** and the ***Madison County Historical Society Museum*** at 210 West Third St. This is a great little museum with a touching display about native-son Baseball Hall of Fame member Richie Ashburn. Another touching display tells the story of the Orphan Train riders, abandoned and orphaned children from New York City who were given new homes in communities throughout the Great Plains, like Madison. And check out the pencil collection; there's a zillion of them. It's open Mon through Fri from 1 to 5 p.m. On Tuesday evenings, volunteers keep the museum open late to show off and play with the extensive model train collection. The phone number is (402) 992-1221; the website is madisoncountyhistory.org.

go the distance

You may have noticed towns getting farther apart. Many towns in rural areas are between 7 and 10 miles apart. Back when farm families traveled to town on horses or in wagons, it took one day to travel the distance to town, pick up or unload goods, and then get back to the farm before dark. Think of that when you cover these distances in just a few minutes.

Southeast of Norfolk on Highway 121 is **Battle Creek,** with its spectacular city park. Within the one park you'll find fourteen smaller parks encircled by paved People Trails. You'll enjoy the Enchanted Forest minipark, the Heritage Park, with a life-size statue of the Ponca Tribe's Chief Petalsharo, and a carved wooden bear in Sandbox Park created by the late cowboy and chainsaw artist Joe Serres (mentioned earlier in the section under Winnetoon in Knox County), to name just a few. Historic buildings from the community have been moved onto the Heritage Park grounds. Battle Creek, with a population of a little less than 1,000, is the winner of the Tree City USA award every year since 1990, as well as numerous other honors for community engagement., A visit here will demonstrate why the community has been so honored.

Platte County

In **Columbus,** located on Highways 30 and 81 in Platte County, you'll find two good eating places. The first is the beautiful **Gottberg Brew Pub** and adjoining **Dusters** restaurant, 2804 Thirteenth St. (402-564-8338), which is known for its Lahvosh, a reflection of the Armenian heritage of this area. You'll also want to visit **Glur's Tavern,** 2301 Eleventh St. (402-564-8615), which first opened in 1876 and is said to be the oldest continuously operating saloon west of the Missouri. All are definitely worth a stop.

A man born in Columbus invented something that saved the lives of untold soldiers during World War II, the Korean War, and the Vietnam War. Andrew Jackson Higgins invented the LCVP (Landing-Craft, Vehicle, Personnel) boat that carried American soldiers ashore, most notably on D-Day. A full-size steel replica of the boat can be seen at **Andrew Jackson Higgins National Memorial** in West Pawnee Park at US 81 and Thirty-third Avenue. Three bronze statues of soldiers representing the aforementioned wars have been installed, as has a piece of steel from the World Trade Center. Also located in Pawnee Park is the Quincentenary Bell Tower, celebrating 500 years since Christopher Columbus, this community's namesake, landed in the Americas. Take note of the murals along the sides of the five towers, each one showcasing an aspect of the journey across the ocean. The bells themselves were collected from long-forgotten churches that once welcomed worshippers in Platte County. Call (402) 564-2769 for more details.

Platte County offers an abundance of water recreation at **Lake North** (a 200-acre lake 4 miles north of Columbus on Eighteenth Avenue) and **Lake Babcock** (a 600-acre lake 4 miles north on Eighteenth Avenue and 1¼ miles west).

Platte County is perhaps the only site in the continental United States that was bombed during World War II by the U.S. Army Air Corps. On August 16, 1943, the tiny community of *Tarnov* was peppered with several one-hundred-pound test bombs filled with sand and small charges. Some fell through a roof and passed inches from two sleeping young sisters. The *Omaha World Herald* reported it thusly: "The good people of this little Polish village (population 70), who were bombed accidently by an army plane early Monday, went to bed early Monday night. It

chickensand cattleand pigs,ohmy!

This is one of the greatest agricultural states in the country, and we have the numbers to prove it! Nebraska has far more farm animals than people. For every human being there are four cows, two pigs, and eight chickens residing in the state at any given moment.

has been a tremendous day—the biggest day for continuous excitement they had ever known." No one was hurt, not even the man who was deep in "an alcohol-induced slumber" inside his car after a harvest festival the night before. A bomb landed a few feet from the car; he woke up only when the sheriff roused him into a hung-over incredulity. It is speculated, but no one knows for sure (the results of the military investigation remain a secret to this day), that the bombs were intended for a test-bombing range outside of the community of Stanton, 25 miles from Tarnov.

Colfax County

If you love to garden and work in your yard, a stop in the community of *Clarkson* is most decidedly worth your time. The *Bluebird Nursery,* in southwest Clarkson at 519 Bryan St., is the largest perennial plant grower between Chicago and the Pacific Northwest. To give you an idea of the magnitude of its operation, it employs 110 people in a community of 700 people. The nursery specializes in, but is not limited to, hardy perennial plants native to the Plains that are able to withstand the wild vagaries of four complete seasons. Bluebird Nursery has more than 1,000 perennial and ground-cover plants, with a large selection of annual plants as well. Each year, the nursery ships millions of plants (up to 1,800 different varieties) from its massive greenhouses to nurseries, garden centers, and botanical gardens in the United States, Canada, England, and Australia. During the summer months make a stop at the Bohemian Gardens, on Main Street, and the All-American Display Gardens and Proving Ground, at 521 Cherry St., to be amazed at the plants and to garner gardening

aprayeron theprairie

The **Saint Benedict Center,** north of Schuyler in Colfax County, offers you a chance to slow down and get in touch with your quiet, spiritual side. Overnight accommodations are offered for those seeking out opportunities for spiritual growth. If you're not the praying kind, you can still ponder, or at least shop. There's a great bookstore and gift shop with greeting cards, religious gifts and statues, icons, rosaries, CDs, cassettes, and videos. Or take home some of the nice pieces of art from Africa, Peru, and Korea. Artisans from throughout North American are represented as well.

The store hours are Mon through Sat from 10 a.m. to 4 p.m. and Sun from 1 to 4 p.m. Sunday mass is held at the Mission House across the street at 8:30 a.m. The complex is ½ mile east from Highway 15 (4 miles north of Schuyler) on St. Benedict's Road. Call (402) 352-8819, ext. 358, or visit christthekingpriory.com for more information.

ideas. Store hours vary seasonally: May 1 through June 30, Mon through Fri from 8 a.m. to 5 p.m., Sat from 8 a.m. to 4 p.m., and Sun from 1 to 5 p.m. From July 1 through April 30, the store is closed on Sunday except during the Christmas season, when it sells poinsettias and Christmas trees. Call (800) 356-914 or visit bluebirdnursery.com.

When you're ready to kick up your heels and do a little polka, the **Clarkson Opera House** is the place to go. Built in 1915, this building has been the site of some of the biggest doin's in the area. Completely renovated by a volunteer group in recent years, the Opera House is now the site of monthly polka dances, as well as regular theatrical performances and other special events. Even if nothing is going on, you may wish to stick your head indoors to see the lovely hand-painted backdrops on the stage that date to the 1920s. For a preview and a dance schedule, visit clarksonoperahouse.org.

You can overnight at **Annie's B&B** at 310 Cherry St. in Clarkson. This huge 1890s plantation-style home has three rooms. The second floor has both front and back balconies, and one offers a 4-mile view. Rooms are between $50 and $60. The phone number is (402) 892-3660.

There's a great little museum, the **Clarkson Historical Museum,** at 233 Pine St. It is said to have one of the best collections of historical Czech immigrant memorabilia in the country. It's open by appointment; call (402) 892-3641. When you're in town, do not miss the **Clarkson Bakery** downtown at 113 Pine St. *Kolaches* (a traditional Czech pastry), rye bread, strudel, and a whole lot more are available with coffee to go. It opens at 6 a.m. and closes by noon, so get there early. The phone number is (402) 892-3131; the website is clarksonbakery.weebly.com. Then go over to **Toman's City Market** at 219

Pine St. to load up on traditional, and award-winning, homemade specialties like sausages, wieners, and bacon. The phone number is (402) 892-3452.

Schuyler, on Highways 15 and 30, is home to one of the finest WPA (Works Progress Administration) buildings in the state. Although senior citizens who watched the **Oak Ballroom** being built in 1937 from huge native oaks and stones jokingly refer to the WPA as "We're Probably Asleep," this beautiful structure stands as tribute to the spirit of the Great Depression. Listed on the National Register of Historic Places, the Oak Ballroom is at the entrance to Community Park, which is situated on another historic site, the Mormon Trail. The ballroom is used for local events, and, if you're lucky, you'll be there when there's a big polka dance going on. Located on Lost Creek in the south part of town on Highway 15, the ballroom is open to visitors for free from 8 a.m. to noon on weekdays. Call (402) 352-9972 for details.

Places to Stay in Northeast Nebraska

(All area codes are 402 except where noted otherwise.)

CROFTON

The Argo Hotel
211 West Kansas St.
388-4200
historicargohotel.com

ELGIN

Plantation House B&B
RR 2
843-2287 or (888) 446-2287
plantation-house.com

TARNOV

The Michael House
Third and Robin Streets
246-4807
tarnov.org/house

VERDIGRE

Commercial Hotel
217 Main St.
668-2386
commercialhotelbb.com

Places to Eat in Northeast Nebraska

(All area codes are 402.)

COLUMBUS

Dusters
(American and continental)
2804 South
Thirteenth St.
562-6488 or 564-8338

DIXON

Euni's Place
(burgers, pizza)
Second and Conway
584-9309

HOOPER

The Office Bar and Grill
(American)
Main Street
654-3373

MARTINSBURG

Bob's Bar (giant burgers)
no street address (honest!)
but you can't miss it
945-2995

HELPFUL NORTHEAST NEBRASKA WEBSITES

Northeast Nebraska Travel Council
travelnenebraska.com

Omaha
visitomaha.com

Columbus
thecolumbuspage.com

South Sioux City
visitsouthsiouxcity.com

Fremont
fremontne.gov

Wayne
waynene.com

Norfolk
visitnorfolkne.com

NORFOLK

The Granary
922 South Thirteenth St.
371-5334

ROYAL

Green Gables
(American home cookin')
go north on the road
leading to Ashfall Fossil
Beds between Royal and
Orchard; closed in winter
months
893-5800

STANTON

Uptown Brewery
(American and Continental)
801 Tenth St.
439-5100

Where the West Begins

The Sandhills region comprises approximately 19,300 square miles of grass-covered, stabilized sand dunes, covering roughly one-third of the state. From the air it looks like ocean swells. It has such subtle beauty that persons hurrying through are inclined to miss the wildflowers, the birds, and the glorious expanse of sky, which is matched by the seemingly endless undulating hills. If you're driving through the Sandhills on Highway 2, you're on a road that Charles Kuralt considered among the ten most beautiful routes in the country. Folklorist Roger Welsch is like many Nebraskans who are smitten with the Sandhills. He maintains "that any days you spend in the Sandhills are not taken off your lifetime allotment. It's so restful that God just gives them to you for free." The many small lakes, coupled with the lush grass on the hills, make this prime ranching country. The Sandhills has its share of western history, with military outposts, horse-stealing outlaws, and frontier justice. The rivers of the Sandhills—the Niobrara, Cedar Dismal, Snake, and Loup—are popular with canoeists. Bicycling enthusiasts will enjoy the Cowboy Trail, which when completed will stretch more than 300 miles across the northern counties of Nebraska and will be the nation's longest

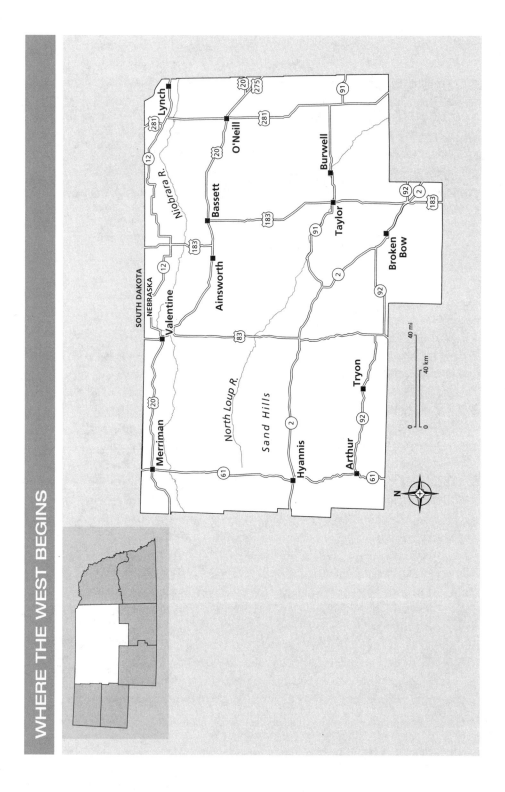

rails-to-trails conversion. Sections of it are open now. An abundance of wildlife refuges, state parks, state historical parks, and reservoirs round out the outdoor offerings of the Sandhills.

Cherry County

You are now in one of the largest counties in the United States. Cherry County is larger than Rhode Island and Delaware combined. You may find yourself frequently checking your watch or phone for the correct time while in these parts. The dividing line between Central Standard Time and the Mountain Time Zone runs right through Cherry County.

You might imagine there'd be a lot of things to see and do in such a large county, and you'd be right. Cherry County is most famous for the Niobrara River, a National Scenic River, and the biological crossroads it represents. The river valley is where several types of vegetation converge. You'll see everything from yuccas to alpine flowers, cacti, and birch trees. What you will see for sure are canoers, tubers, and kayakers on the enormously popular Niobrara River. And there's another waterborne activity in recent years: tanking. Envision one of the galvanized steel water tanks for cattle, horses, and other livestock. Clean it out, jump in it dressed as a pirate, and paddle down the Niobrara in the dead of winter. That's tanking—and that's a darn good time in Nebraska.

FAVORITE ATTRACTIONS IN THE SANDHILLS

Bowring Ranch State Historical Park
northeast on Highway 61
Merriman
(402) 684-3428
outdoornebraska.gov/bowringranch

Happy Jack Chalk Mine and Peak
1½ miles south on Highway 11
Scotia
(308) 245-3276
happyjackchalkmine.com

Heartland Elk Guest Ranch
south of Sparks on a gravel road
(402) 376-2553
heartlandelk.com

Nebraska National Forest
2 miles west on Highway 2
Halsey
(308) 432-0300 or 533-2257

Plains Trading Company Booksellers
269 North Main St.
Valentine
(402) 376-1424 or (800) 439-8640
plainstrading.com.

On Highway 12 in *Sparks,* the Canoe Capital of Nebraska, Dryland Aquatics, (800) 337-3119, drylandaquatics.com, will provide canoes, tubes, camping, and shuttle service, as will several outfitters in Valentine.

Two miles south of Sparks is the *Heartland Elk Guest Ranch.* Log cabins are set in a secluded, heavily wooded area that opens onto an astonishingly beautiful view of the river valley. Owners Kerry and Lisa Krueger have done everything right. The two-bedroom cabins are great—the kitchens come complete with coffeemakers and microwaves, there's a radio but no TV, and an outdoor grill awaits your culinary creativity. And the best thing . . . there are no phones, so this really is a getaway. They've built a horse barn, so you can ride down the bluffs to the valley. A gut-busting breakfast is served in a dining area that provides a perfect view of the elk pasture. Horseback riding through wooded trails and trout fishing at private ponds await. Call (402) 376-1124 or visit heartlandelk.com for reservations.

Valentine, Cherry County's largest community, with a population of just less than 3,000, is located at Highways 83, 12, and 20. Valentine serves the needs of the far-flung ranchers with grocery stores, gas stations, cafes, restaurants, and western supply stores. A great place to browse is a bookstore called the *Plains Trading Company,* 269 North Main Street, which has Nebraska products and a gift shop. This is a wonderful bookstore with authentic human service that makes one ashamed for ever using Amazon. Check out this site instead: plainstrading.com.

Another gift shop with an interesting story is *Cody Foster and Co.* at 227 North Main St. As a little boy, Cody Foster spent a lot of time with both of his grandmothers, who were both very good with needle and thread. To keep him occupied, they gave him some cloth and suggested he "create." The

Team Niobrara

One of my favorite pictures in our family scrapbook is of a canoe trip we took on the Niobrara River. My then eight-year-old son, who was a little guy for his age, was in the front of the canoe commandeered by my husband, who is not so much of a little guy. I was in the other canoe with our nephew. Our weights were more evenly matched, so we worked the river together fairly well. But not so much in the canoe carrying my husband and son. The picture is a perfect example of physics in action—the nose of the canoe plowed down the beautiful Niobrara a good six inches out of the water, while the backend was nearly taking on water. But my little boy, all bundled in his orange life vest, was paddling with all of his might—the paddle nowhere near touching the water. But he and his dad were a team and tackled the wilds of the Niobrara together. The memory is all that matters, right?

result is a business launched while Cody was still in high school that now ships about 50,000 dolls and poly-filled holiday pins to gift shops around the world. You can also find Cody's designs at Tiffany's, Bergdorf Goodman and Anthropologie. Call (402) 376-3369 or check out his creative offerings at cody fosterandco.com.

Smith Falls State Park, 12 miles northeast of Valentine on Highway 12, has the state's highest waterfall. Spring-fed Smith Falls drops 70 feet from a birch-crowned canyon rim to the Niobrara River. You can rent a canoe to cross the river to the falls, and you should do this, as the falls are really quite lovely. Or take a stroll across the footbridge. Picnic sites, restrooms, concessions, tent camping, and showers are available on the north side of the river. The park is open from April 1 through November 30. A park permit is required. The telephone number is (402) 376-1306 or visit outdoornebraska.gov/smithfalls.

So obviously, a number of people come to "the top of Nebraska" in the summer months to enjoy the many pleasures to be found on the Niobrara River on a hot summer day. And there's nothing more pleasant than floating the river here, picnicking by the river, or just sitting under a shade tree watching the river. But when it gets too cold to enjoy the river, there's still plenty to do here. The spring water that flows into the river freezes solid and the resulting cascades of ice make for world-class ice climbing. Simmon's Cliff on the *Niobrara River Ranch* is one of the best places in all of Nebraska to participate in this uniquely seasonal sport. Call (402) 890-1245; nrranch.com.

West of Valentine on Highway 20 is the *Bowring Ranch State Historical Park,* which provides the opportunity to see a working cattle ranch in the Sandhills. The ranch is 1½ miles north of *Merriman* on Highway 61. The cattle industry in the Sandhills began in a serendipitous fashion in 1879, when a blizzard drove many cattle from the E. S. Newman ranch near Gordon, Nebraska, deep into unknown valleys, which had been prematurely judged to be inhospitable to cattle. Hoping to find a few surviving head, ranch hands ventured hopefully into the interior of the Sandhills to discover not only the Newman cattle but thousands more from other ranches that had wandered away and grown fat and content on the rich interior meadowlands. Voilà! A thriving industry was born. Arthur Bowring started ranching in 1894 and married Eve Kelly Forester in 1928. They were successful ranchers and also public servants. He was a member of the Nebraska legislature, and she was the first woman from Nebraska to serve in the U.S. Senate. Eve died in 1985 at the age of ninety-two and, having no living children, donated the 7,202-acre Bar 99 Ranch to the Nebraska Game and Parks Foundation, with the stipulation it remain as a living historical monument. At present the ranch house remains much as it was at the time of Eve's death. It includes a huge collection of glassware and silver, which she gathered on her extensive travels, and also photographs of many of the famous politicians she met, including Haile Selassie, the emperor of Ethiopia. (Eve's experience on the ranch was apparently a whole lot different than that of 1880s pioneer woman Ellen Moran, who wrote that the Sandhills were " . . . a great country for cattle and men, but hell on horses and women.") The barns, bunkhouses, corrals, and other ranch buildings are maintained as workplaces. The visitor center has interesting displays about the Bowrings, the history and geology of the Sandhills, and the ranching business in the state. The center is open from Memorial Day weekend through Labor Day, 9 a.m. to 5 p.m. daily. There is also a sod house, with periodic living-history demonstrations. A park permit, which costs $17.35 for a year or $3.35 a day, is required. The buildings are open from 8 a.m. to 5 p.m. daily from Memorial Day weekend through Labor Day. Call (402) 684-3428 for more information or visit outdoornebraska .com/bowringranch.

Keya Paha County

If shopping malls make you shudder and you can't stomach the thought of another fast-food meal, then **Keya Paha County** will suit you just fine. You'll not find either in this rural area of northern Nebraska. In case you need to pronounce the name of the county you're in, the locals say KIP-a-haw, but other Nebraskans often pronounce it Keya-pawhaw. The name is from the Sioux language and means "turtle hill." Keya Paha County used to be called Mob County because of the notorious Pony Boys, who had a propensity for horses other than their own.

Springview, at Highways 183 and 12, is the largest town in the county; it has 232 citizens. **Burton** has nine. And **Norden** is unincorporated. Springview has everything a traveler could want: a couple of cafes that offer home-cooked meals, a bar and grill, a liquor store, a grocery store, gas stations, and a hotel. Because the county's southern border is the beautiful Niobrara River, Springview offers a couple of canoe outfitters. Fred and Dian Egelhoff will take care of you at Rock Barn Outfitters (402-376-1764) or call Kerry and Lisa Krueger at Rocky Ford Outfitters (402-497-3479).

There are two B&Bs just outside of Springview: At **Larrington's Guest Cottage** you can rent the whole two-bedroom modern house and prepare your own meals, although continental breakfast "fixin's" are provided. There's a dang-wonderful view of the Niobrara River valley from this isolated cottage. Call (402) 497-2261 to make required reservations. The **Big Canyon Inn** also has a beautiful view of the prairie, and the modern home has four cozy rooms and a fireplace. Guests can hike, ride horses, mountain bike, and hunt in season. More than 20 miles of equestrian trails are available, as well as a barn and corral for your horses. Call (402) 497-3170 for reservations. The name Big Canyon is apt; it's adjacent to a seriously deep canyon. A 1939 guidebook about Nebraska, written by Federal Writers Project of the Works Progress Administration, described the terrain south of Springview as "almost mountainous, with cedar and pine trees, rolling hills, and the blue Niobrara winding far below." I'm here to tell you that when you're in that canyon, it's not *almost* mountainous, it *is* mountainous.

When you're about 1½ miles west of Springview on Hwy. 12, you'll see Nebraska's first wind farm. Of course, windmills have been common sites on the prairie since white settlers began making their homes here. Those windmills were used to draw water for livestock as well as humans. The two 296-foot tall turbines furnish up to 40 percent of the electrical power needed in Keya Paha County. The community hosts a charming festival in July called

Exodusters Settlement in the Sandhills

In 1904, a little community was established in the Sandhills of Cherry County called DeWitty, one of several towns that sprung up as a result of the 1904 Kinkaid Act, which opened the Sandhills to settlement and helped many who hoped for a new life in a new land. What makes DeWitty noteworthy is that it was founded by Exodusters, a name given to freed slaves from the south who, like so many others attracted to the Great Plains, were looking for opportunities to build a better life. DeWitty has disappeared from the landscape just west of the community of Brownlee in Cherry County, but the town does hold a place in Nebraska history. The town was named DeWitty after the first postmaster, and after he left the community, it was called Audacious. Later on the town was known as Garden. In 1909 a group of black homesteaders led by William Walker and Charles Mehan took out homestead claims, and other black homesteaders joined them until the population reached a peak of about 175 people. They constructed sod houses, a post office, a grocery store, a church, and a school. There was a baseball team called the Sluggers. They lived just as the white settlers did, working the land, raising families, praying for good weather, and taking part in rodeos. DeWitty dwindled in population, and by 1940 there were no African Americans left in Brownlee.

Another small group of black settlers claimed land west of Westerville in Custer County. Three brothers, Moses Speece, Henry Webb, and Jerry Shores, all of whom had taken the last names of the slaveholders who once owned them, were the first to settle there. The Speece family, whose sixteen living children enjoyed music, was said to have worn out two pump organs and a piano in the twenty-five years they lived in their sod house. Both the Speece and Shore families were photographed by Solomon Butcher, whose work has been widely published. Their homes are gone and their families are scattered, but their images remain forever.

Wind Turbine Days that includes a donkey race, bicycle rodeo, and watermelon eating contest.

Before you leave Keya Paha County, you could check out a ghost town called *Meadville.* Keya Paha County had a wild and wooly western past. More than ten killings are documented, with grisly tales of many more. Meadville had its share of colorful characters. Things slowed down considerably over the next several decades to the point in 1960 that the post office was closed; no mail for anyone, character or not. The community is now enjoying a little resurgence. There's a refurbished general store with food and drinks that's also known to host a rowdy Karaoke night now and then. The park is used by campers, hikers, anglers, hunters, bird-watchers, and outdoor enthusiasts. Also in the area are Bottomless Lake (Perhaps some of the murder victims ended up here?); Oxbow Bayou, the largest and fastest moving fault line in Nebraska (there are occasional reports of small earthquakes in northeast Nebraska); and an old bridge over the Niobrara River. Brochures also tout the Meadville onions, "known far and wide for their flavor and extreme mildness." There's a great big Fourth of July blowout every year. On January 1 at least some people plunge into the icy river. Call the Meadville General Store at (402) 497-2440, for more information. Go north from Ainsworth on a little spur (watch for signs) to get there. Or go south a couple miles west on Highway 12 from Springview.

Brown County

South of Keya Paha County is *Brown County,* with the three communities of Long Pine, Ainsworth, and Johnstown strung along Highway 20 from east to west. *Long Pine* has great fishing on the Long Pine Creek and at the nearby Long Pine State Recreation Area. For lodging in Long Pine, try the *Pine Valley Resort,* which has seven housekeeping cabins (the honeymoon cabin has a Jacuzzi). Rates range from $95 to $125 for two people. Pets are welcomed. The telephone number is (402) 273-4351, and the website is aboutpinevalley resort.com.

There's something about the water in the Sandhills. Perhaps it's so pure because it filters down through so much sand. In any case, the water around Long Pine is so naturally pure that Coca Cola was once made here. A homegrown company called *Seven Springs Water* bottles up Mother Nature's elixir. Watch for it in stores. Or if you stop by the plant (go south on the main street past the old railroad tracks, turn west, and watch for the blue building with the red flagpole), you can buy some there. The number is (402) 273-4295. You can take a quick tour of the plant to see the bottling process and taste this perfectly pure water.

FAVORITE ANNUAL EVENTS IN THE SANDHILLS

(Call ahead to verify dates.)

Polar Bear Tank Race
Thedford to Mullen on the Middle Loup River
first weekend in March
(888) 278-6176

St. Patrick's Day
O'Neill
(402) 336-2355

High School Rodeo
Thedford, early June
(308) 848-3204

Ainsworth Carnival Days
Ainsworth, late June
(402) 382-3537

Nebraska Star Party
(a gathering of stargazers from around the world at Merritt Reservoir)
Valentine, mid-July
(402) 333-5460
nebraskastarparty.org

Nebraska's Big Rodeo
Burwell, late July
(308) 346-4092 or 436-5205
nebraskasbigrodeo.com

Kite Flight (stunt kite competition)
Callaway, early Sept
(308) 870-2808

Beaver Creek Knap-In & Primitive Skills Gathering
12 miles south of Stuart, mid-Sept
(402) 924-3180

Junk Jaunt
300 miles along Loup River and Sand Hills Journey scenic byways
last full weekend in Sept
(308) 346-5151
junkjaunt.com

Old West Days
(with cowboy poetry)
Valentine, early Oct
(800) 658-4024
oldwestdays.net

Evelyn Sharp Days
Ord, mid-Oct
(308) 728-7875

Another great fishing spot is *Keller Park State Recreation Area,* which is west and north of Long Pine on Highway 183. Keller Park has five ponds and is one of the few spots in Nebraska where anglers can catch both cold- and warm-water species. Pond #5 has rainbow trout. It's a really pretty area, with canyons and lots of trees, making it ideal for hiking and camping as well as fishing and bird watching. A park permit is necessary. Call (402) 684-2921 or visit outdoornebraska.gov/kellerpark.

Johnstown, west of Ainsworth on Highway 20, is forever immortalized on film. Many scenes from the Hallmark Hall of Fame made-for-TV movie *O Pioneers!* were shot here. The movie has a couple of Nebraska connections; it was based on a book by Nebraska author Willa Cather, and Hallmark Cards was founded by three brothers (William, Rollie, and Joyce Hall) from Nebraska.

Boyd County

If you enter **Boyd County** from the east on Highway 12, you'll soon come to the tiny community of **Monowi.** Very tiny, indeed. With a population of three, it is the smallest incorporated town in Nebraska. Boost the population temporarily; stop in for a burger and a brew at the **Monowi Tavern,** open from 8 a.m. to 1 a.m. every day, the only business in town. Call (402) 569-3600.

The town of **Lynch** in Boyd County, 7 miles west of Monowi on Highway 12, has become an attraction for Lewis and Clark fans. Just north of town on a dirt road (keep going straight on the main street through town) is **Old Baldy.** Old Baldy, a tall hill naturally devoid of trees and grass on the Missouri River, is where the expedition members came upon their first prairie dogs. They didn't know what they were; they called them "barking squirrels" and were determined to capture a couple of them. Capturing a prairie dog is not easily accomplished. After digging down fruitlessly several feet into a mound, they decided to form a bucket brigade to drown one of the critters out into the open. They succeeded and, ultimately, that prairie dog was sent back alive to President Jefferson. There's a public viewing area in a field near Old Baldy. It's fun to imagine the expedition members struggling up that hill with water-laden buckets to capture a fat little hairy prairie dog. And there's a great vista of the Missouri River from the viewing area, too. The ladies of Lynch, in a promotional effort, get together weekly to sew little stuffed prairie dogs, called Lynch Dawgs, to sell and raise money for the new RV park in town. If you're in Lynch on a weekend, plan on going to the **Lynn Theater.** The theater, which is run totally by volunteers, is a great old structure that looks from the outside like it hasn't been touched in sixty years. For more information on Lynch, call (402) 569-2706 or visit lynchne.com.

Are you in the mood for a Gross Burger? Then you're in luck! In the Boyd County community of **Gross** you'll find the **Nebraska Inn.** Don't worry about finding the building; it's just about the only building in town, and it will be the one with pickups parked outside. On Friday and Saturday evenings, the inn also serves steak dinners ranging from $8.50 to $15. Coffee, if you can believe this, is only 25-cents a cup. The inn is open every day at 9 a.m. until about 11 p.m., or later if the place is jumping. There are two more good things about the Nebraska Inn: The ceiling is plastered with dollar bills that are collected by the owner when people say dirty words, damn it all. To get to Gross, turn north from Highway 12 from Bristow, go for a few miles, and then watch for signs to turn east. It's best to bring a map since it's a little hard to find, but it's well worth the drive. The number is (402) 583-9922.

In the beautiful Niobrara Valley, 5 miles south and 1¾ miles east of **Naper** from Highway 12, there once was a ranch that seemed to be from another world—a gentle world, where a devoted but childless couple, Cal and Ruth Thompson, started a riding school for disadvantaged youths and taught them how to ride and train the graceful white horses that were bred on the ranch. The **White Horse Ranch** closed in 1963 after owner Cal Thompson died. But during the 1940s and 1950s, the ranch was famous for the White Horse Troupe, which performed all over the United States and Canada. The ranch was featured in a photo-story in *Life* magazine in 1945. The horses, which were ridden bareback, dazzled audiences with their many spectacular routines. Ruth Thompson was inducted into the Cowgirl Hall of Fame in 1990. The white horses, known as American Albino or American White, are the only horse breed to be developed in Nebraska. The White Horse Ranch is on the National Register of Historic Places. The current owners no longer accept visitors, but the horses are still there, and you may often see them being ridden in area parades or just basking in the summer sun in a meadow on the ranch.

Holt County

The wide open spaces of Holt County make wind farming a big business in this area. Just north and east of O'Neill is the **Grande Prairie Wind Farm.** With more than 200 turbines and growing, this is the largest wind farm in Nebraska. The annual output is about 400 megawatts or enough to power 120,000 homes all year long. According to the American Wind Energy Association, Nebraska is ranked fourth in the U.S. in wind energy resources.

O'Neill, b'gosh and b'gorra, is the Irish capital of Nebraska. It was established in 1874 by Gen. John O'Neill, a native of Ireland, of course, and a Civil War veteran. General O'Neill founded three colonies in Nebraska for Irish Americans: one at O'Neill, one at Atkinson, and one in Greeley County. Before starting these colonies he was involved in the Fenian invasion into Canada. For this he was jailed, which apparently gave him time to think about his actions. In any case, he moved to Nebraska to start his colonies for Irish Americans. The town gained notoriety in 1892 when Barrett Scott, the county treasurer, disappeared about the same time some county funds disappeared. He was found in Mexico, brought back to face trial, and was kidnapped while out on bail. Frontier justice prevailed; Scott's body was found wrapped in a blanket, the rope from which he was hanged still around his neck and a nasty boot-heel mark on his forehead. By the 1930s, the town of O'Neill seemed safe enough to Mr. William Froelich of Chicago. He was the state's attorney who successfully prosecuted Al Capone and, fearing retribution against his family, moved them to O'Neill. Today O'Neill, at Highway 281 and Highways 20/275, is a thriving, pleasant community of just less than 3,700 people and is home to the Irish Dancers. There are plenty of places to find meals and lodging, and the world's largest shamrock has been painted on the street. If you're in town on St. Patrick's Day, enjoy a meal of corned beef and cabbage provided by the church ladies. And if you stick around into the wee hours, you might see one of the Irished-up locals ride his horse right into a bar. If you're ever in O'Neill at any time, do stop at a great Irish import store, **Saints and Shillelaghs,** at 112 South Fourth St. You can get high-quality Irish goods of all sorts, from clothes (the hand-knit sweaters are to die for) to china, crystal, jewelry, linen, and foods. You can even get Irish tin whistles and a handmade chess set with the "little people" as pieces. It has a whole lot of Irish music, too. Hours are 10 a.m. to 5 p.m. Mon through Sat. The telephone number is (402) 336-2324.

There's a wonderful old hotel in O'Neill called **The Golden Hotel** that's been around since 1913. It's a great place to stay any time, but if you want a room near St. Patrick's Day, well, get in line. These rooms book up fast. The Golden has one bright red room dedicated to the Nebraska Corn Huskers, probably the only thing in all of O'Neill that isn't green. Rates begin at $65 a night. Call (800) 658-3148. The website is historicgoldenhotel.com. If you're looking for a street address—well, it's right there by the world's biggest shamrock.

From O'Neill continue on Highway 20 northwest for 18 miles to **Atkinson** in **Holt County.** Go into the 1950s five-and-dime called **R. F. Goeke** at 110 South Main to buy a soda or sundae. That is, if you can tear yourself away from looking at the notions (lots of notions) and old-fashioned candy. Owners Randy Goeke and Mike Skulavik wanted to re-create a true five-and-dime, and they've succeeded admirably. A sundae will cost between $2 and $4, unless you really go hog wild (for a humongous sundae providing a gut-busting experience). The recipes are all original from old, no-longer-existing soda fountains. A favorite sundae is the Klown, which was invented at a soda fountain in Fremont, Nebraska. They named the restaurant for Mr. Goeke instead of Mr. Skulavik because they thought "Skulavik's" might lead one to think it was a Jewish deli. But if you've got a hankering for a good egg cream, you could do a lot worse at a Jewish deli than at this store. If you're a quilter, you might want to stop in for the really large selection of fabric they carry. The store is open Mon through Sat from 9 a.m. to 6 p.m. The phone number is (402) 925-2263.

Just west of Atkinson is **Atkinson Lake State Recreation Area,** and adjacent to it is the **Bluebird Trail.** Just as everyone loves ice cream, everyone loves bluebirds. Bluebirds, once common in Nebraska, have been making a comeback in the state, thanks to the efforts of people like those who created this trail. Stroll along the half-mile trail and pick out a bench on which to sit quietly and observe. Twelve bluebird boxes are occupied by twelve bluebird families. It's pure magic to see them. You owe it to yourself to catch a glimpse of them.

Garfield, Loup, and Rock Counties

Burwell, at Highways 11 and 91 in *Garfield County,* is most famous for *Nebraska's Big Rodeo,* held each July since 1921 at the rodeo grounds/arena, which is a National Historic Site. The rodeo grounds are active all summer long, with colorful, action-packed ranch rodeos, open ropings held twice weekly, an old-timer's rodeo, and professional rodeos. If you've never been to a rodeo, or even if you have, check out the action at Burwell. Each April and October Burwell is host to two of the few fox hunts in the state.

Six miles northwest of Burwell is the *Calamus Reservoir State Recreation Area,* encompassing nearly 12,000 acres in both Garfield and Loup Counties. There is a huge lake, with 196 million gallons of fresh spring water entering it daily. The lake is great for fishing, sailing, boating, skiing, sailboarding—well, all those water-related things you'd expect to do at such a lake—plus there are sandy beaches. There's a modern campground with restrooms and showers. A park permit is required. If you get tired of cooking out, the *Calamus River Lodge* (308-346-4331; calamuslodge.com) is near the lake, as are a motel and a golf course. The telephone number at the Calamus Reservoir is (308) 346-5666.

The *Calamus State Fish Hatchery,* Nebraska's largest hatchery, produces an estimated forty million fish each year. It is located at the Virginia Smith Dam, 7 miles northwest of Burwell. Visitors are welcome daily from 10 a.m. to 4 p.m. seven days a week in the summer months. Between Labor Day and Memorial Day, the hatchery is closed on weekends. Hatchery activities can be seen from the visitor center. Call (308) 346-4226 or visit outdoornebraska .com/hatcheries for more information. Tours can be scheduled forty-eight hours in advance.

For an abundance of uninterrupted Sandhills scenery, many Nebraskans would recommend the drive from *Taylor,* in south-central *Loup County,* north on Highway 183 to Bassett, in north-central Rock County. This highway is a good place to practice your finger wave on the driver of the in-all-likelihood rare car you'll meet. In the days of the Wild West, the cattle-rustlin', hard-drinkin', and gamblin' Pony Boys, led by David C. "Doc" Middleton and Albert "Kid" Wade, frequented the Martin Hotel in Bassett. Wade was hanged east of town in 1884 by masked vigilantes who dragged him from jail, thinking this swift justice would put an end to horse stealing in the area. Middleton died an old man in the county jail of Douglas, Wyoming, in 1913, while serving a sentence for bootlegging.

Greeley and Valley Counties

Spalding, in *Greeley County,* will welcome you to the town where "a river runs through it." The spring-fed Cedar Creek flows into this valley town, and its 1910 Light Plant still provides up to 10 percent of the electrical needs of the community. A hand-dug millrace and waterwheels were originally constructed to power a flour mill. The dam over Cedar Creek is on the National Register of Historic Places. Tours of the original waterwheels can be arranged. A river might run through your golf game, too. A diversion of Cedar Creek cuts through part of the nine-hole course. If you'd rather be on the water than playing golf near it, the *T&T Canoe Service* will provide canoes, safety gear, and transportation back to your car from downstream. The telephone number is (308) 497-2120. As you drive into town on Highway 91, you'll see the Gothic spires of *St. Michael's Church,* an enormous Catholid church built in the Gothic Revival style that is listed on the National Register of Historic Places. You're welcome to visit the church. The doors are open all the time, but the lights won't be on at night. Call (308) 497-2662 for more information.

In the opposite corner of Greeley County, southwest of Spalding, you'll find the *Happy Jack Chalk Mine and Peak* just 1½ miles south of *Scotia* on Highway 11. Take a tour of the place where chalk was mined from 1887 until 1932. The chalk, used for paint, cement, whitewash, polishes, and chicken

OTHER ATTRACTIONS WORTH SEEING IN THE SANDHILLS

(All area codes are 402.)

LONG PINE

Long Pine State Recreation Area
1 mile north and 1 mile west of
Highway 20
684-2921
outdoornebraska.gov/longpine

VALENTINE

Fort Niobrara National
Wildlife Refuge
5 miles east of Valentine on Highway 12
376-3789

Valentine National Wildlife Refuge
south of Valentine on Highway 83
376-3789

feed, is comprised of the fossilized remains of tiny sea creatures from the time when much of Nebraska was an inland sea. The mine is named after "Happy Jack" Swearingen, a fur trader who built a dugout dwelling for himself near the peak. The mine fell into dangerous disrepair when it closed, the kind of place that draws teenagers who want to scare themselves silly with ghost stories in the dark of the night. A group of Scotia citizens acquired it, fixed it up, made it safe, and turned it into a sweet little tourist attraction. The guided summer tours, the hike to the peak, and the picnic area are well worth your time. Around Halloween there's a haunted house (or I guess it would be a haunted cave) that even grown men say is truly scary. This is the only mine of its kind in the U.S. Call (308) 245-3276 or visit happyjackchalkmine.com.

Aviation fans are encouraged to head north on Highway 11 into **Valley County** and the **Evelyn Sharp Airfield,** on the north edge of **Ord,** to view the touching mementos of Nebraska's most famous aviator. Evelyn Genevieve Sharp was born in 1919, earned her commercial pilot's license when she was sixteen, and three years later became one of the nation's first female airmail pilots. At the age of twenty, she became a flight instructor and taught more than 350 men to fly. At the onset of World War II, Sharp joined the Women Airforce Service Pilots (WASPs), which was organized by Gen. H. H. (Hap) Arnold to deliver airplanes from the factories to shipping points. Sharp died in 1944 at the age of twenty-four in a crash of a P-38 in Pennsylvania. At the time of her death, she was a squadron commander just three flights shy of her fifth rating, the highest certificate available to women pilots at the time. The display about her career contains newspaper articles, photographs, and the propeller of the Curtis Robin airplane that was purchased for her by the businessmen of Ord in 1937. Read her story in the book *Sharpie* by Diane Ruth Armour Bartles. Evelyn Sharp's story is also recounted in a piece of fiction, *Silver Wings, Blue Santiago* by Janet Dailey.

Six miles north of Ord on Highway 11, you'll come to the town of **Elyria** and the exit to **Fort Hartsuff State Historical Park.** Fort Hartsuff was built in 1874 as a buffer between homesteaders along the North Loup River valley and the Native Americans who had lived there for a lot longer. The troops also assisted local authorities in catching horse thieves and train robbers until the fort closed in 1881. Its nine main buildings were built of concrete, which has made the task of restoration somewhat easier than at other abandoned prairie outposts. Although it seems a strange adjective for a military post, Fort Hartsuff can easily be described as lovely. All the buildings around the parade ground are picture perfect, and when you walk into the enlisted men's quarters, you can almost hear them chatting around the stoves before crawling into their lined-up cots. The jail looks exceedingly uncomfortable and, one suspects, served as a silent admonition for good behavior. Staff and volunteers are often outfitted in period uniforms, and the baker turns out crusty golden loaves of bread for guests to sample. There's a picnic area shaded by big old trees. The grounds are open daily from Memorial Day weekend to Labor Day from 8 a.m. to 8 p.m. and from 9 a.m. to sunset the rest of the year. Buildings are open daily from Memorial Day weekend to Labor Day from 9 a.m. to 5 p.m. Call (308) 346-4715 or visit outdoornebraska.gov/forthartsuff for more information.

Wheeler County

The *Starving Stallion Saloon* in *Ericson,* 7 miles off Highway 281 on Highway 70, is a great place to stop for a burger or a brew. You can't miss it; there's only one bar in town, and the Starving Stallion looks just the way you'd expect a western bar to look—wonderfully weathered, just a little worse for wear, and on an unpaved street. It's dimly lit, as a good bar should be, and it offers great burgers. On weekend nights they rustle up a great steak, just like the kind you'd expect from a saloon in ranch country. The interior of the bar is rough wood paneling, and the restaurant is separated from the bar by a partition of authentic barn siding. You can tell this ain't one of them snooty wine-drinker bars. For one thing, there's a decided dearth of hanging ferns, and the wine glasses hanging above the bar look slightly dusty and little used. For more than twenty-five years, the Starving Stallion has sponsored the hilarious Sandhills Turtle Races on the first weekend in August. You don't happen to have a turtle in the car? No problem—you can rent one. But remember, the use of steroids is strictly prohibited! The Starving Stallion is open every day from noon to 1 a.m. The telephone number is (308) 653-3100.

North of Ericson on Hwy. 281 is the little community of Bartlett. Once included in Bartlett's population of about 100 people was Herb Mignery, whose family has been ranching in Wheeler county since the 1800s. Herb is indeed passionate about the ranch life, but chooses to express himself as one of this country's most prolific artists and sculptors. He lives in Estes Park, Colorado, now, but Herb has donated 15 bronze sculptures to his hometown. They are now displayed on the grounds of the Wheeler County Courthouse in what is known as the Mignery Sculpture Park. It's one of the largest collections of its kind in the U.S. and here it is out in the middle of Nebraska. Because it is an outdoor exhibit, you can visit anytime you like. But if you come during business hours at the courthouse, go visit the county clerk's office and ask to see the video about Herb Mignery. It's about 45 minutes long, but he describes each of the pieces outside and what moved him to create the work. The county clerk's phone is (308) 654-3308. Learn more about the artist at herbmignery.com.

Hooker and Grant Counties

If you fancy yourself a good golfer, you will find the next few sentences frustrating. That's because you'll be reading about the **Sandhills Golf Club,** south of **Mullen** off Highway 97, a private membership club where you can play only if you're a sponsored guest or you make written arrangements well in advance of your arrival. Now is the time to plan ahead and consider how to make those arrangements. This golf course, one of the finest natural courses in the country, was designed by Ben Crenshaw and Bill Coore to take advantage of the contours of the Sandhills on a plateau above the Dismal River. Magazine and newspaper articles have referred to the eighteen-hole, 7,000-yard, par-71 championship course as a "masterpiece" and a "work of art" and in other terms generally reminiscent of a mother talking about her favorite child. The owners and managers are intent on maintaining the high-quality atmosphere of the club. If you are a golfer, you'll understand why the club prefers not to have casual tourists. If you are not a golfer, think of something you are passionate about and how much better it is in the company of persons who share your passion. To make golfing arrangements, call (308) 546-2237.

Many of the first white settlers in this part of Nebraska lived in sod huts—basically a house built from slabs of sod held together by the rich prairie grass. Most of them have long disappeared, but a visit to the Double R Guest Ranch allows you the rare opportunity to see a well-maintained sod hut. Relatives of owners Jim and Pat Bridges not only built and lived in this soddie, but people actually lived in it until 1994. The land also contains a one-room school house that dates to the early 1900s. It is still used for weekly piano lessons for children in the area. There are plenty of activities you can participate in that have to do with the real operation of a ranch. Come sometime between March and May to see calves being born. You might be able to help out with the feeding. Check out all of the activities on this family-owned ranch at sandhilldoublerranch.com or call (866) 217-2042.

Hooker County has plenty of other outdoor activities for non-golfers, however. The Middle Loup and Dismal River are great for canoeing, kayaking, and tanking. If you want to rent any of the above, stop at the Sandhills Motel in Mullen on West Highway 2. The number is (308) 546-2206 or (888) 278-6167. Be forewarned that the Dismal River is not for a beginning canoer. It is tricky, and it can be hazardous for the inexperienced. Fishing and hunting in the county are excellent, but again, heed a word of advice: always get a permit, and always get permission from landowners before crossing onto private land.

The drive along Highway 2 in **Grant County** provides still more spectacularly serene Sandhills scenery. And Grant is another county where the cattle easily outnumber humans. ***Hyannis*** has 185 people; ***Whitman*** and ***Ashby*** are both unincorporated. Just a little way west of Whitman there are lakes on the north side of Highway 20, and, yes, those birds you see are pelicans, right here in landlocked Nebraska.

Blaine and Thomas Counties

Have you ever heard of a Sandhills monkey? It's closely related to the jackalope and just as rare. You can see one in Blaine County, albeit stuffed, at ***Uncle Buck's Lodge*** in ***Brewster.*** Uncle Buck's is a big log-cabin lodge, restaurant, and lounge in this community of twenty-two people, at Highways 7 and 91. You can learn a lot about local history by reading the displays and looking at the pictures on the walls. The three-story, 15,000-square-foot, cedar-sided building is surrounded by a deck, and the rooms are comfortable. The dining room has huge windows that open onto a view of the North Loup River. Plus it's got light fixtures made of horns and animal heads on the wall. The food is fine, and the pastries are great (guests have been known to make midnight raids on the pies). It's a popular place for hunters in season and a pleasurable getaway for anyone at any time. The Rhoades family, which operates Uncle Buck's, offers eco-tours through the Sandhills, where you can learn all about the flora and fauna of the region, including the Sandhills monkey. The number is (800) 239-9190; the website unclebuckslodge.com. Oh, about that Sandhills monkey—it's the rear end of a deer, disguised to look like a scary toothsome creature you'd never ever want to meet. And about those jackalopes—well, ask anyone where you can see one. If they tell you that your leg has been pulled mightily, just tell them you know they exist because you saw one on a postcard. While you're at it, ask someone of the opposite sex for the best place to snipe hunt.

You could opt to stay at the ***Sandhills Guest Ranch B&B*** a few miles east of Brewster on a ranch operated by Lee and Beverly DeGroff. You have three choices in accommodations: the bunk house, which is a bunch of bunk beds (think college frat party); a little rustic cabin in a meadow (think romance); or a guest house called Doc's Hideout, named for Doc Middleton, a horse thief in these parts in the 1880s. The rate is $85 per couple, no matter which building you choose, but only the cabin and the guest house have private baths. Beverly fixes a huge country breakfast (they even make their own syrup). After breakfast, spend the day tanking or tubing on the river. Call (308) 547-2460.

You might wonder why you're seeing more trees in ***Thomas County*** than you have in other Sandhills areas. It's because they've been planted, by hand, to create the 93,000-acre ***Nebraska National Forest,*** the largest hand-planted

TREEmendous!

Now, please consider the gentle irony of Nebraska, a state that has the bad (and incorrect) reputation for being flat and treeless, producing trees for reforestation in other states. The Bessey Nursery, in the Nebraska National Forest, produces millions of seedlings to be planted in forests all across the United States. During the first fifty years of the nursery's existence nearly 200 million of its seedlings were planted. Seedlings are still distributed across the country to provide shade and shelter for farms, schools, parks, and other forests, which have suffered from overlogging or fires. Call (308) 533-2257 for a tour. So let's not hear another word about Nebraska being treeless. Well, even if some parts of it are fairly treeless, somebody is probably busy planting a tree or two right now as you read this. Also, keep in mind that those fairly treeless places are good for growing the food you eat—without clearing forests or digging up a bazillion rocks.

forest in the country. The forest was established in 1902 by Teddy Roosevelt, and by 1921 more than thirteen million seedlings had been planted. You can see the forest better when you drive in and look around. The entrance is 2 miles west of **Halsey** off Highway 2. It's quite pretty, and you can climb to the top of the lookout tower in the summer between 2 and 4 p.m. to see off into forever. If you climb to the top, you'll realize how big the forest is, and, seeing the contrast between the forest and the Sandhills, you'll be able to judge for yourself how much work it must have been to plant all those trees. Remember, this is not an old-growth forest, but it's pretty darn impressive just the same. There's a swimming pool, picnic areas, some great hiking, and you can camp year-round. For more information call (308) 432-0300.

Arthur County

The tiny community of **Arthur** is located at the junction of Highways 92 and 61. Even though it's quite small, with a population of 128, Arthur has two attractions you should see. The first is a church made of bales of hay, which was built in the late 1920s. It is said to be the only baled-hay church in the world. If you find another, do let the people at *Ripley's Believe It or Not* know. The bales of the **Pilgrim Holiness Church** have been plastered inside and out, so you'd never know by looking that it's made from hay, except for the plexiglass display that shows the hay and the construction method. In case you tend toward the more critical approach to life, ask yourself if you could do a more ingenious job of devising a structure in a country where hay is more common than trees. If the door isn't open, there's generally a note on the door giving you a number to call to get inside. You should also see the no-longer-in-use, one-room courthouse, which remains the smallest courthouse in the United States. It's in the front yard of the actual working courthouse. Again, if it's not open, there should be a note on the door. If all else fails, call (308) 764-2201.

May's Place, in a restored older home in Arthur, has some fine items made by craftspeople in the Sandhills. Of particular note are silver jewelry and silver belt buckles made by Hanna Silversmiths. Actor Danny Glover has a Hanna buckle, as do several people who've crewed on his movies. You'll also find hand-woven items; a tour of the weaving shop can be arranged. Other items included in the inventory are goat milk soaps, quilts, collectible dolls, crafts, and lots of old stuff in an Antique Room. May's Place is worth a visit, but you have to call and schedule an appointment; (308) 764-2367 or 764-2450.

trivia

South of Arthur, on Highway 61, you'll notice well-worn cowboy boots upside down on fence posts. No one can say with absolute certainty how this custom originated, but some people contend it's because cowboys like their soles facing heaven.

If you're hungry or thirsty or just want to get caught up on the local gossip, stop in at the Bunkhouse Bar & Grill on the main drag through town. It's where everyone comes for lunch or dinner, for the great burgers and good conversation. The ceilings are covered with burlap bags and all sorts of weird things hang on the walls. It's just a place with personality. The Bunkhouse is open Mon–Sat 11 a.m. until about 8 p.m. Call (308) 764-2476.

Logan and McPherson Counties

The best attraction in these two counties is what makes them so eminently qualified to be in a book about off-the-beaten-path places. The whole of both counties is off the beaten path and comprises only three communities, with a grand total of fewer than 350 people. (It's a pretty safe bet there are metropolitan areas where more people than that live in just one building.) All of Logan County has fewer than 750 residents. Of the twenty-five least-populated counties in the country, eight of them are in the Sandhills. Take the time to slow down, see the scenery, hear birds sing, and breathe clean air. Stop for a meal, stop for a soda, or just stop and enjoy a slower pace of life than usual. Take a stroll around *Gandy, Stapleton,* or *Tryon* and let the kids play in the park. It's also a pretty safe bet you won't get mugged and the kids won't get abducted; you won't even have to lock your car. If you want to see small-town America, you're looking at it. Oh, one more thing—when you're driving in the Sandhills, make sure to watch your gas supply. Not every one of these widely-spaced-apart towns has a gas station, and, even if they do, it might not be open when you need it.

Custer County

It seems like all roads lead to **Broken Bow,** which is located at the junction of Highways 2, 21, 91, and 70, in Custer County. A good place to stay is the **Arrow Hotel,** across from the town square. It's a great old hotel that dates to 1928, but has been modernized without compromising any historic integrity. It has twenty-two suites with full kitchens. The cozy little restaurant, the Bonfire Grill, has great food seven days a week, but the Sunday brunch, from 10 a.m. to 2 p.m. really draws a crowd. The telephone number is (308) 872-6662 or (866) 972-6662, and the website is arrowhotel.com.

Power to the People

Working together to achieve a common goal is a time-honored tradition. But how do you organize far-flung farmers across the country to obtain a fair price for farm products and a good value for money spent? If the year is 1867, you start a movement called the National Grange of the Patrons of Husbandry. The Nebraska State Grange was organized in 1872. (In case you're wondering what a grange is, the dictionary defines it as a farm with outlying buildings and as a national fraternal organization of farmers.) During the 1870s the Grange played a huge role in farmers' lives and offered political, social, educational, and fraternal activities. "Granger Laws" put in place by state governments set the pattern for modern America's regulated free-enterprise economy.

Within a decade the Farmers' Alliance, and the Farmer's Equity Union after that, replaced the Grange as the farmers' organization of choice. By the time of the Depression, the Farm Holiday Association became the political arm of the farmers' movement. Other movements supporting farm owners have come and gone as the economic pendulum has swung. However, the Grange Movement was reestablished in 1911 in Custer County and is the oldest Grange organization in the state. The State Grange, likewise, was reorganized in the same year. At present, local granges are important to community life and sound farm policy.

A Nebraska State Historical Marker about the Nebraska Grange is located northwest of Broken Bow on Highway 2 in Custer County.

Kinkaider Brewing Tap Room, located about a mile north of Broken Bow at 43860 Paulsen Road, is open Wed and Thursday 4–10 p.m.; Fri and Sat from 11 a.m. to 11 p.m.

Just east of town on Hwy. 2 is the new *Sandhills Scenic Byways Interpretive Center* and it's worth a stop to better understand this area. For example, you see those old-fashioned windmills, along with modern wind turbines, everywhere in Nebraska, but have you ever wondered how they work? The working windmill here explains that and other secrets of life on the prairie. The hours are 9 a.m. to 5 p.m., Mon through Sat and noon to 5 p.m. on Sun from May 1 to Sept 30. Call (308) 872-5691.

Northeast of Broken Bow, near *Comstock,* is the *Dowse Sod House,* one of the few original intact sod houses in the county; at one time Comstock was known as the Sod House Capital of the World. In this area wood was scarce, and settlers were forced to build shelter from the very ground on which they stood. Sod, known as Nebraska Marble, housed many pioneers until they could afford to build wooden homes. The Dowse Sod House was built by William Dowse for his bride-to-be in 1900. The original house had three rooms and a sleeping loft. For fifty-nine years the Dowse family lived there and overcame drought, blizzards, grasshoppers, prairie fires, rustlers, and isolation. Many of the furnishings in the house are period pieces and similar to those used by the family. Ron Dowse, the grandson of William, owns the house now and, although he never lived in it, he remembers visiting his grandparents there and larger family gatherings at Christmas. You can stop by on your own, but Ron is glad to give a tour with a little advance notice by calling (308) 215-0365. There is no charge, but do leave a donation if you go on your own. To get there, take Highway 183 and go east at the COMSTOCK sign; continue on 21C to the DOWSE SOD HOUSE sign; then turn south and east for 3½ miles to the home place.

Northwest of Broken Bow is *Victoria Springs State Recreation Area.* This secluded sixty-acre park, called an oasis in the Sandhills, is located 6 miles east of *Anselmo* or 9 miles north of Merna. It is named after the mineral springs in the park, the water from which was said to have restorative powers and which was bottled and sold by homesteader and judge Charles Mathews. Log cabins he built are still on the site. The recreation area has two modern housekeeping cabins, camping, picnicking in wooded areas, fishing, and boating. A park permit is required. Reservations for the cabins are a very good idea. Call (308) 749-2235 or visit outdoornebraska.gov/victoriasprings.

Places to Stay in the Sandhills

BROKEN BOW

Arrow Hotel
509 South Ninth
(308) 872-6662
arrowhotel.com

O'NEILL

The Golden Hotel
Fourth and Douglas
(402) 336-4436 or
(800) 658-3148
historicgoldenhotel.com

SPARKS

Heartland Elk Guest Ranch
rural
(402) 376-2553
heartlandelk.com

SPRINGVIEW

Big Canyon Inn
rural
(402) 497-3170

Larrington's Guest Cottage
rural
(402) 497-2261

STUART

The Sisters' House B&B
412 Garfield
(402) 340-4922
thesistershouse.com

Places to Eat in the Sandhills

BREWSTER

Uncle Buck's Lodge
(American)
Highways 7 and 91
(308) 547-2210

BROKEN BOW

The Bonfire Grill
(American)
in the Arrow Hotel
509 South Ninth
(308) 872-3363

ERICSON

Starving Stallion Saloon
(American)
(308) 653-3100

ELYRIA

The Country Neighbor
(American)
½ mile south of Fort
Hartsuff
(308) 346-5049

GROSS

Nebraska Inn
(steaks, burgers)
about the only building in
town—you can't miss it
(402) 583-9922

SPENCER

Angel's Strawbale Saloon
(American)
2 miles south of the
junction of Highways 281
and 12 on the south side of
the Niobrara River
(402) 589-1017

VALENTINE

Peppermill
(American)
112 North Main
(402) 376-2800

HELPFUL SANDHILLS WEBSITES

Ainsworth
ainsworthchamber.com

Broken Bow
brokenbow-ne.com

Burwell
visitburwell.org

Long Pine
cityoflongpine.org

O'Neill
oneillchamber.com

Valentine
visitvalentine.org

Land of Cowboys and Indians

The Pine Ridge area of northwest Nebraska is a land where the drama of the landscape is more than matched by the drama of events in western history. This canyoned, pine-covered territory was home to the Sioux, who occupied it permanently beginning in 1810. This is where the Oglala Sioux warrior Crazy Horse was killed in 1877 and where fur traders set up early trading posts. This is the land of novelist Mari Sandoz, who wrote about history and the incontrovertible effect the land had on shaping the destiny of the people who lived here. Although there is a Cowboy Museum in the Pine Ridge, you'll find cowboys around every corner, still making a living from cattle and the land. And, if you're lucky, you'll catch a glimpse of the lake "monster," which rivals the Loch Ness Monster in its elusiveness. Prehistoric wonders and paleontology digs round out experiences for travelers in the Pine Ridge.

Sheridan County

Sheridan County is where the Sandhills meet the Pine Ridge. The northern part of the county has the topography of the Pine Ridge, with Beaver Wall, a nearly vertical rock cliff that

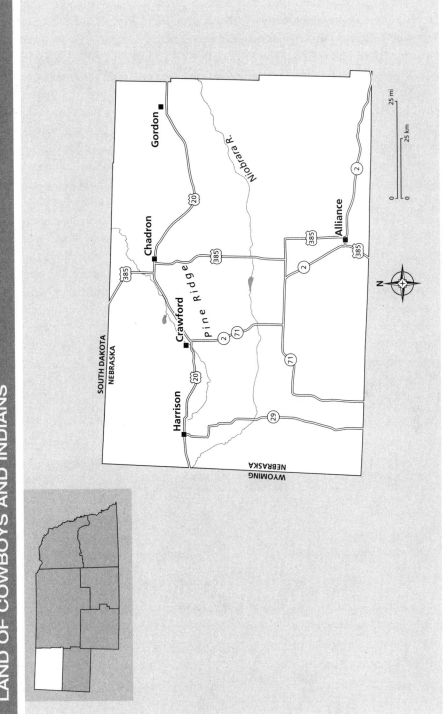

extends for several miles north of Hay Springs. The central and southern areas of the county are prairie country. In **Gordon,** at Highways 20 and 27, is the **Tri-State Oldtime Cowboys Memorial Museum.** It's located in a city park 1 block west of Main Street between Third and Fourth Streets. This log cabin contains a collection of cowboy artifacts from the late 1800s to the present day. The collection includes tools and gear such as saddles, hats, and boots, plus a chuck wagon, with more than 200 cattle brands. If you think branding cattle is barbaric, bear in mind the words of South Dakota rancher/writer Linda Hasselstrom, who wrote in her book *Land Circles* that she'll "consider another method of marking my cattle when we stop licensing cars to identify them and prevent their theft." The museum is open from Memorial Day through Sept 15 daily from 1 to 5 p.m. Admission is free. The phone number is (308) 282-0749.

Sheridan County is also known as Sandoz Country for novelist/historian/biographer Mari Sandoz. Sandoz, who grew up on a ranch south of Gordon, has been credited with creating a Great Plains legacy with sensitive portrayals of pioneer men and women and Native American history and culture. Not bad for a woman whose taciturn (and some say downright tyrannical) father kept her out of school until she was nine years old. Some of her most famous novels are *Old Jules* (pioneer stories; some describe life with her father), *Cheyenne Autumn* (it's been made into a movie), and *Crazy Horse*. Four of her books have been included in the 100 Best Books about the West, which are selected by the Chicago Corral (the parent group of the Westerners). Sandoz died in 1966 and is buried on her beloved land south of Gordon, at the privately

FAVORITE ATTRACTIONS IN THE PINE RIDGE

(All area codes are 308.)

**Agate Fossil Beds
National Monument**
24 miles south of Harrison or
34 miles north of Mitchell
668-2211
nps.gov/agfo

Carhenge
2½ miles north on Highway 87
Alliance
762-3569
carhenge.com

Olde Main Street Inn
115 Main St.
Chadron
432-3380

Toadstool Geologic Park
northwest from Highway 2
Crawford
432-0300

Believe It or Not: The Mouth That Roared

Try to catch of glimpse of the fabled, elusive *Walgren Lake Monster* at the *Walgren Lake State Recreation Area* near Hay Springs. This benign, Loch Ness–like creature has been the subject of spirited local legend and debate for decades. Verified sightings have yet to be confirmed. Some locals insist on the authenticity of sightings; folklorist Roger Welsch says the creature has been seen only by fishermen who've been out too long in the sun without a hat, while others say it's seen by teenagers on a toot. Here are some of the things that have been written about the monster: it eats a dozen calves when it comes ashore; it flattens the cornfields; its flashing green eyes spit fire; the gnashing of its teeth sounds like a clap of thunder. Newspaper accounts from the mid-1930s claim that a skeptic from Omaha bravely spent the night alone at the lake. He returned home haggard, white-haired, and voiceless with fear. Three days later, upon regaining speech, he said the monster was 300 feet long and its mouth was big enough to hold Omaha's Woodmen of the World building. It's a great legend (although a great big hoax), and you'll enjoy the peaceful surroundings of this beautiful lake, where you can camp, hike, and fish. A park entry permit is required and can be obtained from stores in town. To try your luck at seeing the creature, go 3 miles south of Hay Springs on Highway 87 and then 2 miles east.

owned ranch where she grew up. Several miles south of Gordon on Highway 27, near the ranch, a historical marker commemorates her life and work.

Beaver Road, north out of *Hay Springs,* is located in Beaver Valley and extends the length of *Beaver Wall.* Beaver Wall is an escarpment with breathtaking views. You can see for nearly 150 miles from the Black Hills to the buttes at Crawford. According to Sioux legend, if someone made a wish and spent the night in the cavelike depressions in Beaver Wall, the wish would be granted the next morning. The drive is pretty spectacular. If you must get out to hike, always find a landowner to ask his or her permission. Or if you want to climb Beaver Wall, seek out the owner and ask permission. Beaver Wall is 10 miles north of Highway 20 on a county road at the west end of Hay Springs.

South of Gordon on Highways 27 and 2 is the tiny town of *Ellsworth,* with a ranch store called *Morgan's Cowpoke Haven* that is also the post office. The store has been here since 1898 and in 2010 was placed on the National Register of Historic Places. The store has maintained its authenticity with a tin ceiling inside and a hitching post outside. You'll find all kinds of horse gear as well as cowboy hats and boots. A lot of the equipment is made on-site from a wear-like-iron modern fabric known as cordura. In the store you can buy luggage, from garment bags to backpacks, boot bags, saddlebags, sports bags, ditty bags, hat bags, bridle bags, pistol cases, outfitter packs, panniers—well, the list goes on and on. Ask to see a mail-order catalog if you don't want to schlepp stuff around on your trip. The store is open Mon through Sat from 8:30 a.m. to 5 p.m. The telephone number is (308) 762-2666. The bathroom has this no-nonsense poem on the wall: "With these two rules to live by, / You've got it put' near skinned:/Never whittle towards you, / And don't spit against the wind."

Just west of **Antioch,** north of Highway 2 across the railroad tracks, you'll see some ruins that look as though a very small, bizarre cathedral once stood there. These are the ruins of a potash plant. Potash was a component of a fertilizer used in the Cotton Belt of the United States. When World War I broke out and cut off the supply of European potash, a plant was built near Antioch to extract potash from the alkaline lakes in the area. Five plants were built by 1918, and the potash was used for fertilizer, epsom salts, soda, and other products. When peace was achieved, the European potash was again imported, and at a cheaper cost than that needed to keep the plants open. The last of the plants closed in 1921.

Dawes County

Three miles east of **Chadron** on Highway 20 is the **Museum of the Fur Trade.** This fascinating, one-of-a-kind museum features an extensive collection of items associated with the fur trade and the daily lives of traders, trappers, and Native Americans. The museum does not limit itself to the American fur trade; there are also displays of international fur trading. Plan on spending a long time here viewing trade goods like knives, beads, cloth, traps, blankets, and other items used either for trade or treaty payments. The collection of guns made for the Native American trade from 1750 to 1900 is the largest and most complete in the world. You'll see all types of fur, from buffalo robes to beaver, mink, wolf, badger, and sea otter. (Shoppers take note: I always leave some of my money at the gift shop.) On the grounds is the site of the re-created Bordeaux Trading Post. Built in 1837, the original trading post was part of the American Fur Company until 1849, when it became an independent post operated by James Bordeaux for trade with the Sioux until 1872. Four years later, with the Indian Wars in full cry, the U.S. Cavalry confiscated illegal ammunition being sold to the by-then-hostile Sioux, and the post was abandoned by the subsequent owner, James Boucher. The trading post is built on the original foundations. Inside you'll see evidence of the far-from-fancy life of the frontier trader. Imagine sleeping on the willow bed, cooking in the kettles hung over the fire hearth, and selecting from the store shelves stocked with trade goods. There's also a garden of fruits and vegetables grown by American Indians.

FAVORITE ANNUAL EVENTS IN THE PINE RIDGE

(Call ahead to verify dates; all area codes are 308.)

Henge Days
Alliance, late June
762-3569

Intertribal Gathering
Crawford, early July
207-0510

Old West Trail Rodeo
Crawford, early July
665-2594

Fur Trade Days
Chadron, mid-July
432-4401

Willow Tree Festival
Gordon, mid-Sept
282-9972
willowtreefestival.com

This museum is a must-see for anyone interested in western history. Admission price for those eighteen and older is $5; children seventeen and younger are admitted free when accompanied by parents. The museum is open from May 1 through Oct. 31 from 8 a.m. to 5 p.m. The museum is not heated, so consider that if requesting an off-season tour. Call (308) 432-3843 in advance. The Web address is furtrade.org.

A great place to stay in Chadron is the *Olde Main Street Inn,* at 115 Main St. Chances are you'll find owner Jeanne Goetzinger at her spinning wheel in the evening. This eclectic B&B, now listed on the National Register of Historic Places, has ten rooms on the second and third floors. Some are charmingly restored to reflect the original days of the 1890 hotel; others are awaiting renovation. On the first floor is the Longbranch Saloon, where locals and guests gather to swap stories. There's a pool table, too. If you don't like bars, you can enter by a private outside door, to which you'll get a key when you register. If you decide to forgo the bar, however, you'll miss the chance to meet other guests, who have ranged from rodeo stars to barnstorming pilots, foreigners who come for the nearby Sioux Sun Dances, and people who are riding a mule-driven wagon across the country. If you ask, Jeanne will turn back the guest book pages to show you Dick Cavett's name, who has stayed here four times, as well as the late Senator George McGovern and country music singer Michael Martin Murphy. The history of the hotel is the history of the area as well. In December 1890 and shortly into the following year, the hotel was the military headquarters for Gen. Nelson Miles, who commanded the Wounded Knee operations in the Native American campaigns. Jeanne will make breakfast pretty much to your order, and, if she has the time and you have the inclination, might join you for stories of the area and to share insights on life. Reservations aren't necessary but are encouraged. Rates range from $70 for one person to $105 for the three-room General Miles suite. The telephone number is (308) 432-3380.

Before you leave Chadron, spend some time at the **Mari Sandoz High Plains Heritage Center** on the Chadron State College campus. The center is devoted to the culture and history of the High Plains as well as the personal and professional life of Mari Sandoz. You can hear oral histories from local ranchers and of course, see original manuscripts and more from the life of Mari Sandoz. The hours are Mon through Fri, 8 a.m. to 4 p.m., Sat 9 a.m.–4 p.m. Admission is free The phone number is (308) 432-6401; the website is sandozcenter.com.

Just 8 miles south of Chadron on Highway 385 is **Chadron State Park.** This heavily wooded retreat can come as a surprise to persons unfamiliar with the rugged terrain of the Pine Ridge's Nebraska National Forest, which compares favorably to many forested areas of Colorado. There are several housekeeping cabins tucked among the ponderosa pines of this 972-acre park. Or you can pitch a tent or park your RV. Established in 1921, this is Nebraska's oldest state park, but the campgrounds are modern, as are the showers and restrooms in the camping areas. Trail rides and jeep rides can be arranged. There are tennis and sand volleyball courts, paddle boats, a swimming pool, a craft center, horseshoe games, and picnic shelters. Cabin reservations must be for a minimum stay of two nights in peak season. However, if you happen to show up without a reservation and there are availabilities, you can stay for one night. Even if you can't stay, stop for a hike or unload your bikes. The park is at an elevation of nearly 3,500 feet; mountain bikers sing the praises of the park and surrounding trails. The required park permit is available at the park office. To make reservations for a cabin (from $80 per day) or to get more information, call (308) 432-6167. Reservations can be made online at outdoornebraska .org/chadron.

Since we're on the topic of mountain biking, the Pine Ridge is an excellent place to do so. There are approximately 70 miles of marked bike routes that will challenge even the scoffers who say that mountain biking isn't possible in Nebraska. The trails might not be as rocky as in neighboring Colorado, but there's a little creature here called a puncture vine that will do just that to your tires if you aren't careful. The Nebraska Game and Parks Commission and the U.S. Forest Service have produced a wonderful weatherproof topographic map for bikers. It is available from the Chadron Chamber of Commerce (call 308-432-4401) or from local bike shops. **Soldier Creek Wilderness Area** (to find it, follow Soldier Creek Road at the entrance to Fort Robinson State Park) is a particularly wonderful place to bike. It's off-limits to motorized vehicles. No matter where you bike in the Pine Ridge, whether in state parks or U.S. Forest Service land, follow these rules: Stay on the marked and visible trails; don't scare the slower-moving hikers and horse riders; don't trespass; always leave any gate as you found it; take water; and wear your helmet. And remember, prickly pear cactus and puncture vines are common in the area. If you get off the trails, your tires are in peril. If you go too fast and take a spill, your body is in peril.

Fort Robinson State Park is just about five minutes west of town. It's hard to say enough good things about this park. Not only is it Nebraska's largest state park (with 22,000 acres of incredibly beautiful scenery), but it's simply dense with history and great things to see and do. It was an active military post from 1874 to 1948. Chief Crazy Horse was killed here in 1877, at a site now marked by a simple stone monument outside the guardhouse. He had freely agreed to come into Fort Robinson for negotiations with the military; when he realized he had been betrayed and was about to be imprisoned, his struggle ended when he was bayoneted and lay bleeding to death on the floor of the Adjutant's Office. Fort Robinson was a post for the Ninth Cavalry's famous black "Buffalo Soldiers" and, in later years, was a training ground for the Army's Olympic equestrian team, a World War II K-9 Corps, and a prisoner-of-war camp for German prisoners.

Today guests can stay in any number of original and reconstructed historic buildings: the ranch house, the lodge, cabins, and officers' or enlisted men's quarters. Primitive and modern camping facilities are available. There is a long list of things to do: ride horses in the buttes, hike, bike (you can rent bikes there), fish, see the buffalo herd, swim in the indoor swimming pool, see a free rodeo, take a hayrack or stagecoach ride, or go to the evening buffalo-stew cookout and campfire sing-along. As for biking, don't miss nearby Smiley's Canyon. If you're a theater buff, each season the Post Playhouse Summer

Tunnel Vision of a Ghost Town

If you want to see a ghost town, go to what was once *Belmont.* It's near *Crawford,* 1 mile east of Highways 71 and 2. This former town once had fifty buildings, most of which are gone except for the brick school building and a few others. The town was established in 1886 by a dairy farmer who used a pooch-powered treadmill to separate the cream. (Do you suppose townspeople back then thought the business was going to the dogs?) A short walk north from Belmont takes you to the only railroad tunnel in the whole state. Built in 1888, it was used for nearly a century until 1983.

The Mysterious Burial of Crazy Horse

When **Crazy Horse** was killed at Fort Robinson in 1877, his family came to get his body, taking it away on a horse-drawn travois. Apparently they placed the body in a tree on a scaffold in Beaver Valley. After a period of mourning, the body was removed. But to where? The site of his final resting place remains a sacred, and decidedly secret, place. Historians, professional and amateur alike, have tried for more than a century to find that place. Some say Crazy Horse's remains are in a crevice near Scout Point in Beaver Creek Valley. A book called *To Kill an Eagle: Indian Views on the Last Days of Crazy Horse* by Edward and Mabell Kadlecek supports this view. Other theories support likely burial places in South Dakota, such as Wounded Knee, Eagle Nest Butte, Pepper Creek, or Porcupine. Many believe his remains were divided and placed in several locations so as to avoid discovery by unscrupulous profit-seekers. Charles Trimble, himself an Oglala Sioux and a former board member of the Nebraska Historical Society, has been quoted as saying, "To us, he's all over. That's where his spirit is. Your spirit is what is important. Your body is not."

Repertory Theater offers three really good productions that include musicals, comedies, and melodramas. The Lodge has a nice restaurant for all three meals. Fort Robinson is immensely popular with Nebraskans and residents of nearby states, so rooms are often booked in advance for the summer. But you might get lucky if there's been a cancellation. Cabins are available only from early April through mid-November. Even if you can't stay at the park, you can stay in motels at Crawford and take advantage of Fort Robinson's activities. Call (308) 665-2900 for reservations. The web address is outdoornebraska.gov/fortrobinson.

Also on the grounds of Fort Robinson is the ***University of Nebraska State Museum at Trailside.*** The Trailside Museum has paleontology exhibits that include a giant mammoth, a fossil rhino, and a giant tortoise, plus geology exhibits of rocks and minerals. Special demonstrations include flint knapping, and there are temporary exhibits and traveling art shows. The museum's gift shop has a good selection of educational (and fun) games, toys, and books for children of all ages, as well as Native American crafts from nearby reservations. Hours are daily June through Aug, 9 a.m. to 6 p.m.; Sept, Oct, April, and May, Mon through Fri, 10 a.m. to 5 p.m. Admission is (with a valid park permit) $3 for adults. Call (308) 665-2929 for more information or to arrange field programs.

The ***Fort Robinson Museum,*** on the grounds of Fort Robinson, is operated by the Nebraska State Historical Society. The interpretive exhibits are housed in the 1905 Post Headquarters building. The museum's wonderful collection, which spans the entire history of the fort, is nicely designed and curated. Of special interest is a Sioux Ghost Dance shirt (the shirts, believed by some Sioux to make the wearers invisible and impervious to soldiers' bullets, were worn during the Ghost Dance in a spiritual effort to make the white man go away and the buffalo, as well as all Sioux ancestors, come back). Also of interest to visitors is a collection of McClellan saddles, which were designed for use by the military. The McClellan saddles are very lightweight, with a slot down the middle. If you're hoping to see a photograph of Crazy Horse at the museum, prepare for your hopes to be dashed, for Crazy Horse never allowed his photograph to be taken by anyone. Hours are Memorial Day through Labor Day, Mon through Sat, 8 a.m. to 5 p.m., Sun, 1 to 5 p.m.; Sept through May, Mon through Fri, 10 a.m. to 5 p.m. Hours may vary a bit during the off-season; call ahead at (308) 665-2919. The admission is $2 for adults; children accompanied by adults are admitted at no charge.

It might take you a while to follow these directions (and I assure you— you'll think you're way lost en route) to the ***Hudson-Meng Education & Research Center,*** but you'll be glad you did. And if you think you'll just use the GPS on your phone, there's a good chance that won't work here. GPS on your automobile will serve you well. Go 4.2 miles north of Crawford on Highway 2 to Forest Development Road 904, turn left on 904, and go for 7.4 miles to Sand Creek Road; then turn left on Sand Creek Road and go 6.3 miles to the Hudson-Meng turnoff—you'll be truly off the beaten path. Be forewarned that after a rain, the roads turn into what the locals call "gumbo." Also, don't drive fast unless you're adept on gravel roads. At the end of the road is the final resting place of more than 600 bison who died en masse about 10,000 years ago. What, you might ask yourself, caused so many bison to die in one place at one time? The answer is literally being unearthed. Archaeologists and paleontologists at first thought the place might have been a buffalo jump where Native Americans stampeded the beasts over a cliff. But if it had been a buffalo jump, there would have been more arrowheads and tools unearthed; there have only been a couple, and those might have been dropped at a later time. There are other theories: a prairie fire may have trapped the bison around a watering hole, or a fierce winter storm could have covered the grass with snow too deep to paw through, causing the bison to starve to death. The prairie-fire theory is the most probable. The visitor center allows you to watch the continued excavation under way and ask questions of the staff. There's a pretty little pond with cattails there, and lots of hands-on activities. Call for more information at (308) 665-3900. Hours from mid-May through Sept 30 are 10 a.m. to 6 p.m. daily. Admission is $5 for adults; $3 for children aged seven through twelve.

When you leave Hudson-Meng, stop by for a meal or a piece of killer-good pie at the ***Drifter's Cookshack.*** Or if looking at all those old bones made you tired, then just stay the night at the adjacent ***High Plains Homestead Bunkhouse.*** I swear this is one of the coolest places in the whole state. Not only is the food good (I have dreams about the sour-cream raisin pie), but the whole dang place looks like a movie set that has been perfectly placed on a windswept plain surrounded by buttes. The Cookshack is full of antiques and neat stuff to look at while you wait for the food. Do not fail to look up at the really creepy enormous dried and intact hornets' nest hanging from a rafter. The rooms at the Bunkhouse are cozy, with private baths and no phones or televisions. If you're coming from Hudson-Meng, you'll drive right past it. In addition to the room, overnight accommodations include RV hookups and primitive camping. You can even bring your horse for a restful overnight stay. If you're coming from Crawford, take Highway 2 north and follow the signs. The phone number is (308) 665-2592, and the website is highplainshomestead.com.

North of Crawford is ***Toadstool Geologic Park.*** This awesome landscape is absolutely lunarlike. Take a walk through these badlands and watch for fossilized tracks of ancient creatures. The "toadstool" formations were created when erosion affected the different strata of sediment deposited by ancient volcanoes. Toadstool Park is 4 miles north of Crawford on Highway 2 and then 15 miles northwest on Toadstool Road (an all-weather road). Toadstool Park is on federal land, is open year-round, and is free. You can even camp here, but that will cost you $5 a night. The phone number is (308) 432-0300.

Now we're headed 10 miles south of Crawford to the ***Ponderosa Ranch.*** This working cattle ranch offers visitors a variety of experiences. From May until October you can do ranch work such as rounding up cattle or riding fence (riding along the fenceline to make sure it is in good repair). Rent a cabin year-round; they have full kitchens, plus a woodstove for that rustic ambience. In the winter there's cross-country skiing through some pretty spectacular scenery. The cabins rent for $50 a night. To get there, go south of Crawford on Highway 2/71, turn east at Saw Log Road (you'll see a sign for the Ponderosa Wildlife Area), go 2 miles, and cross a railroad track. Turn south and go 3 miles to where the road divides; here there's a sign for the JX Ranch, so go 2 more miles to the headquarters. The phone number is (308) 629-7733 and the website is ponderosaranch.net.

Sioux County

When you look at Sioux County on a state map, you'll see lots of boxes filled with what look like little green dots in the northern tier of the county. This is the 95,000-acre **Oglala National Grasslands,** a veritable ocean of prairie administered by the U.S. Forest Service. The area is great for hiking, wildlife viewing, photography—and great for the soul. The grasslands begin approximately 15 miles north of **Harrison** on an unpaved road. It is open year-round, and admission is free. A request: If you find a fossil bit, leave it there, and please don't pick any wildflowers. Leave the place as you found it for future generations. The phone number is (308) 432-0300, and the web address is fs .fed.us/r2/nebraska.

A lovely 24-mile drive on the high plains of Sioux County, south of Harrison on Highway 29 (or 34 miles north of Mitchell), will bring you to **Agate Fossil Beds National Monument.** Start at the visitor center. It has exhibits on the now-extinct animal life of nineteen million years ago, whose fossilized remains are part of a permanent diorama. Other exhibits feature the current plant and animal life of the region. Fossils were first discovered by Capt. James Cook on the land in 1878. Cook was a colorful character who counted many people as friends; among them was his close friend Chief Red Cloud, who gave him many beautiful handmade items. Many of these items are on display in the Cook Collection. This display, beautifully curated, is honestly one of the nicest Native American collections I've ever seen. There's a piece of pipestone

A Bellyful of Scenic Wonder

You must, without fail, take a drive through **Sowbelly Canyon.** If you could visit only one place in Nebraska, this is the place to go. All the adjectives in the world cannot describe the sheer, jaw-dropping beauty of this canyon, so I won't even try. You decide for yourself which words best describe it. Take your time, relax, enjoy the view. Pull off the road when you can, because you will want to firmly fix the view in your memory.

The canyon was dubbed Sowbelly when some soldiers were trapped there by unhappy Native Americans. The soldiers ran out of food, and when they were rescued, they were fed dry salt bacon, or sowbelly, which probably seemed downright tasty.

You won't find Sowbelly Canyon on a state map, so pay attention. If you're coming from the east on Highway 20, turn north at Hillside Service in **Harrison** and watch for signs. If you see signs for Coffee Park, that means you're on the right road. When traveling from the south on Highway 29, go straight through town (the highway ends at Harrison), then watch for Hillside Service and the SOWBELLY CANYON sign. Or you can go 3 miles east of Harrison on Highway 20 and turn north on Pants Butte Road. If all else fails, ask someone in Harrison how to get there. For more information call (308) 668-2466.

Buffalo Bill and the Cheyenne

Warbonnet Battlefield, in northern Sioux County, was the site of an 1876 skirmish between the Fifth Calvary, with Buffalo Bill Cody serving as chief scout, and a group of 800 Cheyenne, mostly women and children, who were fleeing the Red Cloud Agency. This battle took place not long after the Battle of Little Big Horn. At Warbonnet, Buffalo Bill fought a duel with Yellow Hair, sometimes referred to as Yellow Hand. Buffalo Bill killed and scalped Yellow Hair, whereupon he is said to have held the scalp aloft triumphantly and declared, "The first scalp for Custer."

that Crazy Horse had on his person when he was killed. A 2-mile trail leads to the Fossil Hills, which was the site of the early 1900s excavations. Another trail, the 1-mile Daimonelix Trail, will take you past some "devil's corkscrews," or preserved burrows of an ancient beaver called the paleocaster. If you take a hike, watch for rattlesnakes (yes, it's true, but they often want to avoid you just as much as you want to avoid them) and take water with you. There are sheltered picnic areas near the visitor center, where you can gaze for miles at the scenery. The monument is open daily, year-round except Christmas, New Year's Day, and Thanksgiving. Hours from Memorial Day to Labor Day are 8 a.m. to 6 p.m. The trails are open from dawn to dusk. Admission is free. The telephone number is (308) 436-9760. The website is.nps.gov/agfo.

Box Butte County

Alliance, with a population of nearly 10,000, is the largest community in Box Butte County. In fact, it's one of only two communities in the county. A mustsee attraction near Alliance is ***Carhenge,*** a wonderfully whimsical re-creation of Stonehenge—but instead of giant stones, it's made out of old cars. One imagines that the builders of Stonehenge would be pleased by this modern-day version. It's been featured in several magazine stories and on *Good Morning America* and *The Today Show;* it was the answer to a *Jeopardy* question, and it graces the cover of Steely Dan's *Greatest Hits.* There's a summer solstice gathering each year when a new sculpture, made, of course, of car parts, is installed on the grounds. (My favorite one is of a giant fish.) At the visitor center you can learn more about the crazy people who build Carhenge. Or you can sit down in some bucket seats to enjoy a hot dog and drinks from the snack bar. Kids are invited to play a game of car-quet. It's like croquet, only the mallet is made from car cylinders and the balls are knocked through miniature Carhenge-type structures. Come the last Saturday in September for the Stone Soup Supper, just another crazy get-together for fans of Carhenge. It's open year-round and admission is free, but do leave a donation. Carhenge is 2½ miles north of Alliance on Highway 87. Call (308) 762-3569 for more information. The web address is carhenge.com.

What do a bordello, a Chinese laundry, a mortuary, and a bootlegger's cabin have in common? They are just a few of the buildings at ***Dobby's Frontier Town*** in Alliance, at 320 East Twenty-fifth St., just east of Box Butte Avenue. A local resident named Kenneth Dobby Lee began preserving buildings and gathering artifacts in an effort to create a frontier village that is now managed by his son and daughter-in-law. Other buildings include a general store and meat market, a post office, a saloon, a blacksmith shop, an original home of a black homesteader, a bank, a jail, and more. All the structures have antique furnishings, tools, and appliances. April through October hours are

No Tears Allowed

While driving the back roads of Nebraska, I invite you to stop and explore a rural cemetery. It sounds morbid, I know, and you may experience a feeling of inappropriateness or an invasion of privacy. Those are legitimate emotions, but stop nonetheless. These small country church cemeteries are museums containing the strength and spirit of Nebraska, a history lesson for those who feel overwhelmed by life's modern and momentary challenges.

Sometimes the graves are without identification, or stones so faded and neglected that the individual's life story may appear to have become lost to the eons. Even though you may not know the circumstances, appreciate that this person has known love and happiness and pain and melancholy. It's the human experience. What makes this story special is that the individual has chosen Nebraska as a final resting place.

My friend Mary Ethel Emanuel was fond of the remote *Montrose* church cemetery among others, for what she described as the achingly beautiful view of the valley here and buttes in the distance, and clusters of deep-purple irises surrounding the nameless headstones. Although she was not necessarily a religious person, she was moved by the spiritual power of this place.

My friend now rests in another remote country cemetery on the back roads of Nebraska. Each time I've stopped to visit her, I am overwhelmed by the simplistic beauty of the location. Perhaps no more than 100 souls share this tender spot of Nebraska soil, shaded by a huge oak tree, surrounded by corn fields, and swept with fresh scents of the region carried on a breeze as soothing as the warm Nebraska sun. This is as sacred a place as any in the land and my hope is to rest eternally in a destination equally filled with the beauties found in these remote, yet meaningful settings of Nebraska.

Mon through Sat from 10 a.m. to 6 p.m., and winter hours are dependent upon the weather. Admission is free, but donations are accepted. Call (308) 760-3574 or visit dobbysfrontiertown.com.

The **Sallows Arboretum and Conservatory** is a good place to learn about western Nebraska's indigenous plants and those that have come to Nebraska from other parts of the world. The greenhouse measures 1,800 square feet, and a conservatory houses forty different types of tropical and subtropical plants that are not typical to western Nebraska. An arboretum has sixty-four types of woody plants that will thrive in the local climate. A cacti garden featuring thirty-five different types of catci has been added recently. Besides seeing lots of colorful plants, you can learn ways to landscape your yard to conserve energy, supply shade, and reduce wind velocity. In this part of the country, the matter of reducing wind velocity is important. There's an old story that a turn-of-the-twentieth-century traveler, remarking on the wind, asked if it always blew that way. He was told, "No, sometimes it blows real hard." The arboretum and conservatory are in Central Park, at Eleventh and Niobrara Streets. They are open most days from 1 to 4 p.m. Call (308) 762-2384. Admission is free.

The arboretum is adjacent to the **Sallows Military Museum** that tells the story of the Air Force base located in Alliance during World War II. There are other artifacts that date back to the Revolutionary War. Hours are Mon through Fri 1 p.m. to 4 p.m., and most weekends during warm weather. Call (308) 762-2384 or visit sallowsmilitarymuseum.com.

HELPFUL PINE RIDGE WEBSITES

Alliance
alliancechamber.com

Panhandle Area
westnebraska.com

Chadron
chadron.com

Sioux County
visitnorthwestnebraska.com

Gordon
gordonchamber.com

Places to Stay in the Pine Ridge

(All area codes are 308.)

ALLIANCE
Grandma LaLa's B&B
1232 Box Butte Ave.
762-2925

CHADRON
Olde Main Street Inn
115 Main St.
432-3380

CRAWFORD
High Plains Homestead Bunkhouse
Old West Cowtown Museum (with lodging, corrals, fossil collecting)
263 Sandcreek Rd.
665-2592
highplainshomestead.com

GORDON
Horse Thief Cave Ranch
(private building on 2,000 acres)
282-1017
horsethiefcave.com

Places to Eat in the Pine Ridge

(All area codes are 308.)

ALLIANCE
Martin's Family Restaurant
(Mexican)
1307 West Third St.
762-8548

Sauced BBQ
324 East Third St.
760-1256

CHADRON
China House
(Chinese)
1240 West Highway 20
432-4080

77 Longbranch Saloon
(American)
115 Main St.
432-3380

GORDON
Italian Inn
(Italian)
200 North Main St.
282-0247

Highway to History

When you're in the Panhandle of Nebraska, you'll be reminded again and again of the many historic trails that crossed the region. The Oregon Trail, the Mormon Trail, the Pony Express, the Sidney-Deadwood Trail, and stagecoach routes all had major roles in the development of the area and of the Old West. Several excellent museums will show you how the West was won, and numerous historical markers dot the Panhandle like porcupine quills. The Panhandle is also dotted with recreation areas and wildlife refuges, where you can enjoy the great outdoors in uncrowded settings.

Scotts Bluff County

Four miles west of Morrill on Highway 26, you'll come to a historical marker. This marker will tell you about the 1851 *Horse Creek Treaty* and the largest gathering of Native Americans in history. More than 10,000 people, representing the tribes of the Sioux, Blackfeet, Crow, Assiniboin, Mandan, Gros Ventre, Arikara, Cheyenne, and Arapahoe, assembled near the North Platte River and Horse Creek to sign the first Treaty of Fort Laramie. The treaty's purpose was to ensure the safe passage

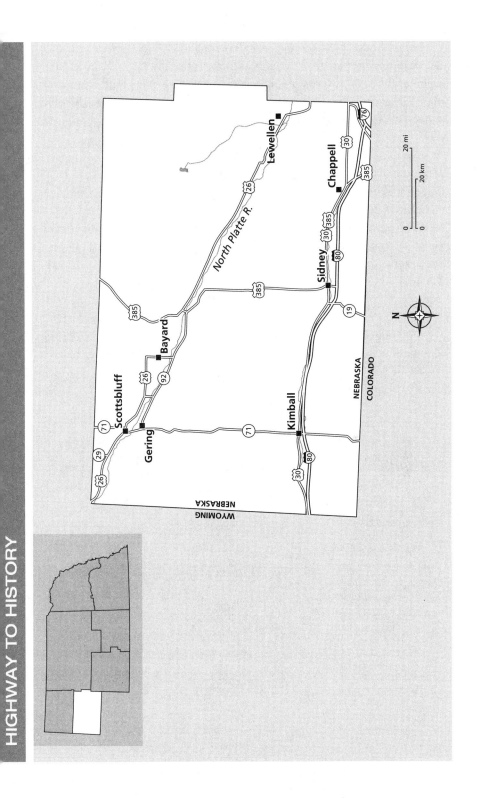

of westward-bound pioneers and to end intertribal warfare; however, the treaty was broken by the United States almost immediately after it was signed. While imagining the land covered for miles in all directions with Native Americans camped in unprecedented numbers, one wonders how history might be different if the thousands of Indians there had decided to fight instead of sign that treaty.

If you continue southwest from *Mitchell* on Highway 26, you'll come to the communities of *Scottsbluff* and *Gering.* The most outstanding attraction in the area is *Scotts Bluff National Monument,* which is 3 miles west of Gering on Highway 92. Scotts Bluff was a famous landmark along the Oregon Trail. The Sioux name for this geologic formation meant "the hill that is hard to go around." You'll soon see why this is an appropriate name. Scotts Bluff got its current name from Hiram Scott, a fur trader who was abandoned by his expedition and whose remains were found in the area the following spring. Several theories exist about where he died (near the river or at the base of the bluff), why he died (Indian attack, broken leg, or illness), and when he died (1828 or 1829). Although there are mysteries about the demise of the unfortunate Hiram Scott, there is no mystery why you should see the place named after him.

The visitor center has fascinating displays about the Oregon Trail, and wagon ruts are still visible. You can drive to the top of the bluff on Summit

FAVORITE ATTRACTIONS IN THE PANHANDLE

(All area codes are 308.)

Barn Anew B&B
170549 County Road L
Scottsbluff
632-8647

Cabela's
north of I-80 at the junction of 385,
exit 59
Sidney
254-7889

**Chimney Rock National Historic Site
and Visitor Center**
1 mile south of the junction of Highways
92 and 26
Bayard
586-2581

Scotts Bluff National Monument
3 miles west on Highway 92
Gering
436-9700

**Wildcat Hills State Recreation Area
and Nature Center**
10 miles south on Highway 71
Gering
436-3777 or 436-3743

Road for a spectacular 100-mile view, or you can hike to the top on trails. There's also a bike trail, but it doesn't go all the way to the top. Summer hours are 8 a.m. to 7 p.m. daily. From Labor Day weekend through Memorial Day, the hours are 8 a.m. to 5 p.m. daily. Admission is free, but donations are accepted. For more information call (308) 436-9700 or visit nps.gov/scbl.

Not far from the monument is the ***Legacy of the Plains Museum,*** at 2930 Old Oregon Trail Rd. in Gering. This little museum has a lot of old equipment that was used for planting and harvesting crops in the region. They have an 1831 reaper that is probably the oldest reaper in existence. There's also an 1863 hay baler that could, with lightning speed, crank out seventy-two bales of hay a day. (Modern balers can produce up to 2,500 bales in the same amount of time.) You can see plows, corn pickers, drills, grinding equipment, tractors, corn shellers, threshing machines, and a giant steam engine used to power the equipment. All the equipment is donated, and all the enthusiastic staff are volunteers. This museum is open year-round, Tues through Sat, 9 a.m. to 5 p.m.; and Sun, 1 to 5 p.m. with extended hours in the summer. Admission is $10 for adults; $5 for students and seniors. Call (308) 436-1989. The website is farmandranchmuseum.com.

From the Legacy of the Plains Museum, take a hike at the ***Wildcat Hills State Recreation Area,*** 7 miles south on Hwy. 71. This picturesque, 935-acre setting with rugged buttes and pine-covered canyons has walking trails, stone shelters with fireplaces, picnic tables, and water and toilets for your convenience. Camping is also available. The Nature Center has great displays on the flora and fauna of the region, plus raptor displays and murals. There is a bee colony that you can view from inside the Nature Center. (Don't worry—you can see them, but they can't get near you.) There also is a large aquarium with some fat fish; visiting children often catch grasshoppers outside and come in to feed the fish. It's pretty fun to watch the fish leap up out of the tank for this tasty treat. A park permit is required. The trails are open year-round, and the Nature Center is open daily in the summer and Mon through Fri in the winter, from 8 a.m. to 4 p.m. Call (308) 436-3777 or visit outdoornebraska.gov/wildcathills/.

The ***Riverside Discovery Center*** in Scottsbluff, is a combination children's museum, zoo and natural history museum. The beautifully maintained zoo, the largest in western Nebraska, has more than 175 exotic and regional animals in natural-looking habitats. There are endangered species, such as vultures, chimpanzees, spider monkeys, and Amur tigers. Other animals in the cat family include bobcats, mountain lions, lynx, and a black leopard. Kids love this zoo and enjoy the splash pad playground where they can run through water spraying from the ground. The zoo is 1 mile west of Broadway Street on

FAVORITE ANNUAL EVENTS IN THE PANHANDLE

(Call ahead to verify dates; all area codes are 308.)

Banner County Museum Annual Open House Event
Harrisburg, early June
436-5074

Sugar Valley (Car) Rally
Scottsbluff/Gering, early June
632-3381
sugarvalleyrally.com

Ash Hollow Pageant
Lewellen, mid-June
778-5548

Oregon Trail Days
Gering, mid-July
436-3304
oregontraildays.com

Cabela's Sidewalk Sale
Sidney, late July
254-7889

Farmers Day Off Golf Tournament
Kimball, mid-Aug
235-3782

Greek Festival
Bridgeport, mid-Aug
262-0281

Chimney Rock Pioneer Days
Bayard, mid-Sept
586-1846 or 672-1683

Octoberfest
Sidney, early Oct
254-2932

Old West Weekend
Scottsbluff/Gering, mid-Oct
632-5667

the South Beltline Highway. From Mar through Nov, the hours are 9:30 a.m. to 4:30 p.m. Winter hours are 10 a.m. to 4 p.m., weather permitting. Admission is $6.50 for adults. Call (308) 630-6236 or visit riversidediscoverycenter.org.

Two miles east of Scottsbluff on Highway 26 you'll see a historical marker for *Rebecca Winters' Grave.* Rebecca was with a group of Mormon families traveling to New Zion to flee religious persecution. She died near here on August 15, 1852, one of thousands who died on the Mormon Trail. For years her grave was tended to by the Norman DeMott family, who homesteaded there beginning in 1887. Her grave was relocated when the land was sold to the railroad. Stop and appreciate the price too many people have paid for intolerance.

A great place to stay in the area is the *Barn Anew B&B.* A few years back this B&B was a huge, crumbling old barn without a roof but with about forty years' worth of debris. Now the four rooms are comfy and have private baths, and there's a sitting room upstairs with a balcony view of the back of Scotts Bluff National Monument. All rooms are $140 per night. If you like Native American art, you'll be happy here because the owners taught school on a reservation for nearly 30 years and have acquired some beautiful pieces. Call

(308) 632-8647 or visit barnanew.com. Directions are complicated, so call and ask. Your phone's GPS might not work in these parts.

South of Gering, in Carter Canyon, is the **Robidoux Trading Post,** a beautifully reconstructed trading post made from one-hundred-year-old, hand-hewn logs. The post is 1 mile south of Gering on Hwy. 71 and then 8 miles west on Robidoux Road. Tours can be arranged by calling (308) 436-6886. Or follow the marked 23-mile Robidoux Loop, which begins here. Admission to the post is free, and it's open year-round. Nearby are **Robidoux Pass, Blacksmith Shop, and Pioneer Grave Sites** in the Wildcat Hills. The graves of Oregon Trail travelers can be found here, including the grave of twenty-six-year-old F. Dunn, who died of cholera on June 13, 1849. Robidoux Pass is 1 mile south of Gering on Highway 71 and 8 miles west on Robidoux Road. For more information about Robidoux Trading Post and other sites, call (308) 436-6886.

A lighthouse in a landlocked state? Yes, and you'll find it just 5 miles east and 4 miles north of Scottsbluff at **Lake Minatare State Recreation Area.** The recreation area is accessible on a paved road from either Highway 26 or Nebraska 71. The 55-foot-tall lighthouse was built in 1937–39 entirely of native stone by the Veterans Conservation Corps. It's the only structure of its kind in the state and one of only seven inland lighthouses in the country. It is open to the public, and you can climb to the top. If it's locked, you can get the key from the Game and Parks office, just down the road, and besides, you'll need to stop there to get a park permit. As the brochure says: "Those with the stamina to climb its winding staircase to the top will have a spectacular view of the lake and the river valley." But you really don't need all that much stamina; it's an easy climb. If you've ever climbed a winding staircase in one of those massive cathedral towers in Europe or to the top of the Statue of Liberty, this is a piece of cake in comparison. The lighthouse is open from April through mid-Sept, Fri through Sun, 9 a.m. to 8 p.m. Call (308) 783-2911 or visit outdoornebraska .gov/lakeminatare/ for more information.

Morrill County

You are now within sight of the **Chimney Rock National Historic Site and Visitor Center.** Chimney Rock, a compelling spire jutting up into the landscape, was visible for days to Oregon Trail travelers and was mentioned in journals and diaries more often than any other natural formation along the entire stretch of the trail. It still amazes and delights travelers. The visitor center has wonderful displays about the geology and history of Chimney Rock (including the fact that the Native American name for it was Elk Penis). There's a great interactive exhibit for children, with a miniature wagon and miniature supplies with the number of pounds marked on them. Children can learn the realities of pulling up stakes and traveling west by deciding what to take on the trek. If they pack too much, the oxen or horses can't pull the weight. Do they pack tools at the cost of leaving behind treasured heirlooms? Do they pack supplies to start a new crop, or do they pack a lot of extra food in case wild game is not in abundance? This is a great museum, and you should stop. Admission is only $3 for adults age eighteen or older; young people age seventeen or younger visit free. The visitor center is open from 9 a.m. to 5 p.m. daily. It is closed on Veteran's Day, Thanksgiving, Christmas, and New Year's Day. The telephone number is (308) 586-2581. Although it is a National Historic Site administered by the National Park Service, the Nebraska Historical Society operates the visitors center. Learn more at nebraskahistory.org/sites/rock.

Two more impressive natural formations along the Oregon and Mormon Trails are **Courthouse** and **Jail Rocks.** The site, open year-round and free, is just a few miles south of Bridgeport on Highway 88. It is under the jurisdiction of the National Park Service, so call (801) 741-1012 for any specific questions.

Banner and Kimball Counties

The **Banner County Historical Museum and Village** in **Harrisburg,** at 200 North Pennsylvania, has a fascinating collection of historic structures, particularly when you consider that Harrisburg is the only town in the county and that the population of the entire county, according to the latest census, is 759. Consider further that Harrisburg isn't even located on any highway; it's 4 miles west of Highway 71 on S4A. Seventy-five people live in Harrisburg, and they are justifiably proud of their museum. It has a sod house, a church, a log schoolhouse, and a log house. The buildings are full of well-designed displays, and the museum building has a spectacular collection that ranges from Native American to pioneer artifacts. The official hours at the museum are Memorial Day through Labor Day, Sun from 2 to 5 p.m. However, if you'd like to visit at another time, just call Vicki at (308) 575-0808. For a preview, visit bannercounty historicalsociety.com. Please leave a donation. Harrisburg and the museum are well worth a stop.

Another reason to take yourself to this part of Nebraska is a place called Double L Café and Country Store. Laura Lee Whelchel opened this homey little business in 2016 and people now drive hours for the food. Most of the beef and pork is raised on the Whelchel's ranch. The potatoes are all grown locally, as are the eggs. Laura and her staff make all of the bread, including the hamburger buns. People go nuts over the selection of pies, especially the sour cream and ranch. The Country Store sells homemade candy. Take time to belly up to the bar to count the pennies. The bar top is covered with 8,617 pennies, or at least that's what Laura says. You count them all, just to double check. The Double L is just outside of Harrisburg on Highway 71. Open every day but Sunday from 8 a.m. to 3 p.m. On Fridays, Laura stays open late for dinner and music. Call (308) 241-2266.

The highest point in Nebraska is in the extreme southwestern corner of *Kimball County. Panorama Point* is 5,424 feet above sea level. On clear days you see almost forever—to the Rocky Mountains to the southwest, anyway. You can drive to Panorama Point from I-80 by getting off at the Bushnell exit, and then going 10 miles south, 4 west, 1 south, 2 west, and 2 more miles south to the entrance road. There's a guest book to sign, and if you "rappel" the marker, the Chamber of Commerce in Kimball will happily send you a certificate. Better yet, stop in at the chamber office, at 122 S. Chestnut St. in Kimball, to get the certificate. Call (308) 235-3782. And make a stop at *Gotte Park* to see a 100-foot Titan missile on display. The park is on Highway 30, 9 blocks east of Highway 71.

Kimball is in the middle of the largest complex of intercontinental ballistic missiles (ICBMs) in the world (more than 200 are deep in the earth in the immediate tristate area, although they have been decommissioned since 2005), and the town has declared itself to be Missile Center, USA.

Also deep in the earth is oil; more than 1,400 oil wells have been discovered since 1951 in Kimball County. The brochure for Kimball says it's "a place where strangers are greeted on the streets, and senior citizens are respected." Don't you just love that? There's also a brochure with "101 Ways to Satisfy Your Curiosity About the Kimball Area." Some suggestions: Pet a goat; go bowling;

OTHER ATTRACTION WORTH SEEING IN THE PANHANDLE

(All area codes are 308.)

OSH KOSH

Crescent Lake National Wildlife Refuge
28 miles north of Osh Kosh between Highways 26 and 2; 762-4893. Forty thousand acres serve as a nesting site and stopover for migratory birds.

tee off on the highest tee box in Nebraska; play cards or dominoes at a corner bar; pull weeds at the arboretum; watch the wheat grow; hug a tree; plant a tree; or climb a tree. Ya just gotta love it.

Kimball is also the southern post point of what has become known as the Fossil Freeway. This unofficial roadway, that starts on Hwy. 71 in Nebraska zigs and zags north via Hwys. 20 and 29 until reconnecting with Hwy. 71 leading into South Dakota, includes seven sites where fossils have been discovered and are available for viewing. The first point is Wildcat Hills State Recreation Area. Among the many cool things in the visitor center is a 25 million year old fossil discovered in this area. Find out more about what to see and do at Wildcat Hills at outdoornebraska.gov/wildcathills or by calling (308) 436-3777. To learn more about the Fossil Freeway, visit fossilfreeway.net.

Cheyenne County

Little Sidney Nebraska, population 6,879, is known around the world as the birthplace of *Cabela's,* one of the world's largest outfitters of hunting, fishing and outdoor gear. The company launched here in 1961 when Jim and Dick Cabela placed an ad in the newspaper for 12 hand-tied flies for $1. The company grew to nearly 100 stores in 49 states and Canada. Although BassPro Shops purchased Cabela's in 2016, this original store remains a popular destination for those who know and love the Cabela's brand.

This massive building, measuring 85,000 square feet, contains more than 100,000 products. There's not nearly enough space on this page to tell you everything you can buy, but, trust me, if it concerns the outdoors, you'll find it here. You'll also find more than 500 wildlife mounts from around the world, an 8,000-gallon aquarium with Nebraska game fish, an art gallery, a gun library, a bargain center with first-quality merchandise no longer listed in the catalog, a great gift selection, and even a snack area with smoked meats—including buffalo, ham, and turkey—and roast-beef sandwiches. Outside you'll see the amazing Royal Challenge, a larger-than-life bronze sculpture of two battling elks (it's so big it had to be shipped in on two separate trucks). You should stop here even if you think you already have every outdoor item you'll ever need. Cabela's is open Mon through Sat from 8 a.m. to 8 p.m. and Sun from 10 a.m. to 6 p.m. The telephone number is (308) 254-2619; the Web address is cabelas.com.

You'd never know by looking that the pleasant town of *Sidney,* just north of I-80 at Hwys. 385, 30, and 19, used to have the reputation as one of the roughest towns in the West. When gold was discovered in the Black Hills of South Dakota, the town became a jumping-off place for miscreants and reprobates of all sorts. (Historical note: Gold was discovered when a group led by Gen. George Custer violated an agreement with the Sioux that kept whites from even setting foot in the sacred Black Hills. Some scientists in the group discovered gold, and whoops—there goes another promise.) At one time there were twenty-five bars in just a 1-block area. Citizens became inured to the frequent murders. Railway passengers were advised not to disembark in Sidney because thieves had grown bold enough to smack them on the head and throw them, robbed and dazed, back onto the train. Historians recount an episode when a dance was interrupted briefly by one murder, the unfortunate victim of which was dumped in a corner. The dancing went on, briefly interrupted by another murder and another corpse in the corner. It wasn't until a trio of corpses graced the corner that the dance came to an end.

Visitors today can quite safely venture into Sidney to see the interesting *Fort Sidney Complex,* on Sixth Avenue and Jackson Street. The original mission of the fort was to protect the people who were building the Union Pacific railroad from Indian attack and later to protect travelers against "depredations" inflicted by these same "hostiles." Soldiers at the fort also played a role at Wounded Knee. The complex has a powder house, officers' quarters, and the restored post commander's home. The museum is open daily May 1 to Labor Day from 9 to 11 a.m. and 1 to 3 p.m. The post commander's house is open daily Memorial Day to Labor Day the same hours as the museum. There is no admission fee. The telephone number is (308) 254-2150.

A final note about Sidney: Calamity Jane is said to have given birth to an illegitimate child in Sidney. Others say this was impossible; she was really a man, or at least a hermaphrodite. Who knows?

This book is about getting you off the beaten path, but, if you are driving on I-80 about six miles west of Sidney, you'll cross a section of brass plates embedded into the interstate pavement. This is called the *Golden Link,* commemorating the last segment of I-80 poured here in 1974.

About 20 miles west of Sidney on I-80 is the cute little community of *Potter.* People who love to bowl travel from across North America to Potter because the bowling alley here, which opened in the 1920s, is one of only two bowling alleys in the country where the pins are still set by hand. *Duck Pin Bowling* is the name of the business, but it is also a lesser known style of bowling. The balls are smaller and the pins are shorter and fatter. This is a

trivia

Lodgepole Creek, which meanders through Cheyenne County adjacent to Highway 30, is the longest creek in the world. It stretches more than 200 miles through Wyoming and Colorado before dumping into the South Platte River in Nebraska.

America's Main Street

If you've traveled on Highway 30 across Nebraska at all, you should be aware that you were on the historic **Lincoln Highway.** The Lincoln Highway, which stretches all the way across the state from Omaha on the eastern border to Bushnell through to the Wyoming border, was the first transcontinental highway across the United States. It all started in 1903, when a Vermont physician accepted a fifty-dollar bet to prove he could drive a car from San Francisco to New York.

Sixty-five days later the physician, his mechanic, and a stray bulldog named Bud arrived in New York. In 1913 the Lincoln Highway, named after President Lincoln, came into being. For many years the route across the country seemed to be comprised either of mud or choking dust. One early traveler called the Lincoln Highway "a red line connecting all the worst mudholes in the country," but now the paved route provides a delightful alternative to I-80. If you're interested in learning more, there's a great book entitled *The Lincoln Highway, Main Street Across America* by Drake Hokanson. There's also a book by Gregory Franzwa, *Nebraska's Lincoln Highway,* that includes incredibly detailed maps and the history of the Lincoln Highway in Nebraska.

Nebraska State Historical Site. Located at 328 Chestnut Street and it is open for a few hours every day. If it's not open when you come by, walk next door to the Potter State Bank and ask for Drew Enevoldsen. He'll let you in and set up the first game. Call (308) 247-2858 or 207-5908.

Plan your visit to Potter the last week in June and you'll be in for an additional treat. That's when the **Potter Melodrama** puts on its annual family-friendly production at the American Legion Hall. It's a dinner theatre and a fundraiser for the Potter Public Library. Follow their production schedule on Facebook or once again, call Drew Enevoldsen over at the bank. He's also the director of the Potter Melodrama. Call (308) 247-2858 or 207-5908.

Garden County

In the southeast corner of Garden County, you'll find **Ash Hollow State Historical Park** 3 miles southeast of **Lewellen** on Highway 26. This park is chock-full of history: fossils, the cave where prehistoric native peoples lived, Oregon and Mormon Trail lore, and Plains Indians conflicts. The Bidwell-Bartelson group was the first emigrant train to pass through Ash Hollow in 1841. Early emigrants commented on the sweet spring water and abundant ash trees that made the hollow so attractive to them. Before too many years passed, the water became less sweet, due to the sheer number of people and animals who used the stream, and the ash trees all but disappeared as they were used for fuel. The grave of the newlywed, eighteen-year-old Rachael Patterson, a victim of cholera, is in the cemetery, just ½ mile west of the park entrance on Highway 26. It's sure to strike an emotional chord as well as make you ponder how easy life is for modern travelers. The visitor/interpretive center is located on a bluff that offers a marvelous view, and it has displays that describe the history of the area and a video you can watch, too. The gift shop has great books about western and plains history. Take the time to have a picnic in the wooded grassy area at the entrance to the park, or walk down to see the cave where native people lived. Do make a stop at Windlass Hill, just 2½ miles south of the park entrance on Highway 26, which can be easily hiked. Try to imagine the difficulty of coming down this steep hill with a team of animals and a fully loaded wagon. For the emigrant trains, this tricky descent was the first frightening inkling of the increasingly arduous journey ahead into the mountains, after the relatively flat crossing of the plains along the Platte River valley. The visitor center is open 9 a.m. to 4 p.m. Tues through Sun from Memorial Day to Labor Day. A park permit is required. Call (308) 778-5651 or visit outdoornebraska.gov/ashhollow.

Deuel County

A mystery exists in the public library in a small town called **Chappell** on the high plains of western Nebraska, just north of I-80 at exit 85. The **Chappell Memorial Art Gallery,** in the Chappell Public Library at 289 Babcock St., has three pieces of art that might be original works by Rembrandt. Or they might not. The staff is quick to point out that the works have never been verified as authentic and they don't really know the genesis of this story, but everyone can agree that the work is important. The pieces are called *Self Portrait, Rembrandt and Saskai,* and *Dr. Faustus and the Magic Disk.* If you're an art historian, or in a position to shed some light on the mystery, stop in for a look. The works of art, and the money to build the library itself, were donated by Mrs. John Chappell, a wealthy resident of Chicago's Lake Shore Drive. Mrs. Chappell seems to have adopted the town of Chappell after seeing it from the train and appreciating the fact that they shared a name. The library also has a collection of pieces by a local artist named Aaron Pyle, who studied with Thomas Hart Benton. While you're in the library, you should also see the **Bergstrom Rock and Gem Collection,** which features fossil finds from the area such as mastodon teeth and bones, plus a collection of polished gems and stones. The library is open Tues and Thurs from 1 to 7 p.m. and Sat from 9 a.m. until noon. There's no admission fee. The telephone number is (308) 874-2626.

Big Springs, just north of I-80 on Highway 138 in Deuel County, was the site of the first and greatest robbery of a Union Pacific train. In 1877, Sam

chappell
remembers

During World War II, Nebraska was home to eleven air bases that filled the sky with air crews in training. On June 7, 1944, fifteen B-24 bombers departed from the Lincoln Army air base en route to the West Coast. One of the planes caught fire during a thunderstorm and began circling Chappell in Deuel County. It exploded 2 miles southeast, resulting in the tragic loss of life for all ten men on board. A historical marker in Chappell commemorates their supreme sacrifice.

Bass and five other men stopped the UP express train, stole $60,000 in gold and currency, and relieved passengers of their cash and watches. They split up the booty and went their separate ways. Legend has it that some of the twenty-dollar gold pieces are still buried in the area. After the robbery, Bass returned home to Texas and resumed his larcenous ways. He formed a new gang and robbed four trains within a few months. Bass was generous with his ill-gotten gains and earned the nickname of the "Robin Hood of Texas." He was mortally wounded and died on his twenty-seventh birthday, ten months after the Big Springs robbery. His headstone in Round Rock, Texas, was erected by his grieving sister and reads: A BRAVE MAN REPOSES IN DEATH HERE. WHY WAS HE NOT TRUE? Indeed, why was he not? In the park at the south edge of downtown, near the railroad tracks, you'll find a charming, chain-sawed wooden folk-art memorial to this historic Big Springs event.

Not What You'd Call a Fair Fight

A historical marker near **Lewellen** tells the story of the **Battle of Blue Water.** In 1855, a 600-man expedition commanded by Col. William Harney attacked and destroyed a small Lakota village 3 miles north of Blue Creek. The fight, if you want to call it a fight, is also known as the Battle of Ash Hollow, or more appropriately, the Harney Massacre. Eighty-six Native Americans were killed, seventy women and children were captured, and all the tepees were looted and burned. The battle was fought to avenge the death of Lt. John Gratton, which took place near Fort Laramie the year before. Lieutenant Gratton went into a large Indian encampment where a lot of hungry Native Americans had taken and eaten a cow belonging to passing Mormons. Retribution was called for. Lieutenant Gratton, an interpreter, and three others tried to arrest High Forehead, the man responsible for the theft. Chief Conquering Bear offered a mule to take the place of the cow. No dice. More talking led nowhere, and Lieutenant Gratton decided a show of force was in order. In fact, it was his last order. He ordered the infantry to fire a volley, and this resulted in a skirmish in which he and all of his party were killed. The marker is located in a turn-off area ½ mile west of Blue Creek, west of Lewellen, and 3 miles from the battle site.

Drive up the main street through Big Springs and look for Buffalo Joe's five buffalo, all made of barbed wire.

Places to Stay in the Panhandle

(All area codes are 308.)

BAYARD

Flying Bee Beefmaster Ranch
(4,000-acre working cattle ranch. Cabin, RV, or tent camping. Bring your hiking boots and even your horse.)
Route 2
783-2885

SCOTTSBLUFF

Barn Anew B&B
rural Scottsbluff
632-8647
barnanew.com

Places to Eat in the Panhandle

(All area codes are 308.)

BAYARD

Corner Cafe
(American; giant cinnamon rolls)
602 Main Street
586-1666

LEWELLEN

The Most Unlikely Place
205 Main Street
778-9557

SCOTTSBLUFF

El Charrito
(Mexican)
802 Twenty-first Ave.
632-3534

Rosita's
(Mexican)
1205 East Overland
632-2429

Taco Town
(Mexican)
1007 West Twenty-seventh St.
635-3776

SIDNEY

Dude's Steakhouse
2126 Illinois
254-9080
dudessteakhouse.com

HELPFUL PANHANDLE WEBSITES

Gering
visitgering.com

Kimball-Banner County
kimballbannercountychamber.com

PANHANDLE AREA

West Nebraska Tourism
westnebraska.com

Scottsbluff
visitscottsbluff.com

Sidney–Cheyenne County
sidneycheyennecountytourism.com

Prairie Lakes Country

Just as the name implies, the Prairie Lakes Country in southwest Nebraska has several large lakes, recreation areas, reservoirs, and rivers, which makes it ideal for outdoor activities. The Texas-Ogallala Cattle Trail passed through the area, and history books are full of accounts of cowboy fights and stampedes. Native Americans favored the area for its hunting, and it is still renowned for that same purpose. This is the land that marks the transition from the tallgrass prairie in the eastern part of the state to the short-grass prairie of the high plains. The land is surprisingly hilly, with tree-covered canyons hidden along river banks deep in the hills. If you're traveling on Highway 30, remember that the old Lincoln Highway—the first transcontinental road, which led from New York to San Francisco—followed the same approximate path, beginning in 1913. Only then the road was mostly dirt trails and a bit more challenging. Present-day travelers will find museums, restaurants, guest ranches, and golf courses that early travelers could not have even imagined.

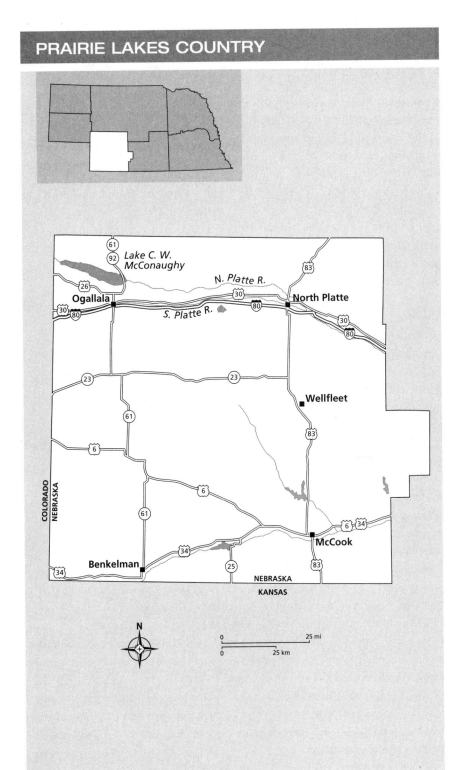

Keith County

Ogallala, just north of I-80, on the terminus of the Texas-Ogallala Trail, was at one time a wild town that earned a well-deserved reputation as the Gomorrah of the Plains. It all began when cowboys finished the cattle drive after weeks on the trail and went looking for diversions. They got paid, got a bath, got a drink (or several), and often got taken by gamblers and businesswomen of easy virtue who were eager to separate the freshly bathed and freshly paid cowboys from their money. The ten-year span between 1875 and 1885 saw Ogallala change from a quiet small town to one where gunshots were not uncommon. One odd fight erupted when a drunken cowboy from somewhere in the South took curious and great umbrage at two cowboys from the North when they ordered baked beans as part of their meal. He kicked over his chair and howled, "Just what I thought! A couple of Yankee bean-eaters." The unarmed Yankees ran for their guns, followed more slowly by the alcohol-impaired but decidedly armed Southerner. As happened in the Civil War, the North won. The Yankees were never arrested because it was clearly a case of self-defense, as anyone who heard the soon-to-be-dead man bellowing about what he was going to do to them when he caught up with them could testify. Ogallala is considerably safer now, and you can order whatever you want at a restaurant without risking the ire of fellow diners.

The frontier history of Ogallala is encapsulated at ***Front Street,*** at 519 East First St. It looks from the outside like an Old West street from the 1800s. Inside is the Livery Barn Cafe, with a western-style menu, a saloon, a free cowboy museum, and a gift shop. In the summer months you should see the family-oriented ***Crystal Palace Revue,*** with dancers, singers, and musicians, and which can only be described as western burlesque. It is Nebraska's oldest summer theater production, and you might be tempted to think that some of the jokes are equally as old. But it's great fun, and you'll enjoy it. There's a nightly shoot-out at 7:15 p.m.; the revue starts at 7:30 p.m. The telephone number is (308) 284-6000, and the website is ogallalafrontstreet.com.

Your next stop should be the ***Kenfield Petrified Wood Gallery*** at 418 East First St. Here you'll find art and music boxes and wall hangings made from teensy-weensy pieces of petrified wood about the size of a baby's fingernail. They're truly amazing. Do take the time to look at the wonderful collection of rocks and stones. It is open in the summer from Mon through Sat from 9 a.m. to 7 p.m. and Sun 1 to 5 p.m. Winter hours are Mon through Sat from noon to 6 p.m. It's free! The phone number is (308) 284-9996. The website is petrifiedwoodgallery.com.

FAVORITE ATTRACTIONS IN SOUTHWEST NEBRASKA

(All area codes are 308.)

Dancing Leaf Earth Lodge and Cultural Learning Center
6100 East Opal Springs Rd.
Wellfleet
963-4233

Fort Cody Trading Post
intersection of I-80 and Highway 83, northeast corner
North Platte
532-8081

Kenfield Petrified Wood Gallery
525 East First St., at the
Front Street attraction
284-9996

Ole's Big Game Steakhouse and Lounge
east side on the main block of downtown Paxton
239-4500

Boot Hill is where both residents and visiting rowdies were buried. A man named Rattlesnake Worley was killed over a $9 poker bet. The most famous and tragic resident of Boot Hill, however, was Mrs. Lillie Miller, who died along with her baby during childbirth in 1861. She and the baby were exhumed twenty-five years later to be moved to a new cemetery. Mrs. Miller, by all accounts, was perfectly preserved and perfectly petrified. Her remains were so heavy that a crane was required to move her. (The baby was neither preserved nor petrified.) Boot Hill is on West Tenth Street, 4 blocks west of Highway 61. It's always open, and it's free.

The **Bayside Golf Course** outside of Ogallala is located on **Lake McConaughy,** a huge reservoir with 100 miles of beaches. Its eighteen holes are tough, but five tee boxes allow those of all skill levels to enjoy the course with its great view of the lake. When you've had your fill of golf, you can go boating or fishing, or play tennis or volleyball. It's a public course, but do make reservations. The Nineteenth Hole Restaurant is a pretty good place to eat as well. They're very proud of their rack of lamb, but the chicken fried steak is darned good as well. To get to Bayside from Ogallala, take Highway 61 north to Highway 26 west. Go west approximately 7 miles to Lakeview Road (watch for a billboard), then turn right and go north 3 miles to Lakeview Road West. Turn left here and go another 2 miles to the entrance. The phone number is (308) 287-4653 or visit baysidegolf.com.

If you didn't know much about Nebraska and found yourself inexplicably transported to the white-sand beach of Lake McConaughy, you'd likely not guess correctly as to your location. This enormous lake, or Big Mac, as it is referred to locally, is 22 miles long and nearly 4 miles wide, and it has 100 miles of shoreline. It's the largest body of water between the Great Lakes and the Great Salt Lake. It is very popular for fishing, and several fish caught here hold state records. In some parts the lake is 142 feet deep, so who knows what lunkers are lurking in the depths? Boating, Jet-Skiing, scuba diving, camping, and sailboarding are also popular. One of the nation's largest sailboarding competitions, the Toucan Open, is held here each Sept. Resorts, marinas, and restaurants are sprinkled around the lake, mostly on the north side. Lake Ogallala is a smaller lake, just below Kingsley Dam to the east; it has camping and fishing, too. The dam is 3.1 miles long, 162 feet tall, and is the second-largest hydraulic-filled dam in the world. The dam complex supplies hydroelectric power and irrigation water for nearly half a million acres. Free tours of the plant are offered daily from Memorial Day to Labor Day, with the exception of Mon and Tues. Big Mac is 7 miles north of Ogallala on Highway 61. Call (308) 284-8800 or visit outdoornebraska.gov/lakemcconaughy/ for additional information or stop by the visitor center/water interpretive center. Learn about the lake, where its waters come from, and where its waters go.

East of Ogallala is **Paxton,** located 1 mile north of I-80, where you'll find **Ole's Big Game Steakhouse and Lounge** on the main street through town. Before stepping into Ole's you might imagine you'd be stepping into the old west. Instead, you'll be back in the era of Hemingway, when men traveled around the world shooting things. In these politically correct times, this is not considered such a cool thing to do, but you'll still be fascinated by more than 200 mounted trophies from every continent, which were personally bagged by former owner Ole Herstedt. When you walk in, there's a behemoth polar bear in a glass case. Everywhere you look there are animals and birds and animal parts. It might be disconcerting at first, but just chill; the animals have been dead for a long time, and they were bagged in a different time, when the world had a vastly different mind-set. Ole's has one of the world's largest privately owned trophy collections. The bar has a colorful history; it opened its doors in 1933, one minute after Prohibition ended. The steak house serves Nebraska grain-fed beef, plus chicken and fish. The food isn't fancy, but it is very good, and there's a lot of it. If you're wondering what Rocky Mountain oysters are, here's a clue: the menu says that you'll go nuts over these. The hours are Mon through Sat, 7 a.m. to 10 p.m.; and Sun, 7 a.m. to 9 p.m. Call (308) 239-4500; olesbiggame.com.

You should change your watch now. Mountain time changes to central time (and vice versa depending on which way you're headed) between Paxton and Sutherland.

For the Birds

Each year some 200,000 cliff swallows fly 3,000 miles from wintering grounds in Argentina to nest in western Nebraska. They represent the largest concentration of cliff swallows in the world. The cliff swallow earned its name from the practice of building gourd-shaped mud nests on cliffs or canyon walls, but these birds also seem to like making their homes on the smooth concrete facing of bridges and culverts. Biologist Charles Brown, fondly referred to as Captain Swallow, and his wife, Mary, a research assistant, have studied the swallows for several years at the Cedar Point Biological Station near Ogallala. They've discovered some fascinating things about cliff swallows' behavior. Like humans, their behavior runs from generous cooperation to mean-spirited competition. They share information about where to find food, and they work together to drive off predators such as sparrow hawks and bull snakes. But, they steal from each other, they're aggressive, and, none of this mate-for-life stuff, they engage in frequent adultery. Females often lay their eggs in another's nest, thereby getting the fun of messing around without the drudgery of raising the little buggers.

Both Keith and Garden Counties are known as hot birding spots. A viewing station at Lake Ogallala gives a great view of lots and lots of bald eagles. Paul Johnsgard, professor of life sciences at the University of Nebraska–Lincoln, has written that there are close to 310 bird species in the region. "It's the best place in the state and third-best in the country to go birding," Johnsgard is quoted as saying in the *Keith County News*. "It has the third-largest local list for any locality in the United States." The others are in Texas and Kansas, but you'll need to read about those in other books in the *Off the Beaten Path* series.

A checklist of birds in the area is available at the Ogallala Chamber of Commerce; call (800) 658-4390. In addition, a sizable number of sandhill cranes gather at the west end of Lake McConaughy every late winter and early spring.

Lincoln County

North Platte, just north of I-80, was home to one of the most famous characters from the Old West. In 1886, William "Buffalo Bill" Cody built an eighteen-room French Second Empire mansion and started his Scouts Rest Ranch northwest of town after he retired from a series of quintessentially "Western" jobs. He was a trail hand at the age of nine, a trapper, a Pony Express rider (he was fourteen years old when he responded to ads seeking riders who were young, wiry, and preferably orphaned), a buffalo hunter (he supplied meat for crews who were building the Kansas Pacific Railroad, and he shot 4,280 buffalo in eight months), and chief of scouts for the Fifth Cavalry during the Plains Indian wars. In 1882, the town fathers of North Platte asked him to plan something special for the Fourth of July. What he came up with ultimately brought him out of retirement and into international fame. He devised what is now thought to be the first organized rodeo in the nation, and it led to the inception of the wildly popular Buffalo Bill's Wild West Show and Congress of Rough Riders of the World, which performed to capacity crowds internationally. His home and ranch are now part of the **Buffalo Bill Scouts Rest Ranch State Historical Park and State Recreation Area.** The house is full of mementos and articles from his life (check out the beaded buckskins), and the huge barn has films from the Wild West Show and even some footage shot by Thomas Edison. Horseback rides on the adjacent 233-acre recreation area are available. The grounds, house, and barn are open daily from Memorial Day weekend through Labor Day weekend from 10 a.m. to 5 p.m. In April, May, Sept, and Oct, the house and barn are open Mon through Fri from 10 a.m. to 4 p.m. A park permit is required. To find the ranch, take Highway 83 north to Highway 30; then go west 2 miles and follow the signs. Basically, follow Front Street for 6 miles through North Platte. The telephone number is (308) 535-8035; outdoornebraska.gov/buffalobillsra.

You must stop at **Fort Cody Trading Post,** at the intersection of I-80 and Highway 83, if you have any intention of buying souvenirs for yourself or for anyone. This place has the most eclectic collection of gifts, from astonishingly tacky trinkets to exquisite jewelry, pottery, western clothing, antiques, and leather goods. There are a zillion too many things to mention, but at one end of the taste spectrum is an ink pen that has Buffalo Bill dropping his trousers to reveal red-and-white polka-dot drawers, and at the other end is an incredibly beautiful Navajo silver story bracelet. The store has a very good selection of western literature, both fact and fiction. Do not fail to see the miniature, hand-carved, mechanized Buffalo Bill Wild West Show, with all its 20,000 pieces. Watch for the teensy woman with the cigarette being flicked out of her mouth by a whip. Words fail me as to how wonderful this place is—just see it. Don't miss the two-headed stuffed calf. Did you notice the raging battle up top on the outside of the building between the cavalry and the Indians? The front facade of the building looks like a stockaded fort with mannequins dressed and posed as cavalry soldiers and Indians. This place has something for everyone. And more seriously, the site includes a museum of western-made clothing items. You'll find vintage Stetson hats, August Buermann spurs, and hand-written documents from Buffalo Bill. The trading post is open from 9 a.m. to 9 p.m. most of the year; winter hours are 9 a.m. to 5:30 p.m. The telephone number is (308) 532-8081, and the website is fortcody.com.

Most people don't give a lot of thought to how and why train cars are connected together, who and how they are routed, and other nitty-gritty details, but you will after you visit the **Union Pacific Bailey Yard** in North Platte.

Oh, Give Me a Home Where the Buffalo Roam

Because Grand Duke Alexis of Russia came all the way to southwest Nebraska in 1873 to shoot buffalo, this chapter is an appropriate place to talk more about them. Two hundred years ago, fifty million **buffalo** roamed the Great Plains. In 1804, Lewis and Clark reported "seeing buffalo in such magnitudes that we cannot exaggerate in saying in a single glance we saw 3,000 of them." Early fur traders who crossed the Plains told stories about seeing so many buffalo they blackened a valley stretching 10 miles across. That's a lot of buffalo. Initially, buffalo were hunted by whites in the millions for their hides and their tongues; their bodies were left to rot where they fell. Later, buffalo were killed to feed crews building the transcontinental railroad. A skilled shooter could kill 300 buffalo in one day.

Killing buffalo also became a political tool. If you want to get rid of pesky Indians on the Plains, get rid of their primary food source. In 1876, Rep. James Throckmorton of Texas said, "I believe it would be a great step forward in the civilization of the Indians and the preservation of peace on the border if there was not a buffalo in existence." We wonder what Mr. Throckmorton would think of the symbol the American bison has become for strength, stamina, and courage in the United States. Look at the various sports teams that use it for a mascot, it's use in coins, and in so many proud images of the American landscape. Ultimately, the Army paid hide hunters to hasten the demise of the buffalo. By the early 1900s, fewer than 500 remained. Five hundred! About 250 wild buffalo remained at Yellowstone National Park, and the rest were mostly scattered in private collections. Today there are an estimated 500,000 buffalo flourishing in their native lands, many of them on ranches in Nebraska and surrounding states. Ted Turner owns a buffalo ranch in Cherry County. The buffalo there, and on Turner's other ranches, come to more than 15,000 in number and are part of the largest private herd in the world. He's been quoted as saying, "I guess I've gone buffalo batty."

This is the largest rail yard in the world—train cars almost as far as you can see—with more than 150 trains put together every day. That's about 10,000 railcars carrying just a little bit of everything you can imagine. If you like trains, you'll be in heaven here. The ***Golden Spike Visitor Center*** opened in 2008 to help explain what happens here. Don't let the name Golden Spike confuse you. The Golden Spike was driven in Promontory Summit, Utah, where the transcontinental railroad met. But now, North Platte, Nebraska, is about the halfway point of goods traveling from east to west in the United States. Retired railroad employees volunteer to serve as tour guides and answer questions. There are also a number of displays that explain what is happening in the rail yard below. Admission is $7 for adults; $5 for children up to age sixteen. Summer hours are 9 a.m. to 7 p.m. Mon through Sat and 1 p.m. to 7 p.m. on

Sun. Winter hours are 10 a.m. to 5:30 p.m. To get there, take exit 177 from the interstate to Highway 83 (Dewey Street) and then watch for signs. Call (308) 532-9920 or visit goldenspiketower.com for more information. You can also learn about activities at Golden Spike, like the annual arrival of the Girl Scout Cookie Train, by following on Twitter and Facebook.

Near North Platte on a high hill is *Sioux Lookout.* Except it's no longer topped by a large statue of a Native American, with his hand raised to his eyes, looking for settlers. The statue was damaged by vandals; it was removed, restored, and placed on the courthouse grounds in North Platte. Visitors used to be able to climb the hill to see the statue, but they can still see for themselves what a great view the Sioux had in scouting for interlopers. If you want to see the hill, take Highway 83 south of North Platte and turn east on State Farm Road. Follow the blacktop road, which curves twice to the right and once to the left. A marker on the south indicates the spot.

Glenn Miller, of big band fame, lived in North Platte as a toddler for one year. His family then moved 30 miles north to *Tryon,* where they lived for five years. Today the stretch of highway linking the towns is designated as the

FAVORITE ANNUAL EVENTS IN SOUTHWEST NEBRASKA

(All area codes are 308.)

Buffalo Commons Storytelling Festival
McCook, late May
345-3200
buffalocommons.com

Nebraskaland Days
(PRCA rodeo and nationally known
country music performers)
North Platte, mid-June
532-7939
nebraskalanddays.com

Wurst Tag Days
Eustis, mid-June
486-3611

Kites and Castles
Ogallala, late July
287-2673
kitesandcastles.com

Chase County Fair
(nationally known performers)
Imperial, mid-Aug
882-4017
chasecountyfair.com

Indian Summer Rendezvous
Ogallala, mid-Sept
284-4066

Toucan Open (sailboarding)
Ogallala, mid-Sept
423-0654

Heritage Days
McCook, late Sept
345-3200

The Road Not Traveled

Shortly after graduating from college and eager to make my mark on the world, I received two offers for job interviews in one day. One was in Fort Smith, Arkansas; the other was North Platte. It was January, I believe, and I tried on several occasions to get to North Platte to impress my potential new employer with my skills and prowess. However, snowstorms, car problems, and other obligations kept getting in the way. Eventually the job opening was filled by someone else and I took the job in Arkansas, which I enjoyed immensely. There was a young man named Bill Clinton running for governor at the time, and I interviewed him often. And there were enough other news items to keep me busy and earning my keep for several months.

I don't regret taking the job in Arkansas, but every time I pass through North Platte, I wonder how my life might have evolved had circumstances evolved differently. I wonder who got the job I had applied for, and if he or she enjoyed the work. I wonder about this road not traveled so many years ago, but am thankful that my work today allows me to visit North Platte again and again. I think I would have been happy here.

Glenn Miller Memorial Highway. Take a little "Moonlight Serenade" drive yourself on Highway 97; the Memorial Highway begins at the intersection of Highway 83 north of town.

To see the ***Dancing Leaf Earth Lodge and Cultural Learning Center,*** take Highway 83 about a half hour south of North Platte to ***Wellfleet.*** Owners Les and Jan Hosick have built an authentic earth lodge in which guests can spend the night. You can also learn about the lives of early native people from the very knowledgeable couple. The site is on an old Boy Scout camp. Tent camping, RV hookups, and rental cabins are also available. The view is spectacular, as is the hiking. You can also go canoeing and hiking. The Hosicks are no longer open on a daily basis in the summer, but if you call in advance, they will do their best to accommodate your interests. It's at 6100 East Opal Springs Rd., 2 miles east of Wellfleet. Call (308) 963-4233.

Two miles south of I-80's Maxwell exit 190 is the beautiful, twenty-acre ***Fort McPherson National Cemetery,*** Nebraska's only national cemetery. More than 6,700 veterans, and some spouses, who served in conflicts from the Civil War to the current wars in the Middle East, are buried under row after row of white marble monuments. The utter silence and peaceful beauty combine to make a visit here a moving experience. Gates are open from dawn to dusk. A visitor center provides an electronic grave locator, if there is a particular grave site you are looking for. Fort McPherson was established in 1863 to protect the Oregon Trail travelers. No buildings remain, but you can see a statue of a cavalryman about a mile east of the cemetery, which is situated on the former parade grounds. The cemetery was established in 1873. Call (308) 582-4433 for more information.

Just a ½ mile west and a ½ mile south is **Fort McPherson Campground,** a serene little area filled with cedar trees. There are a couple of housekeeping cabins or one larger house that sleeps up to eight, and the prices are quite reasonable. You can also pitch a tent or camp in an RV. There are shower and laundry facilities, hayrides, and a playground. If you're traveling with a horse, horses are welcomed here as well. Fort McPherson Campground is open from mid-April to mid-Oct; if the weather stays warm, it stays open longer. Call (308) 582-4320.

Chase and Hayes Counties

Champion Mill State Historical Park, in **Chase County** near **Champion,** is a water-powered flour and grain mill now operated by the Nebraska Game and Parks Commission. It began operation in 1889 and remained open until 1968, when it was the last operating mill in the state. Visitors can see how grain was milled in this cavernous place and can even purchase small bags of pancake flour, whole-wheat flour, corn meal, and bran. The tranquil millpond is a state recreation area, with primitive camping and day-use facilities. It is open from Memorial Day weekend through Labor Day weekend from 9 a.m. to 5 p.m. The interpretive facility is open daily from Memorial Day weekend through Labor Day weekend from 9 a.m. to 5 p.m. and on Sat from 9 a.m. to 5 p.m. and Sun from 1 to 5 p.m. in May and Sept. A park permit is required. The park is located on the edge of Champion, which is southwest of Imperial on S15A. Call (308) 882-5860.

The **Camp Duke Alexis Recreation Area,** near **Hayes Center** in **Hayes County,** was at one time an important hunting ground for Native Americans. It's hard to keep a good thing secret, and, lo and behold, the next thing you know, you have royalty coming to pay a call. In 1872 Grand Duke Alexis, the twenty-two-year-old brother of the Russian czar, came to see the "wild life of America, including the Indians." The hunting party was led by Buffalo Bill Cody and was hosted by Gen. Philip Sheridan. Buffalo Bill persuaded a band of Indians led by Sioux chief Spotted Tail who were camped nearby to give a presentation of Indian-style hunting, followed by a war dance. The whole event was declared a brilliant success, and the Duke was pleased to shoot several buffalo. The recreation area, located 8 miles east and north of Hayes Center, covers 140 acres and includes a well-stocked, one-hundred-acre lake.

Frontier County

Frontier County has some of the reasons that southwest Nebraska is known as the Prairie Lakes Country. Strung along the southern tier of the county are ***Harry Strunk Lake*** and the ***Medicine Creek*** and ***Red Willow Reservoirs.*** These lakes offer a variety of activities and amenities: among them are both primitive and modern camping, boat ramps, fish-cleaning stations (there are abundant fish to catch), hunting in season, picnic tables, grills, shelters, modern restrooms, and vault toilets. For information on these and other southwest reservoirs, call (308) 345-1472.

Right smack in the middle of Frontier County on Highway 18 is the tiny little town of Stockville. A few miles south you'll find a collection of history that

OTHER ATTRACTIONS WORTH SEEING IN SOUTHWEST NEBRASKA

KEYSTONE

Keystone Church was built in 1908 to serve both Protestants and Catholics. Neither group could afford to build their own church, so they pooled their money to build one church with a Catholic altar at one end and a Protestant one at the other. Pews with reversible, hinged backs were installed so they could be switched to whatever group had the floor. The church was used until 1949 and is now on the National Register of Historic Places. It's located on McGinely Street. For tours call (308) 726-2271 or (308) 726-2322.

NORTH PLATTE

In ***Cody Park*** there is an amazingly intricate, life-size bronze statue of Buffalo Bill, donated by a British sculptor in 1998. The park is on Buffalo Bill Avenue, which is lined with flags that promoted the various Buffalo Bill shows around the world. There's also a wonderful old carousel for the kids with hand-carved wooden horses; (800) 955-4528.

Lincoln County Historical Museum and Western Heritage Village is a great little museum. Don't miss the display on the North Platte Canteen, commemorating the effort of the people of North Platte, who met every single World War II troop train and offered the men a treat of candy, cigarettes, cookies, or cake. The museum is at 2403 North Buffalo Ave.; (308) 534-5640.

OGALLALA

Mansion on the Hill is a huge brick house built by a local man in 1887 for his bride-to-be from the East Coast, who decided to forget the whole thing. She never showed up, and the heartbroken groom-to-be never lived in the house; in fact, nobody ever did. The house is on the corner of Tenth and North Spruce Streets, 4 blocks west of Boot Hill. Call (308) 284-0821.

truly speaks to the heart of the Nebraska prairie and the people who settled here. To Letha and Marlin Perks, this land is paradise, thus the name of their place, ***Perks' Prairie Paradise.***

Marlin's grandfather homesteaded this land in 1889, and the Perks have devoted themselves to preserving much of the lifestyle of the frontier prairie. Actually, Letha says it's just a hobby that got out of hand. First you'll see the one-room schoolhouse, built in 1885, that Marlin attended in the 1940s. And then there is a log cabin, a sod hut, a country church, a barn, and other buildings, all furnished according to the simple lives lived on this land more than a century ago. There is no admission, but you might offer to make a donation. You will have to call ahead for directions and to make sure Marlin and Letha are around to let you in and tell you their story. Call (308) 367-8782.

In the northeast corner of Frontier County is ***Eustis,*** on Highway 23.

Eustis, with its strong German heritage, was designated by the Nebraska legislature as the "Sausage Capital of Nebraska." There was a time just about everyone made their own sausage at home. If you drive around town, you'll see many outdoor kitchens in backyards, which were used for sausage making and smoking. The place to buy locally made sausage now is ***H & J Market,*** operated by Annette Juergen, a first generation immigrant from Germany. Yep, that accent is authentic. The store is located at 101 North Main St. or call (308) 486-3251.

For more German treats, stop in next door at Der Deutsche Market. Jan Yeutter stocks the little shop with cuckoo clocks from the Black Forest, Christmas ornaments and nutcrackers and all sorts of German gift items. The pretzels and noodles are handmade by German women in the Eustis area. The hours are limited in January and February, but you can always reach someone at (308) 486-5344.

To learn more about the history of this charming community, stop by the ***Grabenstein Insurance Office*** at 110 East Railroad St. They have a wonderful collection of historic photographs of the region taken by a long-lost relative of owner Bob Grabenstein. The office is open most business hours, or call (308) 486-5615.

Dundy and Hitchcock Counties

In 1867 Lt. Col. George Custer camped in ***Dundy County*** on the Republican River, just south of the present-day community of ***Benkelman,*** at Highways 61 and 34. His camp was attacked one June dawn by a group of Cheyenne and Sioux, led by Pawnee Killer. Apparently the leader was better at killing Pawnee than cavalrymen; a sentry was wounded while an unscathed Custer, according to historical records, "rushed from his tent into the midst of the battle." He lived

It's Bean Wonderful

Besides a whole lot of cattle, hogs, corn, and wheat, Nebraska produces a bunch of **beans**. We're first in the nation in great northern bean production, third in pinto beans, sixth in dry edible beans, and seventh in soy beans. A lot of these beans are grown here in western Nebraska. In honor of that, here are two fun recipes from the *Spilling the Beans* cookbook, published by the **Nebraska Dry Bean Growers Association:**

Black Bean Brownies

½ cup cocoa
½ cup butter or margarine
2 cups white sugar
1 cup pureed black beans*
4 eggs
⅔ cup all-purpose flour
1 teaspoon salt
½ teaspoon baking powder

Mix cocoa, butter, sugar, black bean puree, and eggs together in a bowl until well blended. Sift flour, salt, and baking powder together and stir into bean mixture. Pour the batter into a 9 x 13-inch pan greased with butter or cooking spray. Bake at 350 degrees for 40 minutes. If you wish, sprinkle with chocolate chips and nuts while hot and allow to cool completely before cutting.

*Drain and rinse canned beans thoroughly before pureeing.

Bean Cakes

4 cups cooked pinto beans
½ cup flour
Salsa
Shredded cheddar cheese
Sour cream

Mash beans well and stir in flour; mixture will be stiff. Heat oil in a skillet and fry the patties until golden brown on both sides. Top with salsa, shredded cheddar, and sour cream.

To get a copy of *Spilling the Beans* for your kitchen, contact the Nebraska Dry Bean Growers Association at (308) 633-1387, or order a copy from the website, bean grower.com. It's only $6. There are recipes for bean desserts like Pinto Bean Fudge, Bean Ice Cream, and Pinto Pecan Pie.

The Nebraska Dry Bean Growers Association is based in Mitchell, and the second Tuesday of each January is Bean Day. The bean growers come for information talks from experts and to meet with vendors and the like, but if you are in Mitchell on the second Tuesday of January, stop in the Events Center for a free lunch featuring items made from beans.

a while longer before meeting his death at the Battle of Little Big Horn. Benkel-man's most famous citizen was Ward Bond, who was best known for his role as the wagon master in the TV series *Wagon Train.* The **Dundy County Museum,** at 522 Arapahoe St., has twenty-six rooms jam-packed with historical items. The Doll Room alone contains close to 250 dolls. There's a soda fountain that serves malts, frosties, and sundaes. The museum is open Thurs in summer from 1 to 4 p.m. and on the first and third Sun of each month. Call ahead for tours by appointment during the rest of the year. The phone number is (308) 423-5404.

Just east of **Trenton,** in **Hitchcock County,** is a monument and marker that commemorates the final battle between the Pawnee and Sioux tribes. In 1873 a band of 700 Pawnee (300 warriors and 400 women and children) on a buffalo hunt were surprised by a Sioux attack. The Pawnee were outnumbered, and as they fled along the Frenchman River toward the Republican River, they came to a narrow canyon, where the heaviest fighting occurred. Because the Pawnee were friendlier to the whites than the Sioux, soldiers from Fort McPherson were sent to help, but they arrived too late. Twenty-first-century visitors are invited to the annual Massacre Canyon Pow-Wow, held on the first full weekend of August. Native Americans perform traditional dances. A rodeo, a wagon-train ride, and a barbecue provide additional fun. Pioneer burial grounds can be viewed. A visitor center is open from Memorial Day through Labor Day. Massacre Canyon is one hour south of I-80, at the Sutherland exit off Highway 25, 5 miles north of Trenton.

West of Trenton on Highway 34 is **Stratton.** In 1859 newspaperman Hor-ace Greeley, heeding his own advice to "Go west, young man," was westward-bound on a stagecoach to Denver. He stopped at a temporary station, housed in a tent at Stratton, and wrote, "I would match this station and its surround-ings against any other scene on our continent for desolation." That just goes to show what kind of trained observer he was. This is some of the prettiest country in the state.

Red Willow County

McCook, located at the junctions of Highways 83 and 6/34, has Nebraska's only structure designed by the famous architect Frank Lloyd Wright. This two-story frame and stucco Prairie-style house, at 602 Norris St., was completed in 1908. Other structures similar to this one are in Chicago; LaGrange, Illinois; and South Bend, Indiana. The original appearance was altered a bit after a 1932 fire destroyed part of the veranda roof and it couldn't be determined how to rebuild it. New columns were added, which changed the proportion and location of the roof. World War II saw more changes, when the house was converted to apartments; additional changes came in 1960 when the house was used as a medical clinic. It is listed on the National Register of Historic Places, but it's a private home, so please respect the privacy of the owners.

We all know that Benjamin Franklin's curious nature led to his flying a kite in a lightning storm, which led, in turn, to him being credited with discovering electricity. What not many people know is that electricity was brought to many people in the country because of Nebraska senator George Norris. Most famous as the father of the Tennessee Valley Authority, Senator Norris was also instrumental in creating the Rural Electric Administration. He was a sponsor of a bill that abolished the lame-duck session of Congress and changed the date of the presidential inauguration. The creation of the unicameral (one-house) legislature, which is unique to Nebraska, is another of Senator Norris's achievements. He served Nebraskans for more than 40 years, and, as result, his bust was the first one placed in the Nebraska Hall of Fame at the State Capitol in Lincoln. The *Senator George Norris State Historic Site,* at 706 Norris Ave. in McCook, is now a branch museum of the Nebraska Historical Society. This unprepossessing home is filled with artifacts and items used by Senator and Mrs. Norris in their simple, daily lives. The home is open year-round: Wed to Sat, 1 to 4:30 p.m. or by appointment. The admission fee is $3 for adults. The telephone number is (308) 345-8484. McCook was also home to three Nebraska governors: Governor Ralph Brooks, who served for one year before dying in office in 1960; Governor Frank Morrison, who served from 1961 to 1967; and Governor Ben Nelson, who was elected in 1990 and reelected in 1994, and later served as U.S. Senator.

Heritage Hills Golf Course, at 6000 Clubhouse Dr. on the west edge of McCook, has been rated as one of America's top one hundred public courses by *Golf Digest.* Its 270 acres offer Scottish-style golf on a course that incorporates the natural crests and canyons of the land rather than something bulldozed and tortured into something alien to the landscape. The brochure states that the unsuspecting golfer will find the "gaping jaws of fifty-three bunkers and sand traps . . . prepared to snatch his ball if he chooses to attempt to cut the corner of our doglegs." Despite the challenges of snatched balls, the course is absolutely beautiful, with native prairie grasses and yucca plants. Also according to the brochure, a U.S.G.A. official said that Heritage Hills is among the fastest and best courses in an eight-state area. The eleventh hole is rated as one of the best eighteen holes in Nebraska. An eighteen-hole game is $60 and a nine-hole game is $35. Try to book tee times a week in advance online at golfmccook.com. The telephone number is (308) 345-5032.

While in McCook, stop in at the *Bieroc Cafe* at 312 Norris Ave. for a great cuppa joe and a gourmet sandwich, like the Apple Planter or an Adult Grilled

Cheese. The Bieroc Hamburger is an acquired taste. It has sauerkraut mixed in with the hamburger. The Café shares a building with Tied House, one of the best pizza places you'll find. If you're into German food, you'll love German-style Pie that features beer cheese, keilbasa, sauerkraut and spicy brown mustard. The telephone number for both businesses is (308) 345-6500.

Places to Stay in Southwest Nebraska

(All area codes are 308.)

CAMBRIDGE

Cambridge B&B
606 Parker St.
697-3220
cambridge-bb.com

MCCOOK

Chief Motel
612 West B St.
345-3700
thechiefmotel.com

Places to Eat in Southwest Nebraska

(All area codes are 308.)

MCCOOK

Bieroc Cafe
(gourmet sandwiches; espresso, cappuccino, and latte; Italian sodas)
312 Norris Ave.
345-6500

NORTH PLATTE

Knoll's Country Inn
6132 South Range Rd.
368-5634
knollscountryinn.com

Coppermill Steakhouse
(steaks and seafood)
North Highway 83 and
Coppermill Road
345-2296
coppermillsteakhouse.com

NORTH PLATTE

Penny's Diner
473 Halligan Drive
535-9900

PAXTON

Ole's Big Game Steakhouse and Lounge
Downtown
239-4500

HELPFUL SOUTHWEST NEBRASKA WEBSITES

Big Springs
ci.big-springs.ne.us

Chase County
chasecounty.com

Eustis
eustisnebraska.com

McCook
visitmccook.com

North Platte
visitnorthplatte.com

Ogallala
visitogallala.com

Land of Cather and Cranes

South-central Nebraska is the land that inspired Pulitzer Prize winner Willa Cather to write: "There was nothing but land: not a country at all, but the material out of which countries are made." This is the land that draws the world's largest concentration of sandhill cranes; up to a half million birds come to the Platte River area in the late winter months. This is the land that saw the passing of immigrants on the Oregon Trail and the Mormon Trail, who watched as Pony Express riders raced across the lands. This is where Kool-Aid was created and one-of-a-kind museums, historic forts, water recreation, a round barn, and memorabilia from Hollywood stars such as Henry Fonda and David Janssen await your visit.

Sherman and Howard Counties

Sherman Reservoir, in northeast Sherman County, is popular with boaters, anglers, and campers. There are 65 miles of shoreline, and there is a surface area of nearly 3,000 acres. Drainage areas off the main reservoir provide bays and coves with outstanding fishing opportunities. Walleye fishing is good in the spring, largemouth bass and crappie are good from

LAND OF CATHER AND CRANES

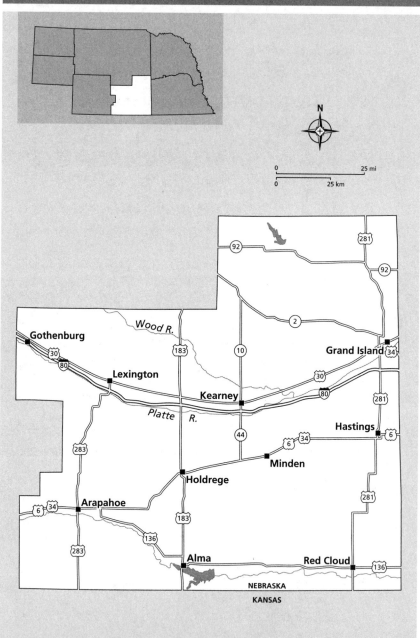

Gothenburg

Wood R.

30

80

Lexington

183

10

2

281

92

92

Grand Island 34

30

281

Kearney

80

Platte R.

283

44

6 34

Hastings

6

Minden

Holdrege

281

Arapahoe

6 34

183

283

136

Alma

Red Cloud

136

NEBRASKA

KANSAS

N

0   25 mi
0   25 km

mid-spring to early summer, and summer brings bites from white bass and catfish. Recreation sites scattered around the reservoir have primitive camping, day-use facilities, drinking water, vault toilets, and shelters. Sherman Reservoir is a good place to get away from it all. It is 4 miles east and 1 mile north of Loup City from Highway 92. A park permit is required. The telephone number is (308) 745-0230; outdoornebraska.gov/Sherman.

Here's an interesting historical fact: *Loup City,* near the Sherman Reservoir at the junction of Highways 58, 92, and 10 in Sherman County, was the site of a Depression-era farm strike led by the famous Communist organizer *Ella Reeve "Mother" Bloor.* On June 14, 1934, violence erupted when rumors spread that female poultry workers at the Fairmont Creamery Plant might strike for higher wages. The Communist group and local supporters clashed with its local non-supporters. The resulting fines and jail sentences levied upon "Mother" Bloor and her group marked the end of this attempt to organize farmers and workers in Nebraska.

From Loup City take Highway 58 south 12 miles to *Rockville.* Stop in for a cold one and a meal at *Jane's Tavern.* They've been serving catfish for many years and lobster for fewer years. It's the lobsters that have transformed Rockville into the Lobster Capital of Nebraska. In the mid-1990s the Rasmussen brothers decided to order up a great big batch of lobsters for a special

FAVORITE ATTRACTIONS IN SOUTH-CENTRAL NEBRASKA

Coney Island Lunch Room
104 East Third St.
Grand Island
(308) 382-7155

Fort Kearney Museum
131 South Central Ave.
Kearney
(308) 234-5200

Harold Warp Pioneer Village
junction of Highways 6, 34, and 10
Minden
(308) 832-2750, 832-1181 or (800) 445-4447
pioneervillage.org

Hastings Museum, Planetarium and Theater
1330 North Burlington Ave.
Hastings
(402) 461-4629
hastingsmuseum.org

Stuhr Museum of the Prairie Pioneer
junction of Highways 34 and 281
Grand Island
(308) 385-5316
stuhrmuseum.org

Willa Cather's Home
tours start from 326 North Webster
Red Cloud
(402) 746-2653

celebration. That event has become "Rockstock," and it draws nearly 3,500 people to feast on Maine lobster on the first Saturday in August. Not bad for a town of 105 people. Then everyone dances the night away at a lively street dance. The phone number at Jane's Tavern is (308) 372-7275.

St. Paul is where you can find the best homemade pies this side of the Mississippi. Stop in at a little cafe called the *Sweet Shoppe* and sink your teeth into a slice of heaven. The fruit pies are quite delicious, but the very best are the sour-cream raisin and the coconut cream. Be sure to thank baker Alice for her magic ways with pies. By all means have a hearty meal, but leave room for pie! The Sweet Shoppe is located at 605 Howard Ave. The hours are Mon through Fri from 6 a.m. to 4 p.m. and Sat and Sun from 6:30 a.m. to 2 p.m. The telephone number is (308) 754-4900.

For a grand slam, check out the *Museum of Nebraska Major League Baseball,* at 619 Howard Ave., which has displays on Nebraska's seven inductees to the Baseball Hall of Fame. These include "Wahoo" Sam Crawford, Bob "Hoot" Gibson, Grover Cleveland Alexander, Arthur "Dazzy" Vance, Don Richie Ashurn, and Wade Boggs. The latest inductee is Billy Southworth, who was born in Harvard, Nebraska. Open all year Mon through Sat 10 a.m. to 4 p.m. On summer weekends open Sat 10 a.m. to 4 p.m. and Sun 1 to 4 p.m. Donations are accepted with gratitude. The museum is at 619 Howard Avenue, 2 blocks north of the *Howard County Historical Village.* The village itself is pretty cool; there's even an outhouse built by the WPA. For more information call (308) 754-5558.

As you drive south of St. Paul on Highway 281, you'll be nearing *St. Libory* and another gift from heaven—the St. Libory melon. On both approaches to town, you'll see roadside fruit and vegetable stands: Helgoth's Roadside Market, the St. Libory Melon Market, and Kosmicki's Market. Stop and buy some of the legendary melons during the summer and fall. People come from miles away to make these melons their own. You should, too.

Hall County

Grand Island, with a population of just under 51,000, is Nebraska's third-largest community, unless you consider the 76,000 fans who attend home football games at the University of Nebraska–Lincoln a community. Located on I-80, at exits 318 and 312 in Hall County, Grand Island offers a grand time to travelers.

First of all, please do not miss the opportunity to eat at the *Coney Island Lunch Room.* This downtown diner, at 104 East Third St., is a step across time, with old-fashioned hot dogs topped with mustard, onions, and chili sauce. The cafe has been tempting taste buds since George Katrouzos bought the place in 1933, and his son and grandchildren continue the tradition of great food at great prices. They sell up to 350 dogs on an average Saturday and many more when people are home during the holidays. They also make mouthwatering chili. On a poignant note, former resident Charlie Hunt's daughter fulfilled his dying wish when she arranged for Coney Island to ship some much-loved chili to her dad in California. Other favorites at the cafe are the creamy malts and shakes. Coney Island is cheerfully decorated in red, pink, and white, and it seats about fifty people in the original wooden booths or at the counter. The cafe also serves breakfast, sandwiches, soups, and salads, but if this is your first or only chance to be here, order the dog, the chili, or both. Take-out is available, too. If you have a cooler in your vehicle, consider buying a pint or quart of the chili and the Coney sauce to go. Coney Island is open Mon through Fri from 8:30 a.m. to 5 p.m. and Sat from 8:30 a.m. to 3 p.m. The telephone number is (308) 382-7155.

After enjoying that fabulous Coney Island dog, chili, shakes, and more, waddle down the street to the ***Studio K Art Gallery*** at 112 West Third St. This cooperative represents the work of about twenty-five Midwestern artists, most of them from Nebraska. The K in the name stands for Karen Neppl, who

Wing It with Lonnie

You know how some people get so excited about something that you just can't help getting excited yourself? Lonnie Logan of Grand Island is like that. A cofounder of a group called Stewards of the Platte, Lonnie gets so excited about sandhill cranes and migrating waterfowl along the Platte River that you find yourself inching closer to him to soak up his enthusiasm and encyclopedic knowledge of these winged creatures. Each spring Lonnie takes groups (children, bird-watchers, retired people, church groups) on tours to teach them about the ecosystem of the Platte region and nearby wetlands. He can tell you why the portions of the Platte suitable for crane habitat have shrunk, and he can tell you what cranes eat, how long they live, how far they can fly, how avian cholera is a serious threat, why little shells are necessary for their diet, and a whole lot more. He will tell you about the many kinds of geese and ducks on the wetlands/lagoons. He can point at an almost invisible speck in the sky and tell you what kind of bird it is. He'll also tell you about competing interests: what's good for the birds might not be good for agriculture, and what's good for agriculture is not necessarily good for birds. Lonnie will have you happily tramping through knee-high grass in boggy marshlands toward a lake covered with ducks and geese and slinking out of a van to see sandhill cranes feeding in cornfields. When he's done with you, your shoes will be muddy and your legs will likely be tired, but you'll have a great big smile on your face and a head full of knowledge. To arrange a tour, you can reach Lonnie through Stewards of the Platte at (308) 382-2521.

is one of those artists. You'll find everything from fine fiber art and wearable art to some wonderful pottery and ceramics. Personally, I fell in love with the repurposed furniture by Donna Ryan. She rummages around flea markets and garage sales for trash furniture pieces and turns them into remarkable works of art. You just have to see it. Prairie Winds hosts a number of special events and launched a First Fridays art walk during warm weather months. You can take classes here in almost any medium. Located in the old bank building that dates back to 1889, Prairie Winds has been given much of the credit for revitalizing downtown Grand Island. Hours are 11 a.m. to 6 p.m. Tues through Sat. It doesn't cost anything to look, but I'll bet you won't be able to resist buying something here. Call (308) 381-4001. You can also order online at studiokart gallery.com.

A couple of other fun things about Grand Island—first of all, there's still a gas station that offers full service. It's Kensinger's Service Station at 1810 Lincoln Highway. I can't remember when, if ever, I've had someone other than my husband or my son pump gas for me. I usually have to do it myself. And, if you happen to get a parking ticket in downtown Grand Island, don't stress about it. Just take it to the nearest business and they'll clear things up for you.

Then there is G.I. Auto Body at 503 East Fourth Street. You'll see it long before you get there, believe me. Not long ago in Grand Island was a fun-loving guy named Fred Schritt, who owned the auto body shop for nearly 50 years. Fred loved cars and cartoons, so when the Pixar movie *Cars* was released, he took leftover car parts in the shop, made a colorful tow-truck, and put it on a pole outside of his shop. Then he put together an old Model T driven by Shrek, and you get the idea. It's a colorful place that demands you stop and take a picture. Unfortunately, the Grand Island city limit for cars on a pole is five, so when that was filled, and after he mounted Snoopy flying his doghouse from the top of the shop, Fred took his talents elsewhere. A lover of animals, Fred put Snoopy and Garfield driving an old Volvo on a pole outside at the Central Nebraska Humane Society at 1312 Sky Park Road. While you're there go on inside and snuggle with the lovable cats and dogs that need a good home. It would make Fred happy.

The 200-acre **Stuhr Museum of the Prairie Pioneer,** located at the junction of Hwys. 281 and 34, is far more than the typical community museum. The main building, designed by world-famous architect Edward Durrell Stone, is a beautiful white structure on a moat-surrounded island. The Fonner Memorial Rotunda has an excellent collection of Native American and Old West memorabilia. One of the very best things about the museum is the forty-acre Railroad Town; stepping into town makes you feel as though you've walked into one of those wonderfully wistful episodes of *The Twilight Zone*. Suddenly you're one hundred years back in time, and you're in a small western town with wooden sidewalks and posts for tying horses. Among the sixty original buildings are a general store, a depot, a doctor's office, a livery, a railroad hotel, a church, a school, Victorian homes, and the small bungalow where Henry Fonda was born. Many living-history demonstrations are held throughout summer and into fall. Railroad Town is so authentic that it's been the location of three made-for-TV movies, *Sarah, Plain and Tall, Home at Last,* and *My Ántonia.* Another nice part of the museum is the wooded arboretum, through which you can stroll, feed the ducks, or have a picnic. This is a day-long experience that you don't want to rush. The museum is open daily except for major holidays. The admission fee in the summer is $8 for adults, $7 for seniors, and $6 for children ages seven through sixteen, but if you go in the winter months, it's $2 cheaper for everyone. Call (308) 385-5316 or visit stuhrmuseum.org.

As you are traveling near **York,** stop at the visitor information centers on either east or west bound I-80. That's where Yvonne Junge, president of the York Area Quilt Guild, volunteers several hours a week, often working on her

FAVORITE ANNUAL EVENTS IN SOUTH-CENTRAL NEBRASKA

(Call ahead to verify dates.)

Crane Watch
Kearney
March 1–April 15
(800) 967-2189

Wings Over the Platte
sandhill crane spring migration
Grand Island, mid-March
(800) 658-3178

Willa Cather Spring Festival
Red Cloud, early June
(402) 746-2653

Hope Blues Festival
St. Libory, late June
(308) 382-8250

Swedish Midsommarfest
Holdrege, mid-June
(308) 995-4444

Central Nebraska Ethnic Festival
Grand Island; late June
(800) 658-3178

Republican River Canoe Race
Franklin, early July
(308) 425-6295

Grover Cleveland Alexander Days
St. Paul, mid-July
(308) 754-5558

Kool-Aid Days
Hastings, early Aug
(402) 461-8405
kool-aiddays.com

Nebraska State Fair
late Aug–early Sept
Grand Island
(308) 382-1620
statefair.org

own quilts during the slow periods. In addition to answering questions about many Nebraska destinations, she can direct you to some of the best quilt shops in the state.

J. Alfred Prufrocks Lounge, at 308 Pine St., is not your typical bar in Nebraska or anywhere really. Little cloth napkins with names of drinks embroidered on them. Beautiful comfy chairs, which I assure you are not standard in Nebraska bars. Astonishing light fixtures. Really cool glasses. The stainless steel counter. Artwork. The women's bathroom is nicer than my house, and they have better hand towels than I do. Oh, yes, those martinis . . . there's a bunch of them. And great wines, bourbon, champagne, double- and single-malt scotch, vodka, cognac, tequila, gin, rum, cordials, a lot of liqueurs, and lots of beers. And they'll bring you a nice cheese-and-cracker tray if you give them money for it. This truly wonderful place is open Wed through Sat from 5 p.m. to 1 a.m. The telephone number is (308) 398-8466.

West of Grand Island at exit 305 is the *Nebraska Nature and Visitors Center,* formerly the Crane Meadows Nature Center. There are 7½ miles of hiking trails on 250 acres that encompass wetlands, woodlands, and prairie. This is a great way to see several landscapes in a relatively small space. On your hike you might see coyotes, deer, turkeys, turtles, ducks, and many other native creatures. There's a huge observation tower over the river that is really worth the climb up the stairs. The visitor center is full of interesting displays

The Threads of Our Lives

The summer prior to my freshman year in high school, my Granny Lambdin decided it was a good time to teach me to quilt. As you can imagine, spending the summer indoors with my arthritic Granny learning to quilt was not my idea of a good time as my friends were at the pool and beginning to drive on their own. But quilt we did, all summer, and I have the ugliest butterfly quilt on the planet as proof of that miserable summer spent side-by-side with my Granny.

All of these years later, that quilt is my most prized possession. I tell my husband if the house ever catches on fire that he should grab the cats and the kids, I'm grabbing my Granny's quilt. I think my Granny would be thrilled that I have taken up quilting as a very enjoyable hobby. So when I travel, I love to stop in quilt shops and at quilt shows, and I naturally gravitate to quilt exhibits in museums.

There are so many quilt-related distractions for me in Nebraska, especially in Grand Island. The Stuhr Museum has about 300 Nebraska-made quilts in its collection that date to the 1850s. The first weekend of February each year is the Stuhr Museum Quilt Show that draws hundreds of fans through potentially wicked winter weather conditions to enjoy the company of other quilters.

OTHER ATTRACTIONS WORTH SEEING IN SOUTH-CENTRAL NEBRASKA

(Call ahead to verify dates; all area codes are 308.)

GIBBON

Iain Nicholson Audubon Center at Rowe Sanctuary
(visitor centers, sandhill cranes tours in season)
44450 Elm Island Rd.
468-5282

GRAND ISLAND

Fonner Park (horse racing)
open mid-Feb to early May
382-4515
fonnerpark.com

KEARNEY

Children's Museum
5827 Fourth Avenue
698-2228
kearneychildrensmuseum.org

on endangered local species, a model of the Platte River, hands-on activities, a gift shop, and art gallery. The hours are Mon through Sat from 9 a.m. to 5 p.m. During the late-winter sandhill crane migration, the hours expand to 8 a.m. to 6 p.m. seven days a week. You can arrange for tours to blinds along the river at a cost of $35 per person, but again, well worth the price. For many people, the Sandhill Crane Migration is a bucket list experience. Call (308) 382-1820 or visit nebraskanature.org.

Do you gotta have art? Then a stop at the *Art Farm* near *Marquette* is in order. This artists-in-residence program in rural Hall County has offered residencies to artists from around the world since 1993. Studio space, workshops, and a gallery have been reconstructed from old farm buildings. Artists live in a century-old farmhouse. Owners and artists Ed Dadey and Janet Williams live in a structure put together from several old barns moved onto the property and joined together. They call it the Mutant Little House on the Prairie. Artists are required to leave one artwork on-site, so the place is sprinkled with pieces, some permanent, some that will devolve back into the prairie. Ed and Janet have turned some of the former cropland back into prairie grasses. It's very fun to wander through the prairie looking at art. The Louvre? MOMA? The Tate or the Prado? Not quite yet, but it's still wonderful. In the fall visitors are invited to the annual "Art Harvest" to see the latest crop. Admission is free, and there are no regular hours; folks just drop by. To get there go 8 miles north of I-80 at Aurora on Highway 14 and then 2½ miles west on West 21 Road. The phone number is (402) 854-3120 or find out more at artfarmnebraska.org.

Buffalo County

Fort Kearny, which was built in 1848 to protect Oregon Trail travelers, was also on the Pony Express route. It is located 4 miles south of Kearney on Highway 44 and 4 miles east on L50A. Before it was abandoned in 1871, it played an important role in the expansion of the American West. It was the base of operation for Maj. Frank North and his brother, Luther, who organized the famous Pawnee Indian Scouts. At present the fort is a state historical park, and it makes an interesting stop. The visitor center has exhibits about the military on the Plains and on the fort itself. The most poignant displays feature ordinary items like uniform buttons and pieces of china that were unearthed during the re-creation of the fort. It makes you wonder what sort of items that belong to you might be unearthed in a century or so. A blacksmith shop, a stockade, and an ammunition storage building are on the site, too. The visitor center is open from Memorial Day weekend through Labor Day weekend from 8 a.m. to 8 p.m. During the rest of the year, it's open 9 a.m. to sunset. The center is also open mid-March to mid-April for sandhill crane tours. The grounds are open daily year-round. A park permit is required. Call (308) 865-5305 or visit outdoornebraska.gov/fortkearny.

Drive into *Kearney* to see the *Fort Kearney Museum,* at 131 South Central Ave. The museum is one of those delightful places that are crowded with the most amazingly curious stuff from all around the world. You'll see a full Samurai warrior costume, a shrunken head, an axe that disconnected people from their heads in the Middle Ages, Zulu spears, an original Ghost Dance shirt, cuneiform tablets, a fragment of a dinosaur eggshell, the first American-made coin-operated music box, Palestinian wedding shoes (they look exceedingly uncomfortable), mummified bread from Egyptian tombs, a Sharp's fifty-caliber carbine buffalo gun, seashells, mastodon teeth—but wait, there's more! After you see the collection, you should ride on the glass-bottom boat (in reality, a boat with a glass panel on the bottom). Underneath it, with the inducement of some fish-food pellets, giant catfish, Japanese koi, and scary-looking gar will gather for your enjoyment. It's pretty cool. Take exit 272 off the interstate, turn north at the first place you can, go 1 block, and then turn 1 block east. The museum is open from Memorial Day through Labor Day, Thurs through Sat, 10:30 a.m. to 5 p.m.; and Sun, 1 to 5 p.m. The number is (308) 234-5200. Admission is $3 for adults; children age eleven or younger visit free when accompanied by an adult.

At 2401 Central Ave. there's a museum that is the polar opposite of the Fort Kearney Museum but equally as wonderful. The collection at the *Museum of Nebraska Art (MONA)* is not from around the world; it all has a Nebraska connection of some sort. Don't even think about smirking when you hear the words *Nebraska* and *art* in the same sentence. MONA is an excellent museum, with twelve exhibition galleries. The permanent collection is admirable, and there is always at least one fascinating temporary exhibit. The museum is housed in a large, elegant, old post office, with a beautiful newer addition and a peaceful sculpture garden out back. The gift shop is sure to tempt even those with the most discriminating of tastes. Hours are Tues through Sat from 11 a.m. to 5 p.m. and Sun from 1 to 5 p.m. Call (308) 865-8559 or visit mona.unk.edu.

Just east of Kearney on I-80, you'll see something you don't see very often, that being a great big huge thing over the interstate. This is called the **Great Platte River Road Archway Monument.** It most decidedly is not off the beaten path, but it is worth a stop. Right about where the Archway is located marks the spot of many important westward expansion factors. Near here is where these things traversed: Native American paths, fur trader routes, the Oregon Trail, the Mormon Trail, the Pony Express, the Lincoln Highway, and the first transcontinental railroad. The museum inside explains all these old things in a very whiz-bang, modern way. It's a nice way to learn about history; you'll like it. There's a restaurant and gift shop on-site as well as gardens that grow ancient varieties of corn used by the Pawnee. Hours are daily 9 a.m. to 5 p.m. Admission is $12 for adults, $1 for over age 62, $6 for children, and free for children five and younger. To get there, take exit 272 north at Kearney, continue north to Talmadge Street, turn right (east) at Talmadge to Central Avenue, turn right again, go to Archway Parkway (or East First Street), turn left (east), and drive for a bit until you see the parking lot. The telephone number is (308) 237-1000 or (877) 511-2724. The website is archway.org.

The **Nebraska Firefighters Museum** is just west of the Archway at 2434 East First St. in Kearney. This museum has lots of the expected old fire trucks and historical information, presented in a very nice way. But it also has a number of programs about fire safety. It's a good place to stop and explore, especially if you have kids—who will get in free if they are under six years old. Admission for adults is $6; for seniors $4; and for children six to seventeen, just $3. In the summer, the museum is open 10 a.m. to 5 p.m. Mon through Sat, and 1 to 5 p.m. on Sun. Call (308) 338-3473 or visit nebraskafirefighters museum.com.

West of Kearney, on I-80 at Highway 183, you'll come to **Elm Creek** and two unique attractions. The first is the **Chevyland U.S.A. Antique Car and Cycle Museum.** Owner Monte Hollertz has one of the largest and most complete collections of Chevrolets in the country. There are more than 115 cars.

A River Runs through It

The *Platte River* has been called many things. It's said to be like a politician: shallow, yet wide at the mouth. It's said to be too thick to drink and too thin to plow. It's also said to be a mile wide and an inch deep. Okay, it's true—it's not your ragin' river, except maybe during the spring thaw, when it can create some highly unpleasant floods. Washington Irving said the Platte was "the most magnificent and most useless of rivers." Well! It does have its good points, though. It was fairly easy to cross in a covered wagon, and it is the major reason why sandhill cranes annually flock here in numbers up to a half million during their northward migration. The shallow river gives them a place to roost overnight on sandbars, where predators can't reach them. They spend their days foraging in the fields, and the young, unmated birds spend time "dancing" to attract lifelong mates. Much has been written about the migration; *Forbes FYI* magazine says it's the number-one place in the world for bird-watchers, and one travel writer called it the "Serengeti of the Plains." The Platte River useless? I don't think so.

The oldest, a Royal Mail Roadster, dates from 1914. There's a rare 1947 Fleet Line Country Custom Club Sedan, with the original wood paneling that came in a kit for do-it-yourselfers. The museum also has a car that was used as the getaway vehicle in a 1965 bank robbery in Big Springs, Nebraska. No matter if running boards on cars from the 1920s or fins from the 1950s put you in mind of your glory days, this is the place to relive old memories. Be sure to check out the fuzzy dice in several of the vehicles. The collection also has about fifty motorcycles and has expanded to include Volkswagens, Toyotas, Audis, Cadillacs, and Fords. The hours are Memorial Day through Labor Day, daily from 8 a.m. to 5 p.m. Monte is in and out the rest of the year, so you can take a chance of him having the museum open, or you can call ahead for an appointment. Admission is $6 for adults, $2 for children age ten through fifteen; kids nine and under get in free. The telephone number is (308) 856-4208. To get there, take exit 257 north on Highway 183 and turn east on the gravel road across the highway from Bosselman Travel Center.

Another worthwhile attraction is the *U.S. **Wild Horse and Burro Facility at Elm Creek.*** This forty-acre facility houses up to 500 wild horses and burros that have been removed from Bureau of Land Management areas in the West and Southwest. The animals rest here before they are adopted by someone who will love and care for them. The facility is open Mon through Fri, 8 a.m. to 4 p.m. You can drive around a road through the pens to get a close-up look at the beautiful animals. There's no admission fee. The telephone number is (308) 856-4498. To get there, travel 3 miles north of Elm Creek on Highway 183.

Dawson County

Lexington, at I-80 and Highway 21, was at one time known as Plum Creek. At present it has a plum of an attraction in the *Dawson County Historical Museum.* For a town with a population of just 8,544, this is one great museum. One of the most popular exhibits is the McCabe Aeroplane, or Baby Biplane, which has unusual elliptical wings and was built here in 1915. Another exceptional exhibit features the preparation and preservation of a Big Al (they thought at first it was Big Alice, but something about the configuration of the hip bones made them change their minds), a 15,000-year-old mammoth that was unearthed in the county in 1993. The main gallery has period rooms, and the military hall contains artifacts from Civil War swords to medals awarded during Desert Storm. There's an 1888 schoolhouse, an 1880 railroad depot, and a 1903 locomotive. A clever photography display shows shots of the same locations in the city, taken every ten years, to demonstrate how the city has changed. There's also a display about the Olive family, who were cattle ranchers, and the trouble they got into with settlers, who wanted to fence the land and farm it. Two settlers ended up hanged in 1878, without benefit of trial, as cattle rustlers. The ensuing legal battle received national attention and is well documented in the museum, located at 805 North Taft St. There's also a nice gift shop and a section of great books. To find it, go north from I-80 over the viaduct and turn east on Seventh Street; then go 5 blocks to Taft Street. The hours are Mon through Sat, 10 a.m. to 5 p.m.; and Sun by appointment. Closed major holidays. Admission is free, but donations are welcome. Call (308) 324-5340 or visit dchsmuseum.com for more information.

The *Heartland Museum of Military Vehicles,* just north of I-80 at exit 237, opened in June 1994 with an exceptional collection of about one hundred vehicles that were used by the military during the last fifty years. The meticulously restored vehicles are still operational. You'll find ambulances, helicopters, one of the first jeeps, tanks, half-tracks, a rare snow tractor, one of the world's few remaining Downed Airman Retrievers, and the only Bradley Fighting Vehicle in private ownership. There's a wrenching display of a Huey UH-1 helicopter perched on a roof with the silhouetted figure of a crew chief reaching a hand to assist desperate refugees aboard the last flight to freedom. If you were a fan of the TV show *M*A*S*H,* you'll love the exhibit that explains the work of the Mobile Army Surgical Hospitals during the Korean War. The museum is open Mon through Sat from 10 a.m. to 5 p.m. and Sun from 1 to 5 p.m. There's no admission fee, but do leave a donation so that they can acquire more vehicles and continue construction. The phone number is (308) 324-6329; the website is heartlandmuseum.com.

Nebraska is blessed to be home to many talented artists whose work brightens the landscape throughout our state. There's a particularly interesting piece in Lexington just outside of **KRVN Radio** at 1007 Plum Creek Parkway. The bronze sculpture by Sondra Jonson was installed in 2001 to celebrate the station's 50th anniversary. It's called Breaking News and immortalizes a family huddled around a radio to learn the news of the day. In this day of instant news via our phones, this sculpture is a humble reminder of a time when the local radio station was a community's primary source of information.

If you like art, the 13-mile drive from Lexington to **Cozad** will be lucky for you. The **Robert Henri Museum,** at 218 East Eighth St., is a restored hotel and the boyhood home of an internationally famous painter. The young Robert Henry left Cozad as a boy, and at present we know him as Robert Henri. His work hangs here, in New York City's Museum of Modern Art, and in forty-three other museums around the world. Henri was one of the founders of a group of influential artists who called themselves the Eight, or the Ashcan School. The adjacent walkway takes you through the Avenue of Flags to a Pony Express station, a pioneer church, and a school. The museum is open daily from May 1 through November 1. The hours are Mon through Sat, noon to 5 p.m., and Sun by appointment. If you go there in the off-season, there's a list of names and numbers on the door of people who will give you a tour. The telephone number is (308) 784-4154; the website is roberthenrimuseum.org.

If you feel as though you're right on the verge of some change, it's because you are: Cozad is located on the 100th meridian, or the geographical line of demarcation between what is considered East and West—you are now right at the spot where the West begins. The **100th Meridian Museum,** at 206 East Eighth St. near downtown Cozad, features pioneer artifacts. The prize of the collection is the antique touring coach used in 1907 by President William Taft and his family on a trip to Yellowstone Park. The museum is open Memorial Day through Labor Day, Mon through Sat, 10 a.m. to 5 p.m. Admission is $2. Call (308) 784-1100 for more information.

Continuing west on I-80, you'll come to **Gothenburg,** home to the legendary Swedish strongman Febold Feboldson, a mythical character akin to Paul Bunyan and Pecos Pete. Feboldson was said to have accidentally carved the Platte River with a plow and to have named the "mugwump" bird as such because, when perched on a fence, its "mug" was on one side of the fence and its "wump" was on the other. Here's some trivia for football fans: another strongman, Jay Novacek, a former tight end for the Dallas Cowboys, is from Gothenburg.

There are two attractions well worth a stop in Gothenburg. The first is the **Sod House Museum,** just north of the interstate on Highway 47 at exit 211.

Owners Merle and Linda Block, descendants of pioneers, built an authentic sod house in 1990 with one-hundred-pound sod rectangles in a labor of love. The sod is knitted together with the roots of bluestem and buffalo grasses. Grass and cacti grow on the roof, and the 3-foot-thick interior walls are whitewashed with lime and water. There's a bed inside with ropes serving as bedsprings under a lumpy, grass-stuffed mattress. This is significant because we've all heard the phrase "sleep tight," and just where do you think that came from? It came from pulling bed ropes tighter for a more comfortable night. Also on the site are two wooden windmills, a life-size buffalo fashioned by Merle from 4½ miles of barbed wire, and a second barbed-wire sculpture of a Native American seated on a horse. Another building at the site contains historical artifacts that pertain to the era of the sod house. The museum is open daily from May through Sept, 9 a.m. to 6 p.m. There's no admission fee. The telephone number is (308) 537-2680. In the off-season, call the Gothenburg Chamber of Commerce at (308) 537-3505 for information.

The second attraction is the ***Pony Express Station,*** which was moved to Ehmen Park from its original location, 15 miles southwest of Gothenburg. The Pony Express operated for only eighteen months, beginning in April 1860, and at that time was called the Greatest Enterprise of Modern Times. The 2,000-mile express route from St. Joseph, Missouri, to Sacramento, California, took ten days to traverse. See if the letters or postcards you mail from here bearing a Pony Express seal get home before you do. If you're around the second week in June, you'll see reenactors riding the entire route, night and day, as they did in the 1860s. Hours at this free museum are the same as those at the Sod

Here's a Line for Ya

The *100th meridian,* which runs smack dab through *Cozad,* is not a line you'll see on a state map, but it's a significant line nonetheless. This is the line of demarcation where the East officially becomes the West, and what some say is the line where the humid East becomes the arid West. You won't notice the difference in the landscape immediately, especially if you're speeding across Nebraska on the interstate. But you can bet this line is as serious as a heart attack to people who make their living from the land; the East gets in excess of 20 inches of rain per year while the West can expect less than half of that. You won't notice the decided change in attitudes if you don't get out of your car and talk to people, and there's a real difference in how people on either side of the 100th meridian view themselves. People west of the 100th meridian are honest-to-god westerners, and they'll tell you so. And anyone east of Cozad, well, they're Easterners and looked at with a bit of curiosity, even if they're from places like Norfolk, Grand Island, or that major metropolis of Omaha.

House Museum, and the telephone number is the same as well: (308) 537-3505. Horse-drawn carriage rides around the park are available from Memorial Day through Labor Day weekend.

Geology buffs will be interested to know that the steep canyon lands southwest of Gothenburg are the *Dissected Loess Plains National Natural Landmark.* It is made up of 200 feet of loess soil, and that's really deep for loess soils, which have been carried in by the wind and have eroded over time into canyons and valleys.

Adams County

The largest community in Adams County is *Hastings,* with a population of just under 25,000. This is an energetic college town, with a great downtown area and plenty of activities for everyone in the family. Hastings is south of Grand Island, at the junction of Highways 281 and 6.

Hastings YMCA is just off Highway 281 at the end of the viaduct if you're coming from the north. You can't miss it; there's a big sign. And you shouldn't miss it because there's a world of things to do. There are three indoor water slides, swimming, basketball, handball, racquetball, volleyball, indoor tennis, a game room, space ball, a weight room, video archery, go-karts, and miniature golf. Costs depend on which activity you select. Hours are Mon through Fri from 5:30 a.m. to 10 p.m., Sat from 8 a.m. to 10 p.m., and Sun from noon to 10 p.m. The telephone number is (402) 462-6220.

The *Hastings Museum of Natural and Cultural History* is not only the premier attraction in Adams County, but it is among the finest attractions in the state. The fully accredited museum features the *Lied Superscreen Theater,* with a screen that's five stories tall and 70 feet wide. Also featured is the *J. M. McDonald Planetarium.* The museum has three floors, with well-designed exhibitions that include natural history, wildlife, Native American culture, a Discovery Center, pioneer history and Americana, local history, and a new fantastic wing about Kool-Aid, which was created in Hastings by Edwin Perkins. (In 1998 Kool-Aid became the Official Soft Drink of Nebraska, whereupon the milk producers of Nebraska had milk designated as the Official Drink of Nebraska.) On the first floor is a very old wooden case with realistic-looking stuffed rattlesnakes. Go stand over there, express loud amazement to your traveling companions, and, when they come over to see what you've discovered, press the secret button and make the rattles buzz. It never fails to elicit a scream. If you're traveling with children, be prepared to press that button again and again and again. Kids love it. This is a must-see museum; there's even someone buried in there. The address is 1330 North Burlington. The museum is open Mon

A Little Flight Music

If you have ever questioned your belief in a higher power, or call it what you will, those thoughts will be forever banished as you crouch in a freezing, riverbank blind to see up to 10,000 sandhill cranes swirl up in a dark cloud to greet the day in an unduplicatable, deafening cacophony. (Check with the Grand Island, Kearney, or Hastings chambers of commerce for information about local events where you can see and learn more about these special birds.) Nebraska is the only state on the migratory route where hunting sandhill cranes is prohibited. My friend Mary Ethel, who loved Nebraska more than anyone I've ever known, often told the story of her encounter with a park ranger in New Mexico. He had witnessed the mate of a freshly killed sandhill crane attack the human hunters as they tried to retrieve her mate's body. The distraught female crane then held a silent vigil by the carcass for several days until hunger and the undeniable pull of instinct called her north. Perhaps that lovely sandhill crane found comfort, as so many of us do, in the peace and protection of Nebraska.

through Sat from 9 a.m. to 7 p.m., and Sun from 1 to 6 p.m. Be sure to take a short walk to the adjacent cemetery, with Oregon Trail–era graves. Admission prices vary greatly depending on whether you want to see a superscreen film, or just the museum, so call (402) 461-4629 or visit hastingsmuseum.org, to decide what works for you.

Murphy's Wagon Wheel, at 107 North Lincoln in downtown Hastings, is a popular watering hole for locals and sports enthusiasts. You'll know you're there when you see the shamrock on the sign and the statue of St. Patrick in the window. Owner Bob Murphy is proud of his Irish heritage. Murphy's serves prodigious amounts of good bar food. In particular, you should try the Macho Nachos; the Murphy Burger with bacon, mushrooms, and Swiss cheese; and the Hot Wings. It's a fun place, and you'll likely make a few new friends from Hastings. Hours are seven days a week, 11 a.m. to 1 a.m. The telephone number is (402) 463-3011, murphyswagonwheel.net.

Take plenty of time to stroll along Second Street in downtown Hastings, enjoying the dozen or more bronze sculptures installed here in recent years. From whimsical images of children sledding in the snow to serious images of the struggling pioneers of this region, these sculptures are an outgrowth of an art festival that was held in Hastings for many years. Now, the city and downtown merchants invest their funds into making these permanent additions to art appreciation in this community. Stop by the Downtown Merchants office at 301 Burlington for a brochure that tells about the artists. Call (402) 461-8415.

Kearney County

In **Minden** you'll see what is best described as a small version of the Smithsonian Institution's National Museum of American History. The Smithsonian calls itself America's Attic, whereas the **Harold Warp Pioneer Village** invites you to "See the Story of America and How It Grew." Minden is 12 miles south of the interstate at exit 279. You'll be well aware of its approach; you'll likely have seen dozens of signs for it no matter what direction you're coming from. There really is no way to begin to describe the sheer magnitude and volume of the exhibits. Twenty-six buildings occupy more than twenty acres, whereas the twelve historic buildings circle a shady commons area that features a steam-powered carousel, built in 1879, with rides that cost only a nickel. More than 50,000 historic items from "every field of human endeavor" are on display. Some buildings are so full of items dating back to the 1830s that you might approach sensory overload. The most famous collections are the 350 antique cars, including one built by Henry Ford in 1906, one hundred vintage tractors, and a huge display of antique farm machinery. In addition, you'll see a Pony Express station, a sod house, a pioneer church, a one-room school, an ocean-going vessel, a steam engine, and lots more. The Home Appliance Building alone has a zillion gadgets and machines designed to "make mother's workday easier." If you take your time and see everything you should see, you'll never make it through Pioneer Village in a single day. Take time to read the remarks in the guest book; one couple from Minnesota described it as "historical overload" while one gearhead wrote, "very good—cars!" One admission fee gets you in for more than one day. Plan on staying at the adjacent motel or campground. And hey, you don't necessarily have to arrive by automobile. The Pioneer Village Field is adjacent to an airport for private aircraft. The museum is open daily year-round from 8 a.m. to sundown. The only day it is closed is Christmas Day. Admission is $14.25 for adults and $7.25 for children age six through twelve. Children 5 and younger are admitted for free. Call (800) 445-4447 or (308) 832-2750, or visit pioneervillage.org.

Phelps and Gosper Counties

The **Nebraska Prairie Museum** in **Holdrege** is housed in a new, two-story building, with well-designed exhibits that cover every facet of the county's development. You can't turn around without seeing something interesting. The Native American collection alone is very impressive. You'll see dolls, bikes, cars, a collection of radios and early televisions, furniture, dishes, clothes, hats, sewing machines, weapons, and all sorts of neat stuff. There's a nice exhibit on the Orphan Trains. One of the more popular exhibits is about Camp Atlanta, a World War II German prisoner-of-war camp, which was located south of town at Highways 6 and 34. All the artifacts in the Prisoner of War Room were donated by former POWs and the military or civilian workers at the camp. There's a scale model of the camp, too. A short video tells the Camp Atlanta story with moving personal stories of German prisoners who became friends with the locals and the farmers for whom they worked. The prisoners were highly important to the area because they worked in many of the businesses and on farms while a lot of American men were off to war. The National Sod House Society is based in the museum, as is a fine genealogical library. You'll find the museum on the north edge of town on Highway 183. Hours are Mon through Sat, 10 a.m. to 5 p.m.; and Sun, 1 to 5 p.m. Admission is free but donations are really appreciated to keep this great place open. The telephone number is (308) 995-5015, and the website is nebraskaprairie.org.

In *Gosper County, Johnson Lake State Recreation Area* has long been a favorite with boaters, anglers, campers, and picnickers. The lake has 2,060 water acres and most everything you'd need for your outdoor adventure. On or near the lake, abundant services are available: boat rentals, boat ramps, camping, cabins, a grocery store, a golf course, gas, bait and tackle, fish-cleaning stations, boat-repair facilities, refreshments, restaurants, lounges, a go-kart track, and even a car wash. Johnson Lake is 7 miles south of Lexington on Highway 283. It is open year-round. The telephone number is (308) 785-2685, and the website is outdoornebraska.gov/johnsonlake.

If you're in the area during the cold winter months, you might consider viewing the *bald eagle population* at the *J-2 Hydro Plant.* Peak viewing times, when you might see as many as two dozen bald eagles, are mid-December through mid-January. The colder it is, the more eagles you'll see. They come to feed on the open water at J-2 when streams and lakes freeze over. It's really quite a wonderful sight. You can observe the eagles from a warm indoor viewing area. Spotting scopes are provided, and attendants can answer your questions. The hydro plant is south of the interstate, at the Lexington exit. Watch for signs that will lead you to the plant. The viewing areas are open from mid-December until the eagles leave in early spring. Call (308) 995-8601 to find out about free Saturday or Sunday viewing on winter weekends.

Webster County

Nebraska's most famous author and Pulitzer Prize winner is **Willa Cather.** She came to **Red Cloud,** at Highways 281 and 136, in Webster County, as a small girl and lived here until she left for college in Lincoln. Cather's experiences, and those of the settlers whose lives were shaped by the land, led her to write extraordinary books about ordinary people. She was awarded the Pulitzer for *One of Ours* in 1922. Six of her twelve novels are set in the Red Cloud of her youth. Her childhood home, now a State Historic Site, is open to the public. Her upstairs bedroom still has the wallpaper she chose and put up herself as a teenager. If you're a Cather fan, this stop is a must. For a tour of the house, go to 326 North Webster in downtown Red Cloud. You can see the house and other buildings associated with Cather, such as the Burlington Depot, St. Juliana Falconieri Catholic Church, and Grace Episcopal Church. The old Opera House has been restored; check out the backstage, where teenage Cather's signature is scrawled on the wall. Hours for daily scheduled tours are 9:30 and 11 a.m., and 1:30 and 3 p.m. Tour prices range from $5 for an adult to tour just the house all the way up to $50 for a narrated driving tour of Willa Cather Country. Call (402) 746-2653 or visit willacather.org.

The **Willa Cather Memorial Prairie,** 5½ miles south of Red Cloud on the west side of Highway 28, is a 609-acre stretch of mixed-grass prairie, the sort of land that inspired Cather to write so movingly about the Plains. See if you have the same reaction to the land as Cather, who wrote this: "That shaggy

Boning Up on History

Historian Will Durant once said that history is lies agreed upon. That may be so, but sometimes once-reasonable, undisputed historical facts are viewed differently with the passing of time. Take the situation of David McCleery, whose great-grandfather, Asa T. Hill, was a Nebraska State Museum and Field Archaeology director who unearthed many a Pawnee burial ground. McCleery's short essay, called "A Brief History of Sacred Places, Archaeology, and Grave Robbing in the Hill Family" (Nebraska Voices, Nebraska Humanities Council), is a sensible, succinct, and poignant statement about historical perceptions, the quest for scientific knowledge, and indigenous peoples. McCleery wrote: "My great-grandfather, Asa T. Hill, was a grave robber. He wasn't known as a grave robber until about ten years ago. Up until that point he was known as an archaeologist. He dug up a lot of dead Pawnee. . . . If A.T. Hill thought folks would be calling him a grave robber forty years after his death, he probably wouldn't have dug so many holes on his farm near Red Cloud, Nebraska. I bet he's rolling over in his grave, but I'm not going to look. As it is, he's safe in a cemetery in Hastings, and as far as I know, no one has any plans of digging him up." He concludes with an apology to the Pawnee tribe, saying he regrets that his great-grandfather "was such a bonehead and fouled so much sacred ground. From the stories I've heard, he seemed like a decent enough guy—he just couldn't stay out of your graveyards." If you'd like to see a historical marker about the Pawnee villages and burial grounds, go east of Red Cloud on Highway 136 and turn south to **Guide Rock** on Highway 78.

grass country had gripped me with a passion that I never have been able to shake." Much of the land has never been plowed due to its proximity to the Republican River and concomitant susceptibility to erosion. The tract is owned and maintained by The Nature Conservancy and is open to the public free of charge. Some of the land is rented out for grazing, so you may see an occasional cow. And sometimes the Conservancy has a controlled "prairie burn," when the dry prairie is deliberately set on fire to mimic the old days, when such fires were natural. It truly helps maintain a healthy prairie. The telephone number is (402) 694-4191.

Five miles east of Red Cloud on Highway 136 is the ***Starke Round Barn,*** the largest in Nebraska and one of the largest of its kind in the world. The three-story barn was built in 1902–03 by the four Starke brothers. It's 130 feet in diameter and is built of 12-by-12 lumber, held together by balanced tensions and stress rather than nails and pegs. It's really a remarkable piece of architecture built at a time and place where tools and other resources were limited. To find it, turn south just at the railroad tracks. The owners live at the site and don't have a phone, so please don't stop at inappropriate times and do conduct yourself accordingly. Learn more at starkeroundbarn.com.

Franklin County

A unique eight-sided, or octagonal, ***church*** was built in ***Naponee*** in 1881. Legend has it that it was built in that configuration to keep the devil out, as there'd be no corner in which to hide. It remains devil-free and now houses the ***Naponee Museum,*** which contains, in addition to the usual historical artifacts, the memorabilia of native son David Janssen, famous for his role as the innocent but hunted man in the original television series *The Fugitive.* It also has memorabilia from Pierce Lyden, another native son who made it in Hollywood. Lyden played the bad guy in his nearly 250 movies with such conviction that he was voted the Villain of the Year in 1944. He played a despicable scout in the movie *Red River,* with stars John Wayne and Montgomery Clift. His scenes, according to a book he wrote, are often cut from television versions of the movie to leave time for commercials. The museum has more than 200 articles that were used in his long movie and television career, which spanned thirty years. The museum is generally open only on holiday weekends in summer, but if you call (308) 269-2791 during the workday or on Saturday morning, someone will likely let you in. Naponee is south of Highway 136 on S31C.

Harlan County

Republican City and ***Alma*** are two communities that are very close to ***Harlan County Reservoir,*** Nebraska's second-largest lake, at 13,250 acres, and surrounded by nearly 20,000 acres of federal land. The lake is popular for boating, fishing, swimming, and camping. There is no entry fee. The six campgrounds range from primitive to those with electricity and showers, from $14 to $26. The Army Corps of Engineers operates three boat ramps here at no charge to the public. Tubing on the nearby Republican River is also popular; you can put in on either side of the reservoir's spillway areas. A 600-acre area is reserved for motorcycle and ATV use. Hunting is allowed in season provided you have a Nebraska hunting license. In the spring months the lake is home to up to 5,000 pelicans who are on their northward migration. Other migratory waterfowl in evidence are a multitude of geese and ducks. The lake can be reached by several exits off Hwy. 136. America The Beautiful Passports are honored here. For more information call (308) 799-2105 or visit harlanlake.com.

There's a nice little museum with a gift and thrift shop on the reservoir called the ***Lighthouse Antique Museum and Flea Market Gift & Thrift.*** Displays include kitchens, living rooms, and bedrooms of the early 1900s through the 1950s. There's even vintage clothing on mannequins to complete the setting. It's not hard to imagine June asking Ward how his day was and telling him of Beaver's latest shenanigans. More than 5,000 pieces of Depression glass grace the tables and china cabinets. There's an extensive toy collection of cap guns and dolls from TV westerns and more than 500 McCoy pieces. The museum is open from Memorial Day through Labor Day on Sat and Sun from 11 a.m. to 5 p.m. Tours can be arranged during the off-season. Call (308) 799-2033.

Step into the former Harlan County Bank building at 710 Main St. in Alma and it's kind of like stepping into a small village in England. Dave Hogeland is the owner of this antiques shop that carries his name. About twice a year, he travels to Swinderby and Newark, England, two little towns in Nottinghamshire, which is located in the east midlands. And oh, the treasures he brings back to this tiny spot in Nebraska. It's truly one of the most elegant antiques shops ever, featuring lots of mahogany and oak from the Edwardian period, estate jewelry, and rare coins. And take a look in the vault. That's where Dave keeps his collection of Flow Blue Pottery. Dave is around most days, but doesn't really keep regular hours, so if he's not there, just give him a call. It's worth it, believe me. His phone number is (308) 991-3172.

Furnas County

Every little town has at least one big showcase of a house that makes you slow down to admire it as you wonder, "Who lives there?" In **Cambridge** the answer is Gloria and Gerald Hilton. The **Cambridge B&B**, on Highways 34 and 6, is heart-stoppingly beautiful inside and out. Outside, the big front porch of the 1910 home invites a good sit. And inside, stained and leaded glass, original hardwoods, and more than thirty-five Greek columns are among just a few of the artistic features. There are five rooms; three have private baths. The Nebraska Room, the home's original master bedroom, has faux painted woodwork that hasn't been touched up in nearly one hundred years. The large, sunny rooms with old-fashioned furnishings all have the most modern conveniences, such as modem access, cable television, and desktop work areas. The inn is open daily for tours, even if you don't plan on spending the night. For reservations call (308) 697-3220 or visit cambridge-bb.com.

If you're a golfer, the **Cambridge Golf Course** is said to be one fine course. All kids under 18 play for free here. Check out the details at crosscreek golflinks.com or call (308) 697-4768 for more information.

Fifteen miles to the east of Cambridge on Hwy. 34 is **Arapahoe** and worth a visit. Few good things came from the horrors of World War II and the Nazi concentration camps, but the **Our Lady of Fatima Shrine** here at Arapahoe's St. Germanus Catholic Church is one of them. Father Henry Denis was a Polish priest and prisoner of war who served time at Dachau, the first of these notorious camps. Father Denis made a promise to the Blessed Virgin Mary that he would erect a shrine in her honor if he lived through the horrors of the Nazi prison camp. He did, and he ultimately made his way to the United States, where he became a pastor at Arapahoe's St. Germanus Catholic Church. It's right on the highway through town.

Before you leave Arapahoe, stop in for an ice cream sundae or old-fashioned soft drink at the **Arapahoe Pharmacy.** Yes, it's still a pharmacy and has been in one form or another since about 1900. Buy your aspirin and other over-the-counter needs here, but sit a spell and enjoy the ambience of this old-fashioned soda fountain. It's located at 507 Nebraska Ave. Call (308) 962-7895.

Places to Stay in South-Central Nebraska

CAMBRIDGE

Cambridge B&B
606 Parker St.
(308) 697-3169

FARWELL

Farwell to Arms B & B
102 Nesbit Ave.
(308) 336-3287

GIBBON

The Suite At George
Spencer Tasting Room
7155 Pawnee Rd.
(888) 273-7739

HOLDREGE

Das Gasthaus B&B
621 East Ave.
(308) 995-2440

Places to Eat in South-Central Nebraska

CAMBRIDGE

Big Mama's Eatery
('50s diner, healthy food,
no grease!)
305 Nasby St.
(308) 697-4808

DONIPHAN

Doniphan Steak House
& Café
113 West Plum
(402) 845-2932

GRAND ISLAND

Bonzai Beach Club & The
Wave Pizza Company
107 North Walnut
(308) 398-9283

Coney Island Lunch
Room
(chili dogs, malts)
104 East Third St.
(308) 382-7155

El Tapatio
(Mexican)
2610 South Locust
(308) 381-4511

HASTINGS

Murphy's Wagon Wheel
(pub fare)
107 North Lincoln Ave.
(402) 463-3011

KEARNEY

Alley Rose
(continental and American)
2013 Central Ave.
(308) 234-1261

New China Express
1304 Wes 24th St.
(308) 238-8858

HELPFUL SOUTH-CENTRAL NEBRASKA WEBSITES

Alma
almacity.com

Cambridge
cambridgene.org

Grand Island
visitgrandisland.com

Hastings
visithastingsnebraska.com

Kearney
visitkearney.org

Lexington
visitlexington.org

Red Cloud
redcloudnebraska.com

Index